stranger here

How Weight Loss Surgery

Transformed My Body

and Messed with My Head

jen larsen

SEAL PRESS

STRANGER HERE
How Weight Loss Surgery Transformed My Body and Messed with My Head

Copyright © 2013 by Jen Larsen

Published by
Seal Press
A Member of the Perseus Books Group
1700 Fourth Street
Berkeley, California

Library of Congress Cataloging-in-Publication Data

Larsen, Jen, 1973-
  Stranger here : how weight-loss surgery transformed my body and messed with my head / Jen Larsen.
    p. cm.
  ISBN 978-1-58005-446-1
  1. Larsen, Jen, 1973- 2. Weight loss—Psychological aspects. 3. Weight loss—Humor. 4. Obesity—Surgery. I. Title.
  RM222.2.L343 2012
  613.2'5—dc23
                                    2012008988

10 9 8 7 6 5 4 3

Cover design by Elke Barter
Interior design by Domini Dragoone
Printed in the United States of America
Distributed by Publishers Group West

For Mary Madeline Theresa Fitzgerald Larsen

part one:
before

secret fantasies . . . an unexpected discovery
. . . a life-altering decision

Here is a fantasy I used to have.

The doctor looks at me gravely. He sets his clipboard down and folds his hands neatly on his lap, one stacked on top of the other. He looks so sad. He says, "It's cancer."

I lift my chin and set my face in brave and stalwart lines. Beside me, my mother bursts into tears, but I don't. I am the bravest person who ever lived, who was ever about to die.

"There's nothing we can do," the doctor says, and his voice cracks. My mother's shoulders shake.

Everyone cares. Everyone regrets every terrible thing they have ever thought about me. Everyone is filled with shame, and loss. Everyone can't believe this is happening. The cancer creeps throughout my body and in the space of months, I lose hundreds of pounds. I am slender, hollow-boned, ethereal. I glow with a light that must be reflected from the eminence of heaven. No one can believe this is happening to such a beautiful girl. I give away everything I own: to people I love, to charity, to the world. I ask for nothing in return.

Sometimes, I go into remission. Sometimes, I make a beautiful corpse. Oh, the thunderous sobbing that lifts the roof off of the funeral home, the tears that flood out the door.

Here's another fantasy.

A terrible car accident. I am beheaded. My body is a ruin, but my bouncing head is swept up off the highway, jammed into a bag of ice and raced to the nearest emergency room. Rushing doctors yell *stat!* and machines wail and gouts of blood splash against the sterile walls. A doctor picks up my head, looks into my quickly clouding eyes, and sees my beautiful soul. I am secreted away for emergency, experimental surgery—my head is implanted on the body of a supermodel! The implant works! The scars heal invisibly.

At first, it is so difficult to walk when I'm six feet tall and my legs are spindly and my ankles are so narrow, but muscle memory is magical. I quickly learn how to walk in four-inch heels. Even better, I don't have to figure out what I want to do with my life, why I am so lonely, why I am depressed, why I feel like I mess up everything I touch—I'm a beautiful supermodel, and my ass is superb.

And another.

There's a switch. I reach inside my rib cage and flick it on, and suddenly everything is different. No—suddenly I'm different. Totally changed, flipped inside out, polarity reversed. I am a good person, a happy person, a smart and dependable and wise person who is never scared of anything. Everything is clear and easy.

And another:

Weight loss surgery.

I found out about weight loss surgery by accident.

For poetry's sake, I want to tell you that I had reached my lowest low. For the sake of the narrative I want to employ irony, and tell you I was eating ice cream right out of the carton, or had my elbows propped up in a pie. That my darkest moment had arrived, and there I was, fat and sad and unaware that dawn was right over the horizon.

But it didn't feel like my lowest point. It just felt like my life. I weighed over three hundred pounds and was the fattest I had ever been in my life. I had been systematically shoving all my friends out of my life because I was almost comically ashamed to be so depressed, out of control, and unhappy. I didn't want to admit to anyone that I was so fat I didn't want to live anymore. It seemed a poor excuse for sadness, and it sounded pathetic in my head. It would sound worse coming out of my mouth.

And then there I was, reading a blog called something like, "Hey I'm Really Fat and I Hate Myself For It." The blogger wrote about she'd never lose weight unless she went on *The Biggest Loser*. I wished I could go on *The Biggest Loser*, except it seemed kind of terrifying to me, all that nakedness—how could they get so emotionally naked on national television? More importantly, how could they stand to be filmed with their shirts off?

I scrolled to the comments. *You could try,* a commenter wrote, *weight loss surgery. The duodenal switch,* the commenter continued, *isn't like most weight loss surgeries.* You lose all your excess weight in a year or less. You can eat whatever you want. It is new and sophisticated. It is the future of weight loss. Here is a link: duodenalswitch.com.

I clicked almost before I finished reading the sentence.

I had heard of weight loss surgery before, because Al Roker had it. Carnie Wilson had it too. She used to have to hide her bulk behind rocks and cars and buildings in Wilson Phillips videos while her skinny bandmates danced. She lost all that weight, but then she gained it all back. Al Roker experienced "dumping," which is what happens when you eat poorly, then you sweat a lot and throw up, or spend hours in the bathroom with a can of odor-killing Lysol, miserable and alone. I always pictured Al Roker eating ice cream on the toilet, and it made me sad.

That wasn't what I was looking for. That kind of weight loss surgery sounded crazy. Not worth it. A panicked last-ditch effort, even.

This, though. Duodenal switch dot com.

It was a very blue web page, very neatly laid out, and I clicked on the link that said "Procedure." What would they proceed to do to me?

A picture of a surgery-altered digestive system popped up. I studied the pastel pink stomach, bisected, half the size of a normal stomach or even smaller. The ghost of the removed part of the stomach was dot-dot-dotted behind it, no longer important. The long white loops of intestines wiggled down the illustration, with arrows pointing out parts that looked exactly like other parts. I couldn't make much sense of it. Somehow I failed to notice—accidentally, on purpose—the arrows that helpfully pointed out where sections of the intestines had been torn from one another and looped around so the surgeons could stitch them to each other. Where one loop ended abruptly, where bits and pieces of the guts were Frankensteined together.

As far as I could tell they just did some rearranging, like the digestive system was your living room and you wanted the couch over by the window, then you were cured. It looked so easy to me, someone who was only vaguely familiar with the workings of a normal digestive system (I always thought my actual digestive system had never really had the opportunity to be normal, really). It looked so *simple.* Could it be so simple? I read sentences like, "The BPD/DS combines restrictive and malabsorptive elements to achieve and maintain the best reported long-term percentage of excess weight loss among modern weight-loss surgery procedures," and I thought *Oh, well, of course it does, that makes so much sense.*

This was weight loss surgery, but it was different. It was weight loss surgery that *worked,* and it was *permanent* and *easy.* They said so themselves, right there on the web page. I didn't understand why the entire world hadn't latched on to this amazing new weight loss technology.

This was me, sitting cross-legged on my futon alone in the dark, my heart beating hard. Me hunched forward over the keyboard, breathing through my nose, deep deliberate breaths, my eyes scanning each link.

Skimming over words like "major surgery" and "three-day post-surgery recovery," and "three-month post-surgery recuperation." Somehow I didn't notice phrases like "loose, foul-smelling stools," and "colostomy bags for the rest of your life." I skipped over the warnings about agonizing death from intestinal complications, "blood clots" and "leaks" and "aneurisms" and "costs up to $35,000, and will probably not be covered by insurance." None of it registered.

Because there were pictures. Pages and pages of "before" and "after" pictures. I flipped through them, quickly at first, and then went back to look at each of them carefully, with a great and terrible sense of recognition pounding with my pulse at the base of my throat.

In the "before" photos, she—it was usually a she—stood there hunched in a question mark with her shoulders pulled up to her ears. An oversized T-shirt, hanging down past her knees, and a skirt to her ankles. A look on her face that said, *I know I am fat. I think I am worthless. I have given up.* I sat and examined their faces, their unhappy, turned-down mouths, their deep-set eyes and the angles of their scruffy eyebrows, their crumpled foreheads, their hands clenched into fists—or loose and open-palmed, as if they had given everything away already, had nothing left and expected nothing in return. I examined every fold along their necks and the curves of their cheeks and slopes of their hips and turns of their ankles and every detail hit me, bang in the heart, like a close-fisted shove.

It made me hate them a little, that they would leave themselves so vulnerable and open. Weren't we already vulnerable, as fat people? Didn't we provide enough ammunition with our size, for anyone who wanted a quick and dirty way to hurt us?

And here they were, their defeat and sense of despair captured forever on film. They looked as though they agreed with every terrible thing that anyone had ever said about them. They were hanging their heads and simply accepting that there was no other recourse—surgery was the only answer, the photos said. Surgery is the only answer, they told me.

Because look. Look what happens—the "after" photos. A picture for every post-surgery month, a record of pounds falling off and vanishing. The dramatic difference in people's sizes and shapes from month to month is breathtaking.

More important is the change in the smaller details over time. The photos seem brighter, the clothes less frumpy. The shoulders straighten. The *smiles*.

Keep flipping to the pictures taken a year or two after surgery and you see hands on cocked hips, heels kicked out, chins lifted, backs straight. These people are thin, and it only took radical major surgery and a single year. A year to lose hundreds of pounds. A year to look so happy.

I flipped through the photo albums of every single person on that site. I spent hours watching obese people shrink magically, rapidly thin. I finally paused at a photo of a woman in an evening gown, her hair shiny, her face bright and open, years and decades and so many pounds away from the sad and slumped "before" to her left. Right there was when I made my decision.

I'm not happy. I want this.

It made *so much sense*. We live in the future. In the future, there is so much medical science can do! It was like correcting a harelip. This was a cure for obesity. Why I hadn't heard about this before? Why had it taken so long?

Everything I knew about the Fat Acceptance movement and Health at Every Size, all my wistful thinking that someday maybe I'd figure out how to be one of those beautiful, happy, confident fat women, vanished entirely. I didn't have to be strong. I just had to get surgery.

I made sure I bookmarked all these sites, the forums, the discussion groups, the doctors' websites, the informational depositories, the piles and piles of promises piled up in my browser tabs just like presents under the tree.

I was alone in my house on the futon, and my foot was asleep. I unfolded carefully, painfully, shifting the weight of my body and the heft of my stomach and I pushed forward off my seat.

At three hundred pounds it was hard to breathe. I couldn't walk more than a block without my back hurting and my knees pinging and my lungs seizing up. My thighs rubbed together with every step. The friction broke the skin, and the moist heat was the breeding ground for yeast infections. Every day I scratched my thighs bloody. When I sat at my desk at the library I worked at, I prayed nobody noticed my heavy breathing. At three hundred pounds, it was difficult to look myself in the eye. I didn't want to be that way.

It didn't have to be that way. This website, these pictures—they all shouted, "It doesn't have to be that way." I didn't have to be strong—just operated on.

I wanted to tell someone. I wanted to fling open the door of my apartment and run from one end of the hallway to the other, pound my fists on my neighbors' walls, shout and turn from black and white to Technicolor, become a part of the picture again, because I could. I would. I could do *this*.

It would all work out. It always did. That is what I have always told people—things work out. Things unknot (sometimes unravel) and everything settles down and you look around and you see that everything has ended up okay and that you couldn't imagine things happening any other way.

I want to tell you that this was the point in my life at which everything finally happened.

the art of the tattoo . . . the foolish conflation of happiness and skinniness . . . lying liar-pants who make up lies

Maybe it didn't all start with the weight loss surgery revelation. I think maybe it started four years before that, with the tattoo. The tattoo was when I started earnestly looking for a cure for myself, for the body I carried around with me, this body that changed without my permission, this body that I couldn't control.

A tattoo is a wound, essentially. Tiny needles dragged through the surface of your skin, digging in and leaving behind a deposit of ink, a trail of blood that wells up and spills over your skin.

"You're a bleeder," Iggy, my tattoo artist, said, in a matter-of-fact way.

"Is that a good thing?" I said.

"Do you want to bleed?" he said incredulously.

"No."

"Then hold still."

I ground my teeth and tipped my head forward. I kept my hands in my lap to hide my belly. The shop was mostly empty and the florescent lights were bright and clear. My friend Jen Wade sat on a rolling chair across from me, her legs crossed at the knee. She had a camera, and I was too embarrassed to ask her not to take pictures.

There was a brief silence, and I braced myself inside it. He set the needle going again. A thrumming burn. I felt it outside my head before it touched my skin, and then there was a feeling like a hot wire being drawn up across my neck. A vibration that burned even deeper. It was in my skull and through my teeth, the back of my throat and across the tops of my shoulders. Sparks scattered down my shoulder blades, raced down an arm, and I twitched and jumped like someone was plugging me in and hand-cranking a generator. I made a low, keening noise that I knew was annoying, but I could not stop myself.

Jen Wade, who we called Jen Wade because she had the kind of gravitas and strength of personality that called for the formal weight of two names, held up the camera. I bared my teeth at it. My skin crawled down my neck and fled along my spine in great waves of goose bumps as Iggy burned the tattoo onto the back of my neck.

This was unchangeable. Irreversible. This was a part of my body that would never alter, a part that I controlled. Iggy's hands were sure as he steadied the machine and swept it down in a long, slow grind through my skin. I closed my eyes and wondered what it would be like when the pain stopped and the feeling returned to the tips of my fingers. I wondered if I would want to start breathing again.

"Breathe," Iggy said. "I don't want you passing out."

"Okay," I gasped. I steadied myself against my knees, and breathed.

You could call my very first tattoo a lie—a lie to myself, a lie to the world.

Lies are so *easy*.

When you lie, you are reshaping the world in the image that burns bright in your head. When you lie to people, when you tell them exactly what they want to hear, you are making the world a better place for them.

You are smoothing down a red carpet and ushering them forward into a brighter reality, a happier one in which you are the person they expect you to be. In which you are exactly as cool as they think you are, before they know any better. Before they catch you in a lie.

In my late twenties, I fled my real life in New Jersey. I exchanged it for San Francisco and an MFA in creative writing. In some strange, indeterminate way that I was afraid to think about too specifically, I thought living in San Francisco really would make me a different person—a better person. In San Francisco, I would be a writer in a graduate writing program, which would make me the interesting person I pretended I was. In San Francisco, after a lifetime of bouncing up and down the scale from large to overweight to fat to obese, I would just stop.

Somewhere along the way, "happiness" and "skinniness" had become hopelessly tangled. Rather than work patiently at that knot with careful fingers and quiet determination, I ignored the snarl and instead pinned all my hopes and the entirety of my dreams on geography. I thought that when the plane passed over the border from Nevada to California, somehow my fat would start streaming off me, get caught up in the wake of the plane and rain down over the hills and the valleys I left behind.

But nothing changed, and I showed up for my first day of graduate school ashamed to be there. I was convinced the first impression I offered was, *hello, I am fat*. It made everything seem impossible. I was so tired of it. I was so tired of myself. I wanted to be happy—such a silly, Disney thing to want, such a sparkles-and-rainbows-and-teddy-bears naïve thing to crave. I didn't think I had ever been happy. I didn't know how to do it. I didn't even know how to be a person who could be happy.

I was tired of bouts of depression. I was tired of them showing up, and I was tired of them hanging around, eating all my cold-cuts and drinking all my beer and leaving crumbs on my couch and thumbprints on my mirrors. I was tired of letting them into the house no matter what coast I was on.

Treatments I tried included medicines, doctors. Going for a brisk walk! Buying myself flowers. Making lists that included the items "get out of bed" and "take shower." Attempts at aerobics. Daydreaming about the bike I'd buy once I was skinny enough to have one. Sunlamps and heat lamps and changes of scenery, from fractions of a mile to three thousand miles. All the methods helped, some more than others, but only briefly; they didn't cure. What I wanted was a cure. What I've always wanted was a cure. Sometimes I wondered what had broken me, and would I ever be fixed. How many more things could I try?

Diets. I will not talk about all the diets I tried, and all the pounds that I lost and all the pounds that I gained. All of the stereotypical, desperate-fat-girl-trying-to-be-skinny scenarios. Sometimes, clichés are clichés for a reason. Sometimes, that's what happens when someone is fat and doesn't want to be. Have you ever seen the failure rates of diets? Has it ever occurred to you that fat is a lifelong, chronic, incurable condition? It occurred to me, over and over. And that's when I tried the just-giving-in and lying-in-bed-and-crying methods of coping. Because I wasn't tough enough for the *fuck y'all, I'm beautiful* method of living. The world is not made for fat people, and I couldn't hack it.

What you need to know about is the feeling of failure, radiating from the outside and filling up the entire inside, because so many people manage to either be thin, or get thin and stay thin. So many people manage to be happy—which is the same thing as thin. So many people manage it, but I failed over and over.

I wanted someone to tell me I was okay. I looked for something outside of me to fix everything. I looked for *happiness* as if someone could hand it to me in a package. I gave up on a part of myself.

My body felt like a lie—I was not the person that my body insisted I was. In my head, I wasn't fat. In my head, I was lovely and bright and sprightly and confident and I could be a happy person. In my body I felt like I was trapped by gravity, earthbound, sure that anyone who saw me believed in all the clichés about fat people—that they thought I was slovenly, lonely, bad-smelling, alone.

And one day, I couldn't stand it anymore.

When I got my first tattoo, I told everyone I was celebrating being close to finished with graduate school—all I had to do was finish my thesis, write a book, and it was done. But really, it was my attempt at making a deliberate, conscious, permanent change to my body. And more than that, it was an attempt to make my body beautiful. It was the white flag I waved at the world. If you are forced to look at me, at least now you have something beautiful to look at. Here's a reason to think I am interesting, beautiful, amazing, lovable. Not a liar.

a personal triumph . . . ominous portents
come from a stranger . . . a relationship

The summer I finished my MFA thesis, the summer after my tattoo, it was cold and my red coat didn't fit anymore. It hadn't closed for a long time, but I didn't have money for another jacket, because graduate students spend all their money on booze. I left a few buttons open on top and a few at the bottom. I wrapped a scarf around my neck to fill in the empty space, and every time I did I thought, with a pang, that I was covering up my tattoo.

Every morning I stood in my closet, surrounded by racks of clothing that were too short and too tight and too impossible. My clothes had somehow gotten small and I had somehow gotten large—it happened at least every year or so. This was the summer I just put on my long T-shirt nightgown, convincing myself it looked exactly like a dress, wrapped my scarf around my neck, and closed as many coat buttons as I could.

My MFA thesis, a book-length work of fiction, was due at the end of the summer, so I took a sabbatical from the library where I worked. Every morning, I went to the University of California's medical school library, where I didn't know anyone and no one cared what I was doing, and I wrote for hours. It was a powerful feeling. I hadn't thought I could accomplish anything like this—getting a degree, writing a full-length novel—when there was still so much wrong with me. When I was still fat. But when I went out to write every morning, I stopped thinking about that for a while.

First, I stopped at the convenience store and I picked up two twenty-ounce bottles of Diet Pepsi, two king-size Kit Kats, and a pack of menthol cigarettes. I smoked nervously, worriedly, at the bus stop. I shivered, waiting, blowing out smoke. Those moments before starting to write were nerve-wracking. The day before, I had written for hours. Good words, words I liked. But would I be able to do it again? That was the terror of writing for me: I wasn't sure I'd ever pull it off again, no matter what I had accomplished previously. It felt like a metaphor for my whole life, but I tried not to think about that too carefully.

I took the bus up the hill, just two stops. Three blocks. I smoked another cigarette in front of the UCSF library, pretending not to notice the signs that called UCSF a non-smoking campus. I went inside and sat at one of the desks on the top floor, in the back corner. I was surrounded by dark shelves. I had an orange chair and a view of the city and complete silence.

I camped out with my snacks spread around me and my laptop open, and I sat and wrote my book in my big navy blue T-shirt nightgown. I didn't have to worry about pinching or pulling or thinking about my clothes or anything below my neck.

Every five pages I took a smoke break, lumbering up and down the sidewalk, thinking about the next word, the next sentence, the next page, the next chapter. Every crevice in my head was filled up by my book, was stuffed and overflowing.

That summer nothing else was important. I put my book together brick by brick in that library overlooking San Francisco, and one day I realized I was a few pages from the end. I headed downstairs with my pack of cigarettes and my laptop under my arm, and I shuffled up and down the block.

"Those things are going to kill you," said a woman sitting on the steps next to the library. She was wearing scrubs and a nametag hanging around her neck. She had big white nurse shoes.

"Probably," I said, and moved away from her so I wouldn't blow smoke into her face.

"You don't want to die," she said. "You don't have that look."

"Thank you," I said, startled. "I don't."

"You better do something about your weight, then," she said. "Or you're going to be worrying about heart attacks. You think you're young now, but that don't last for long. Soon you're going to be old and you're going to have to worry about that heart. And your veins, getting all full of cholesterol. Do you think about your cholesterol?"

"No," I said. "I don't really—"

"No," she said. "I didn't think so. You want to die?"

"I have a book to finish," I said, and I fled. Riding up the elevator, I realized that I had actually answered her question. I didn't want to die because I had a book to finish. I plugged my laptop in, stood up, and went to the bathroom. I splashed my face with water, washed my hands. They smelled like cigarette smoke. I hadn't been thinking about smoking, or eating Kit Kats. I hadn't been thinking about cholesterol, or heart disease. I wrote my book and ate Kit Kats. Three nights a week, sometimes four, my boyfriend Andy came over. We sat on the futon. I laid down and put my feet in his lap, and he tucked the blanket around me. We watched television shows like *Dirty Jobs* and *Mythbusters* and worked our way through the collection of *Babylon 5* DVDs I had. He told me I didn't look like I had gained an ounce after I had gained forty pounds, and then twenty more. I ate before he came over, and then when he came over we ate again: pizza, or sesame chicken, or Pad Thai, or quesadillas. Sometimes platters full of nigiri, sometimes cheeseburgers.

In the UCSF library bathroom, I put my head under the faucet. My hair had gotten so long, falling all the way down to the middle of my back. I hadn't cut it since I moved to San Francisco. I held it in my fist and shoved my face under the stream of water with my eyes and mouth open, and I tried to think about my book, so close to finished. I had a couple of bars of Kit Kat left. I would write, and then I could eat them. I would type THE END, and then I would fold the Kit Kats in half in my mouth, both at once, and crunch down. Then I'd sweep the crumbs up off the library table and wipe away the smears on my keyboard with my thumb and suck my fingers clean. I would have a book. Nothing else had mattered before, so why did anything matter now?

It didn't have to matter. All the weight I had gained over the last semester of my MFA program, all the weight I had gained over the summer. All the weight I had always carried, all the years of my life, all in my face and the thick column of my neck. All the weight I would never lose. All the square inches I could cover up with as many tattoos as I wanted. My tattoos could be the only deliberate change that I made to my body, and the only permanent ones.

Only it did matter. When I was writing my book, I was essentially the brain in the jar I sometimes wished I could be. But it would be over soon, and then what?

I typed slowly at first, but then the words started making a straight shot from the back of my head down through my arms and then I was typing *the end*, backspace backspace backspace, THE END. I scrambled in my bag for my Kit Kat, ripped the package down the center and pushed both bars into my mouth at once. I was finished, and victory tasted like crispy wafers and cheap, waxy chocolate.

I crushed the chocolate against the roof of my mouth with my tongue and swallowed quickly. I saved my file on my desktop, then saved it on my thumb drive, then shoved my thumb drive in my bag. Then I pulled it out of my bag and stuffed it in my bra. If I got knocked down and someone ran away with my bag, at least I'd have a copy of my novel, if not my dignity. Graduate school had taken three years, and now the reason I moved to San Francisco was gone. Not gone—achieved. Right. A goal, achieved.

I took the elevator downstairs and burst out of the library and was disappointed to see that the clouds were low and the day hadn't gotten warmer or brighter, that the sun hadn't burst from its moors and gone hurtling across the horizon, trailing sparks in a victory lap. There are no weather miracles in August in San Francisco; every day is as gray as the next no matter what is inside your heart.

The woman by the door was gone, and I headed down the hill before she could reappear. I wanted to yell about my book. I wanted to yell and to cry.

I called Andy, and he picked up and I yelled in his ear.

"I did it, I did it, I finished my book, it's done." I clomped down the hill, past the rows of pastel houses, and my bag was heavy and my thumb drive was hot in my bra.

"Woo hoo!" he said. "You are awesome."

"I know, right? God." I was seized with a certainty. "I need to celebrate. Where are you? Can we celebrate? I want to drink a lot. And be happy."

"I'm home," he said.

"I'm on my way," I said.

"Finnegan's?"

"That's perfect. I want to smoke, and drink, and be so glad this goddamn book is done." I paused. "When I was working on it, a woman told me that I should quit smoking."

"While you were writing?"

"No, during a smoke break."

"I hope you told her to shove it."

"I did. But I don't know."

"You can do anything you want to, now that the book is done," he said.

"I want to drink whiskey," I said.

"Good choice."

Hours later.

"I'm happy," I said, as we stumbled down the street. I clung to Andy's arm.

"Me too," Andy said.

I stopped in the middle of the street, under a flickering lamp. "But you're not," I said. "You're not."

He pulled a cigarette out of his breast pocket and squinted at me. "What are you talking about?" He stuck it in his mouth and lit up. His glasses were opaque for a moment in the light. "I'm totally happy. Hey we're talking about you here. How awesome are you? You finished a book!"

I swayed. He caught me, laughing, and tucked my arm into the crook of his. He led me home. I stumbled into the bedroom, shedding pieces of clothing as I went, drunk enough to not even consider my nakedness. I collapsed into bed. It was late and my head was swimmy and I was worn out from all the sense of absolute and utter relief, and from avoiding the thought of what might come next and what I would have to do. Andy came in to tuck me in, pull the covers up, and kiss me good night, but I scrambled out of bed, pulling the comforter around me. "I have to save it," I said. I padded out to the living room and sat on the futon. I pulled out my laptop and emailed my book to myself. I squinted at the screen, and carefully typed out a message to my advisor. *I did it*, I wrote. *What do I do now?*

I closed the laptop and Andy was behind me, prodding me back into bed, spreading the comforter back over me.

"I'm going to stay up for a while longer," he said.

I sat up. "Why don't you come to bed now," I said, smiling in a way I thought might be provocative and convincing. "Let's celebrate! We should celebrate!" It had been a long time since I had propositioned him. After a while I had given up, because being told *no* is one of the most embarrassing things in the world. But my head was swimming and I was drunk and I had just finished writing a book and what was I supposed to do next?

Andy laughed. "You need to go to bed."

"Please?"

I was horrified to hear myself say it, because it came out sounding so much less like a joke than I wanted it to.

"I'm sorry," he said. He looked miserable.

"It's okay! It's okay! I'm sorry. I was just teasing you." I pulled the cover all the way up to my chin.

"Have good dreams, okay?"

He left the door a little open, and I could see the light of the television flickering in the living room. I drifted in the dark. The television went off, and his soft footsteps went into the bathroom. The water went on, the water went off. I rolled over onto my back and let the covers slide down to my waist. I closed my eyes and pretended to sleep, an arm over my head, my back arched, naked. Lovers had told me, in tones of awe, *you have magnificent breasts*. Maybe not at this size, the heaviest I had ever been at this point—though the top weight kept creeping up. But maybe it was still true.

Andy crawled into bed, and he didn't notice. He didn't remember that he liked my breasts. He sighed, and settled in with his back to me. Almost immediately asleep, I thought.

I can cry very quietly. The tears slipped down into my ears, trickled through my hair. I lay there breathing quietly for an hour, or more, in the dark, my eyes wide open. Hoping he'd hear me, terrified he would.

He sighed, and turned over on his back. I swallowed. I put my hand on his chest, and his breathing was deep and heavy. I curled into his side. He was warm and comforting even when he was asleep. He was Andy, and we'd figure it out. I reached down to pull the blanket up, and my fingers brushed his erection. I caught my breath. I caressed him slowly, afraid to look up at his face, holding my breath.

His hand knocked mine away as he shifted. He sighed again, and rolled back over onto his side, away from me. I knew I wasn't going to be able to be silent anymore. I crawled out of bed and stumbled into the bathroom in the dark, fumbling with the faucets. I couldn't turn on the light and look at myself. If I turned it on, I'd see my face. I'd see the enormous expanse of pasty skin, the blotchy cheeks, my mouth twisted down and ugly and collapsing. I folded up on the floor of the tub and let the shower run in the dark, water beating down on the back of my neck.

the family buttocks . . . the terrible danger of
genetics . . . an engagement . . . chickening out

My thesis was done and the world didn't seem any different, except for
that too-familiar sense of loss. I went back to work, and nobody noticed
anything different about me—shouldn't they have been able to tell that I
had finished a book and was just inches away from graduating? The days
followed each other, one after another, all the same. Then one day my
brother called me at work to tell me he was engaged. Engaged!

When I was a kid, before puberty, we lived in the Bronx and ate
dinner at my grandparents' brownstone in Brooklyn. One evening, everyone was there—my three aunts, my grandfather at the head of the
table, my mother next to me, my brother squirming on her other side,
and my grandmother next to him at the foot of the table. I don't know
where my father was—working? At home?

My father wasn't there, but everyone who was all agreed that my
brother definitely took after him in looks. My father was very tall and
narrow, and he was famous, in the family, for eating and eating and
eating without gaining weight. Someone said I was beginning to look
like my father, too. My family member's voices took on tones of relief

as they agreed, over a roast and potatoes and over my head, Jennifer does not have the Fitzgerald problem.

"The Fitzgerald *ass*," my mother would say, and Aunt Betty, the most serious one with the upturned nose, would reply, "Oh, *Mary*." Aunt Cealy, the baby with the mass of hair all the way down her back, would smirk, and Aunt Evelyn would say, "Thank *God*." Grandma would say, "What?" and I would take a big bite of my mashed potatoes and wonder what the Fitzgerald ass was, and why I wouldn't want it.

We always had tea after dinner at the kitchen table. At nine I was old enough to plug in the kettle and pour hot water carefully into mugs, and I cut slices of pound cake for all of us and passed it out with cups of tea. My brother mashed his slice with a fork. It exploded it into a crumbled mountain that he'd pick through slowly and sometimes not finish. My mother cleaned her plate and then pressed her fingers against the crumbs that had spilled off her fork and onto the table. I learned that every part of the pound cake was yours and important and ought not to be wasted, because who knew when it would come around again? My grandmother did not allow seconds, and we did not have pound cake at home. I chased the crumbs with my own fingers too, but only when I thought no one else was looking, because I was embarrassed about my small moment of desperation. I was also embarrassed when I watched my mother as she picked the crumbs from the front of her blouse, licked her fingers. Someone was always looking.

Aunt Betty was built like an apple, and looked like my grandmother with her shelf of a bosom. The other sisters were built like Weebles, round around the hips that tapered down to little feet. They were all fat, to varying degrees of Fitzgeraldness, but that's not what I would have thought about them then. They were my aunts, and they looked like my aunts. My mother's ass seemed okay to me. My father said he liked it.

But my mother was afraid I'd get fat. She tried to give me a foundation, a core of self, to prevent it from happening. She said to me, "Do you know how beautiful you are?" That intensity of tone, and the melting way my mother sometimes had, always made me a little bit squirmy. I was pinned down under the force and light and heat of her regard and her love. It was difficult to look her in the eyes, and I sometimes resented her for it, for making me feel overwhelmed and for not knowing exactly how to respond.

My mother said she was too short, but I was nice and tall, with good hands and pretty eyes—sea-green eyes. That was supposed to keep me strong when I turned twelve and my Fitzgerald genes showed up to the party. I got fat.

My mother never said anything about my weight, but she took me to her Weight Watchers meetings. We logged our food together. And we ate ice cream together, dunking our spoons into the gallon tub of Tin Roof Sundae. My mother and I were clearly, obviously, mother and daughter. And I was clearly, obviously fat, and that was the real truth about me.

A picture of us shows everything that mattered about me the summer before I turned twelve years old, when it was clear I didn't really take after my father, after all: I am standing in the yard, looking up at my brother, who is crouched like a tiny blond monkey in the crook of a tree. My polo shirt is baby blue and skin tight, stretched over a round mound of a belly and the soft, prepubescent points where my breasts will eventually be. My butt juts out behind me, and I am wearing very small, thin cotton shorts that are banded with white tape along the hems. My legs look like chicken drumsticks.

I am standing there slouching and poochy and round, an S curve, with no self-consciousness whatsoever. I will learn self-consciousness later, since I will be varying degrees of fat from this age on up. It is something that will become incredibly important to me: an awareness of what I look like at every moment, from every angle, as if someone with a camera is behind every corner and tree, shooting from between the bars of a sewer grate or over top of a brick chimney.

That summer I had no idea what it meant that I had started to look so much like my mother. I had no idea that my brother was the lucky one, skinny—practically scrawny, fearless as he jumped through the trees, fearless for as long as I have known him.

In that picture, I am not a lovely child. I find it hard to look at because I hate that fat little girl for being so stupid as to leave herself vulnerable. There is something raw and painful about her lack of awareness. I envy it. I would never recapture that lack of fear.

In seventh grade, I met the boys in my homeroom who felt they needed to explain to me that I should have been ashamed to go around looking the way I did and thinking it was okay. At first, the knowledge that being fat calls for embarrassment confused me, bewildered me, set me off balance. Years of high school and experiments in trying to hide, in trying to fit in, in trying to stand out, taught me that when you are fat, that is one strike against you. It is a vulnerability that attracts enemies. It is the target toward which anyone can aim confidently and score a direct and palpable hit. A statement of fact was enough to brutalize me: "You're *fat*," spit with a helping of scorn, of disgust, was weapon enough to end any argument, to destroy me.

I wanted to be my invulnerable brother. My skinny, tall brother who looked so much like my father who was always running ahead of me, circling around the park, lapping me again and again.

When he called to tell me he was engaged, I doubled over with the surprise of it. "You're going to get married!" I said. "You proposed."

"In the park. We had a picnic, and I proposed to her. I was so nervous." He laughed his mumbling sort of chuckle. "I spoke so fast. 'CarrieIreallyloveyouandwanttospendtherestofmylifewithyouwillyoumarryme?'"

"Oh my god!" I said. "I can't believe it. You proposed! Did you do it on her timeline? When I met her, she said, 'Ken knows I expect to be married in a year.' Has it been a year already? Are you on time?" I was always slightly alarmed and amazed by Carrie's assertiveness, her willingness to explain exactly what she wanted and needed. She was fearless. Unstoppable.

"Oh," he said, and it was a scoff. "No. I wanted to propose."

"I know!" I said. "I'm so happy for you guys. I'm so happy. It's kind of crazy."

"It's nuts, isn't it?" he observed.

"It is. Have you told Mom?"

"Oh. My. God. She said, 'Ohhhhhhhhh *Ken,*' and then she cried for like, twenty minutes. And she said Dad would be looking down from heaven at the wedding."

"She's going to be a mess," I said.

"Yeah. But you know, it's a wedding."

"It'll be a good wedding. Carrie will make it spectacular. And you ought to bake the cake."

"Jen," he said. "I'm not going to bake my own wedding cake. I have people for that."

For some reason, I didn't tell Andy about the engagement, the wedding we'd have to travel to New York to attend, the fact that I would have to wear a bridesmaid's dress.

I wanted to tell him. At the bar after work, he asked, "How did your day go?" and I turned and felt like I could say something. Anything. *Kenny's getting married. My book is done and I've finished grad school and now I don't know what to do. I'm a bridesmaid and I'm afraid. My brother's getting married.* All these subjects were so perilously close to the things we never talked about. Carrie wouldn't have set up this delicate balance Andy and I had. She wouldn't have to worry about breaking open this bubble we'd been living in so carefully. My relationship with Andy was safe and easy. It had become a comfortable, lovely habit. Sometimes, lonely one.

At work we had hired student assistants, and I said to Andy, "They're so young. They talk about their futures." I was holding a glass of whiskey. It was the first glass I had that night, but it had been refilled and refilled by the bartender so many times I had lost count.

I paused, and I thought, *I'm really going to talk about it, aren't I.*

"As if they had futures," Andy scoffed. "The robot apocalypse is coming."

"But, I mean, they have futures. And we—we have futures, too. But we don't talk about the future." I looked up at him, and then realized I couldn't stand it and looked down again quickly.

He took a long drag of his cigarette, and then a sip of his beer, and he was so quiet. His hands were shaking. They always had a slight tremor. I had to look at his face to figure out what he was thinking. If he had even heard me. Had he heard me? We'd both gotten used to not listening for these sounds of distress. I stared down into my glass.

"That's my fault," he said, finally.

"Do you ever think about it?" I said a little desperately to my whiskey.

"Of course I do. And I know that you're in it." His arm reached around me, and I rested my forehead against his chest.

"I don't know that," I said. I had to say it. "It doesn't feel like you want that. We've been dating for three years, and there are steps, and I feel like we're still at the bottom of the stairs."

"I think about it," he said. "I'm sorry. I—I want to want those things. I'm working on it. I am working on it."

In my mind, things go so many ways at this moment. There are so many alternate histories, splintering off into so many directions. I cry; I lose my temper and rage. I lose my self-respect and beg. I assume some dignity and quietly spell out my emotional and physical needs, explaining that if they are not met, we cannot continue our relationship. I smash my glass and break up with him immediately. I laugh, and he laughs, and something loosens in his chest and he apologizes, he gathers me up, he says that things will be different. Everything changes.

What actually happened: I said, "Okay." And I sipped my whiskey. And nothing changed.

unhappiness everywhere! . . . my sweet fat thing . . . stumbling drunkenly into the dark

The summer disappears, the autumn San Francisco sun burns the fog from the sky, and I graduate. I want more. I am unhappy. It grows, I am not sure how to stop it. My unhappiness is inextricable from the air I move through. It's part of my skin, my reflection, my face.

Nobody knew I was unhappy because I didn't know how to talk about it. There was shame in being unhappy. There was shame in admitting that I knew my own body was my problem, and that my problem was my own fault. That my problem was something I didn't know how to solve.

The less I talked about it, the easier it was to not talk about it. It was even easier to not talk when I avoided the people who might care. I assumed they didn't care if I was unhappy, or even if I was around. I wasn't being unreliable by never talking to my friends, by hiding from the world—*I was doing everyone a favor*. I existed within a special kind of unhappiness that made me think I could read the minds of everyone around me.

And yet, I still had friends—I was lucky. We had a dinner party every month, taking turns hosting at our houses. Somehow, I made it every month. At that month's dinner, I poured myself a glass of wine, and then added some more. I looked around the room at my friends, the people who made me glad to live in San Francisco.

I opened my mouth to say something. Jen Wade. Edith. Monique. You guys. I have to tell you this. I have to tell you that I am unhappy. I have to tell you that I have a problem, and maybe you can tell me what to do? I haven't had sex with my boyfriend in over a year. I am getting so fat. I wrote a book. I also graduated and that's great, but now I'm supposed to do something, and mostly I'm just getting to work two hours late every morning and getting away with it. I'm showing up for my own life late and getting away with it so far, and I don't know how to stop.

I have not yet stumbled on the idea of weight loss surgery. I am convinced I have no viable choices. I mean, I knew all about the Fat Acceptance movement. I knew about the bullshit lies that the media feeds us about skinny being beautiful and beautiful meaning happy. I knew all about calling bullshit on the prejudice, and saying *fuck you* to all the haters who thought they had a right to comment on a fat person's body, on anyone's body. Fat is emotional and biological and psychological and how dare people suggest that there is something inherently ugly about fat and size and weight? I had to stop internalizing these messages, and hating myself and my body.

I knew that. I *knew* it. I loved the Fat Acceptance movement. I loved the beautiful, strong fat women who were proud of themselves and knew how beautiful they were. And I knew I could never be them. It takes strength of character and of personality, a force of will, and some days an entire movement to be a beautiful, confident fat woman. I couldn't do it.

Monique, sitting across from me at the dinner table, did it. She was happy, and she laughed, and she was lovely. She was fat but she kissed boys and walked across the Golden Gate Bridge and wrote poetry. She had adventures. When we were together, we were fat girls together. We had a kind of connection that not-fat people maybe couldn't understand.

We knew that we could say the things to each other that most civilized people would never dare say. I had never had a friend who was willing to talk about being fat—everyone had always participated in the polite fiction that I looked like all the other people in the room. If I said anything to the contrary, there was a rush to correct me—*you're not fat! You're so beautiful!* Sometimes it was even more embarrassing than being the fattest person in the room.

But Monique and I could be fat together, and there it was exhilarating. We drove through the aisles of a supermarket in the motorized grocery carts we called fatty carts. She swung her bag into the basket on the handlebars, cranked the key, and backed out of a space. She swerved around the display of flowers in the front of the store and disappeared down the produce aisle, the tinny, electronic noise of her horn sounding like a war cry. I almost bulldozed the security guard, who watched with a bemused look on his face. Monique trundled back toward me at high speed, her face lit up like Christmas.

"I am coming, my sweet fat thing!" I cried.

"Come to me, my portly beloved!" She held out her arms. I revved up my little engine and chugged to her side. We filled our carts with meats and cheeses and cookies and rolled up and down the aisles. I said, "I want to lather your thighs with Oreos, my porky princess," and she said, "Cover me with the whipping cream of your chubby love!" With every joke, we were saying, *we acknowledge that we are fat. It is shocking. It is hilarious. It belongs to us. We are fat and that is fine.* We tootled our little horns.

We were fat, but there was a difference between us. She was the kind of person who could walk into a room and command attention. She was fat, and people lusted after her. That flew in the face of everything I believed—when you're fat, who wants you? When you're fat, you take what you can get. Monique never just took what she could get. I studied her, because I wanted to know how she did it. I wanted to know how to become someone who was so confident, with a sure voice and a sense of self that appeared unassailable. I thought if I watched carefully enough, I would learn those secrets and ferret out the cause. I could be that person, too.

My secret hope was that people already thought I *was* that person. That people had no idea I was unhappy, a mess, and floundering. I had that tattoo; I had cool hair. I didn't tell anyone, any of my friends there at the dinner party, that I needed—something. And they would have never guessed it, I thought. I was sure. I couldn't tell them, and they'd never know.

By the end of the dinner party I had drank enough wine that I thought walking home was a good idea.

"Are you sure you're okay to walk?" Monique said. She ruffled my short hair.

"Do you need me to call you a cab?" Jen Wade said.

"You're a cab," I said muzzily. I hauled myself up off the couch. I walked very carefully to the hallway. "See? I'm just fine."

Edith was leaving, too, and she said I could get a ride with her. While she called a cab I quietly left the house, closed the door behind me, and carefully stepped my way down the front stairs. I stomped into the dark street, arrowing straight ahead, weaving from side to side and pretending like I knew where I was going and I didn't need any help.

three hundred pounds and counting . . . rules
are for suckers . . . becoming a head in a jar

It was like someone put her mouth very, very close to my ear and said, "I dare you." And very thoughtfully, with great deliberation, I picked up my fifth peanut butter cup, placed it in my mouth, and said, "Mmph mph."

Which meant: Okay. Let's see just how fat I can get.

Six more months out of grad school, and I weighed 279 pounds. That was fatter than I had ever been. I thought about it. The fattest I had ever been used to be 250, in high school. Later, when I was in a terrible relationship, I somehow made it up to 270, and then escaped—the relationship entirely, the weight only briefly.

And now, I was more than 270. I was 275, 279. I was creeping up slowly. And I wondered—could I weigh more than 300 pounds?

I didn't have to diet. I didn't have to think about food. I didn't have to count calories or exercise or give a shit about my cardiovascular fitness. I could just—never stop eating. There was nothing I had to do but go to work and come home and eat. I didn't have to talk to anyone, I didn't have to go anywhere, I didn't have to do anything but put food in my mouth. I could eat whatever I wanted, whenever I wanted. Eat myself *sick*. Binge every day.

And I could see—because I was depressed enough to be reckless, self-destructive enough to be stupid, angry enough with myself to punish my body—just how fat I could get.

Just how large can a human body become? How large could my human body get, and what would that look like? How would it feel when my skin stretched even farther? Would it get thinner and thinner and become like a balloon filled with pudding, until it popped?

There was pleasure in that thought; no, glee. Utter, reckless glee in this mad little secret: I had lifted my hands in the air in surrender, and I was watching myself wreck like a train speeding over a bridge. Skidding off the rails and plummeting, car by car, into an endlessly deep lake. I could let the water close over my head, ripple, and be still.

My switch, my controls, my brakes had broken without me ever noticing. Or did they even ever exist? I mean, what was stopping people from waking up and doing whatever they wanted? There were no real barriers, no physical chains. There was nothing but rules—ephemeral, insubstantial, easily-brushed-aside rules. Rules were so much less real than Oreo cookies.

So I ate.

As I got heavier, everything else did, too. The drag of the earth against my body. Everything so difficult and so slow.

And I ate. That is what I did, and what I became. That is what I became good at.

Text messages—*meet for drinks? Where are you? What are you doing this weekend?* I closed my phone, and I ate.

I ate with absolute recklessness. And a quiet terror, because I didn't know what had caused it; I didn't know how things had gotten this way, how I had gotten this way. And yet I still felt that small sense of glee, because there was such a sense of freedom from moderation, or even the pretense of moderation.

It grew unbelievably easy to stop thinking about my body. Something so large really couldn't be missed, and yet I had perfected the art of not looking at myself directly in the mirror, not actually thinking about the body under my hand when I showered (grunting and twisting to reach between my thighs, clean my back and my feet), when I got dressed. It was gone, and there was such relief in that. I barely felt human.

When I folded my laundry, I wondered at the size of my clothes; I thought about how they were so large, such huge swaths of fabric. But they were getting tight. I would need to order from a special catalog soon because I was outgrowing the sizes in the stores. That was enough to give me a pang, to make me pause.

It wasn't enough to stop me.

When did it stop feeling like freedom, and more like I had become confined by the boundaries of the person I had eaten myself into? I ended up a collapsed, pathetic thing, curled up like a pill bug around my stash of food, afraid of the world.

I didn't want to kill myself, though, because I couldn't bear the idea of someone stumbling upon my enormous corpse. I couldn't stand the idea of that final, foolish, tragic, comic indignity.

Andy had become the only person I could stand to talk to. He became vital to my well-being, my continuance. I was still anchored to the world by someone who held my hand, touched my hair, listened to me speak, would notice if I were gone. He was there, and he was solid, and he was what kept me from flying apart utterly. He put his arms around me, as far as they would reach, and he held me together as best he could.

If I had something to wear that fit, I could go out. If I had something to wear that hid me, every part of me, disguised me and made me an entirely different person, maybe I could work this out. Start over. But first I needed to not be me.

Chapter 7

via *WebMD.com*

For patients who remain severely obese after non-surgical approaches to weight loss have failed, or for patients who have an obesity-related disease, surgery may be an appropriate treatment option. But for most patients, greater efforts toward weight control, such as changes in eating habits, lifestyle changes, and increasing physical activity, are more appropriate. The following questions may help you decide if weight loss surgery is right for you.

- Have you tried to lose weight through conventional methods of weight loss: group classes, one-on-one counseling, calorie controlled meal plans, food journals, and exercise?

- Are you well informed about the surgical procedure and the effects of treatment?

- Are you determined to lose weight and improve your health?

- Are you aware of how your life may change after the operation (adjustment to the side effects of the surgery, including dramatically different eating habits)?

- Are you aware of the potential for serious complications from the procedure, the associated dietary restrictions, and the slight chance that the procedure will not help you lose weight?

- Are you committed to lifelong medical follow-up?

what does a girl have to do around here
to get weight loss surgery? . . . overcoming
inertia . . . the terror of smilestones

This is all to say: It felt like a miracle when I stumbled across the idea of weight loss surgery. Getting surgery would fix everything! Only I had no idea what to do next.

I had found out about the duodenal switch, and then I spent the next month just looking at "before" and "after" photos, because the forums where you were supposed to connect with other patients made no sense to me. People wrote posts in long, unbroken blocks of text that ended with multiple panicked question marks and breathless exclamation points. There were acronyms I didn't understand, and lots of capital letters in places they didn't generally belong, and entire jargon-stuffed sentences that were incomprehensible to me.

And there were no answers. The forums told me that I had to consider many important things: insurance providers, insurance provider coverage, finding a competent surgeon, choosing a domestic surgeon versus an overseas surgeon, filing claims, psychological testing, blood testing, health screens, pre-surgery weight screens, filing for disability, filing for medical leave, filing for medical loans, covering surgeon's fees. Medical necessity, sleep studies, documentation of obesity-related medical issues, forms, form letters, medical receipts, appeal letters, re-appeal letters sent certified, re-re-appeal letters sent certified and return-receipt requested, careful notekeeping, self-advocacy. Self-advocacy. Me, hunched over at home in my nightgown, a self-advocate.

Self-advocacy meant actively formulating plans and carrying them out. It meant talking to people, possibly leaving my house. It meant night after night with a laptop shoved up against the mound of my stomach, scrolling down through the endless pictures of what I wanted, what I could have, what seemed impossible.

I wanted there to be a guy with a gurney and a bucket in an alley somewhere, waiting to go *psst* as I wandered by fat. Or a postcard that mysteriously showed up in my mailbox with a checkbox to check: "WEIGHT LOSS SURGERY: YES," after which a doctor showed up at the door with a laser scalpel and a gallon of hand santizer. Or maybe a big, round, shiny red button on my laptop, labeled with the words: PRESS HERE TO SUMMON NEXT AVAILABLE SURGEON. You know, something simple. Something reasonable. Something less overwhelming than trying to sort through all this information I didn't understand, that made me feel panicked and stupid.

One morning I stood with everything that didn't fit me piled at my feet, almost all the hangers in my closet empty, and I cried, feeling my face twist into something ugly. And then I put my nightgown back on, that ankle-length column of T-shirt cotton jersey, and put a cardigan over it. I'd worn it to write my book, but never to work. It was possible it looked like a plus-size dress they'd sell in mail order catalogs for people who couldn't buy off the rack, but somehow that didn't comfort me. I spent the whole day burningly aware that I had crossed a line.

I spent the day afraid to stand up from my desk, and when it was time to leave work, I couldn't stand the idea of walking outside where everyone could see me. I decided to stay for a few more minutes. I Googled: San Francisco weight loss surgery.

Oh yes, I was so stupid for not thinking of doing it sooner. For not realizing I could just let a doctor tell me what to do. But none of the websites had ever said, "First call a surgeon." There had been no step-by-step list! This is what I had become.

I took the first result and I punched the numbers into my phone. With my finger over the send button, I dove into the stacks, headed for the farthest corner. Maybe no one would answer and I could leave a voicemail.

A click like the flick of sharp fingers against the wall of my heart. The person at the other end of the line said hello.

"I am interested in weight loss surgery." I said the words out loud for the first time.

"Okay!" the woman on the line replied. There was a brief pause, and I was filled with a terror, afraid for a moment she'd hung up the phone. This was where she was supposed to gather me up and smooth out all the wrinkles in my map, and point out the next leg.

"Okay!" she said again. "I've got my screen up. The computers are a little slow this time of day." I politely gave her my name, my address, and my age. I told her my approximate weight with a catch in my voice—I had a sense of the dramatic. She asked me how I had found this surgical group.

"Online."

"Of course. Obesity Help, I assume, or did you find duodenal switch dot com?"

"I don't remember," I said. "I'm sorry."

"Okay!" she said. There was a waiting period, she continued, to get an appointment at the office, and before that you had to attend an orientation session that was only held once a month and sorry, you just missed it.

"But in the meantime," she went on brightly, as if she could hear my panic flare up like a furnace, could see me in my nightgown, "you should join our email discussion list, for patients of the surgeons."

"Email?" I said stupidly.

"It's such a lively community," she rushed on. "Introduce yourself. Everyone is so friendly. They can answer most any question you've got, and if they can't, we monitor the list and pass everyone's messages on to the doctor, and it's like a family where everyone helps each other out."

She loved the email list. She thought the email list was the greatest thing ever. It was populated by survivors of the surgery who could tell me, as specifically as I could ask, every little thing I wanted to know. Meeting people, but in the dark, with my keyboard. I could handle that. I could make that happen.

I spelled out my email address carefully, twice, so that she could send me all the information I needed, with links and instructions. I walked home with my head down, that phone call like an armored shell. *Not for long, not for long, not for long. I won't be like this for long.* Instead of stopping to pick up dinner somewhere on 9th Street the way I usually did, I raced straight home, fired up my laptop, found the email, and signed up for the forums.

And then I put my laptop away. That had been too great a rush of activity. It was impossible to think about it anymore. If I kept thinking about it I'd want to talk about it, and if I talked about it— something else would happen. It was a delicate state of precarious balance between panic and terror, my entire body vibrating until my teeth clacked together.

I woke up the next morning to dozens and dozens of emails from the doctor's email list in my inbox: people asking questions, replying to questions, making jokes, telling stories, requesting help or advice or support or just asking that people out there read their words and send some sympathy and understanding their way, and maybe also an animated gif. Some had traveled ridiculous distances to have their surgeries, and everyone had paid for their surgery in a different way and had different amounts of difficulty getting it approved. Most patients had no complications, but some patients did.

And every one of those patients thought that weight loss surgery was a miracle of the future that had changed their lives. Every one of them thought that the surgeons were celebrities; father figures; minor gods; loving dictators; cold, cruel masters; genius miracle surgeons; and no other surgeon performing any type of weight loss surgery could ever possibly even begin to live up to the level of talent and surgical precision that their—our—surgeons demonstrated.

I clicked through these emails, one after the other, and I wanted to delete them. I wasn't sure that I was ready for that level of enthusiasm. It seemed like work. There were so many inside jokes, and a sense of wild-eyed fervor exhibited for being skinny, taking vitamins, discussing which foods had the most protein and where to find them on sale. And the jargon—the jargon was like a shower of Splenda and sugar-free Jell-O and protein shakes.

They talked about The Weight Loss Journey; how every pound lost was Gone Forever; and how a smaller, non-weight-related goal was a *smilestone*. Everyone carefully documented their Aha! Moments, when they just finally "Got It." Everyone wanted to make it to Onederland—when you dropped below two hundred pounds—was dealing with Head Hunger, and was Hanging on Tight for this Amazing Ride. They kept careful count of how many Months Out they were, and celebrated each of their Surgerversaries. Once you had a certain number of Surgerversaries, you were a Lightweight, with Seniority over the Newbies who were likely to experience a Two-Week Freakout, both before the surgery (what was I thinking?) and after (what was I thinking?).

They were hunkered down behind their jargon walls, cuddled up with other survivors, as if they had been trapped, years ago, by their bodies and did not know any other way to live. The idea that a community could be built around something like weight loss surgery worried me. That some of these people had had surgery three, four, five years ago and were still participating avidly on the email list, that there was so much focus and attention and interest still lasered in on their new bodies and their new stomachs and their whole new lives made me uneasy in a way that I could not pinpoint exactly, then.

But what it was I know exactly, now: I had spent my whole life identifying myself as a fat girl. I didn't want my identity tied up so neatly anymore. I wanted weight loss surgery to be a very specific and useful tool that I would afterwards slot neatly back into my toolbox and leave behind. I wanted to just slink in for a bit of the slice and dice, sneak back out magically skinny, and get on with the rest of my life.

I thought being skinny meant that the worry and stress and anxiety my body had caused me would be over. I wanted to punch my clock, step through the exit door, and be free and clear and with no obligations, in the Land of Eternal Slimness where problems did not exist.

The email-list participants were sending dispatches from there. Why were they still talking about this stuff? Why didn't they shake it all off and go leaping away like gazelles into the hills, forever happy? Could they please stop talking about food like it was their job?

Later I would appreciate that in the end, they were all people who wanted to help each other. They saw themselves as resources, historians. They were people who understood exactly what it was like when you were fat and thought being fat was the end of the world. They knew what it was to think fat was a terrible and permanent part of you, until you learned about surgery for the first time.

They knew what it was to climb up, terrified, onto a hospital gurney and to wake up in a recovery room with a whole new digestive system and no idea what to do with it. They knew how strange it was to go from fat to skinny, and how radically things can change in the wake of such a drastic right turn.

They had never heard of Fat Acceptance, or Health at Every Size, or the possibility that being fat was okay. This was a group of he-man fat haters, advocating for the elimination of fat in everyone's body, campaigning for the miracle of weight loss surgery, giddy with relief that they had escaped a fate worse than most things, into a better life.

And I could be happy too, they were saying. It was easy! It was great! It was the best thing they had ever done! It was so seductive, and their straightforward, black-and-white perspective was so mesmerizingly simple. These were the people who understood not wanting to be morbidly obese, not wanting to work on self-esteem and self-acceptance, who just wanted to be fixed. Who wanted to just be normal. They understood.

I read all the messages and got to work later than usual that day. I was full to bursting on the bus ride there—every time someone didn't sit down next to me, I wanted to tell them it was okay I was thinking about weight loss surgery, and I wouldn't be this way for very long. I didn't tell my co-workers, though my entire body was boiling with the steam-pressure of possibility. I didn't tell my mother—the idea of telling her horrified me; I didn't tell Monique when we emailed back and forth half the day; I didn't tell Andy when I met him at the bar that night, and he had a Maker's there waiting for me.

I was alone in my head with the idea of surgery, surgery, surgery. Every day I had an inbox full of people shouting *surgery, surgery, surgery, it's the best thing I've ever done!*

I started to recognize each person by not just email addresses, but writing styles. I imagined them with skinny bodies and strange, floating auras, coronas of the fat people they used to be. All of them the voices in my head.

a living "before" story . . . little pink flats . . .
making best friends . . . eternal salvation

At the bar that night, after we'd both had a couple of drinks, I looked at
Andy and said, "Hey."

"Hey! What?" he said.

"Do you want another drink?" I finished my last few drops of Maker's.
"Are you okay?" His hands were shaking.

"Fine," he said. "How are *you*?"

I couldn't talk about how I was, he didn't want to talk about how he
was, and we never talked about us.

The next morning I introduced myself on the email list. The post-ops
were kind, welcoming me with open arms and questions—are you coming to the next support group? Are you ready to get started? Next week,
I said. I wrote down the time and day of the meeting in my calendar.

I counted down the days to the meeting, crossing off each one. I
had the odd compulsion to not be the self-loathing slob I thought these

people were expecting, the living "before" photo with the defeated eyes, looking at the skinny people with wonder and envy. I couldn't go in my nightgown. At work I placed an order on Torrid.com, expedited the shipping, and took my package to the third-floor bathroom of the library the moment it arrived. There were jeans and T-shirts and blouses in the largest sizes they carried. Everything smelled chemical-new and stiff. Everything fit. I stood in the bathroom with piles of new clothes heaped on the sink and thought about all the money I had just spent, wondering why I hadn't done it sooner. I looked taller in new pants. My skin looked clearer, my eyes brighter, my hair shinier. Maybe I had a cute butt, in new pants. Maybe I could be me, in new pants.

"I have a doctor's appointment," I reminded my boss the next morning, and I tried not to look significant. Debbie said, "Okay," mildly, and told me to remember to file my time off request. She did not mention how cute I looked, and how terrified. I had dressed so carefully. Lipstick. Pointy pink flats. I'd told the email group about them—*I'll be there this afternoon*, I said. *You'll know me by my pink shoes.*

The surgeon's office was in the hospital down the block from my office, and the surgery survivors threw their support groups in the cafeteria.

I showed up to the hospital forty-five minutes early. I pattered through the glossy linoleum hallways, peering into patients' rooms and wondering if I'd run into someone just returning from surgery, someone whose guts were still in the building somewhere, steaming inside a bucket and about to be dumped into a plastic bin marked MEDICAL WASTE. I'd tiptoe into her room and lean over her hospital bed, take her cold hand and warm it in mine. I'd bend close and whisper, *What was it like? What is it like to finally be on the Other Side they keep talking about? Do you feel strangely empty? Do you feel completely ready? Are you filled with regret? Or are you ready for what's coming next?*

Still woozy from the anesthesia, her defenses would be weakened and she would tell me the truth. She'd be unable to focus on me, to look me up and down to decide if we were kin. She might think it was God talking to her, and I would take her confession.

Along the hallway I passed closed doors, more closed doors. No groggy-looking obese people wandered the halls. I found a bathroom, peed, washed my hands, and reapplied my lipstick carefully, sweeping the tube along the bow of my lip, tracing a perfect arc. I dusted my face with powder, smoothed my eyebrows. I was as armored as I'd ever be. I wound my way down to the cafeteria, getting lost but refusing to ask for directions. No fat girl will ever ask directions toward the food.

Outside the cafeteria, I stopped. I didn't know if I had the energy for this. I had been buoyed by all my expectations for the future, life after surgery, a month out, a year out, three years later, when I would be skinny and well. But this meeting was the present in which I was still fat, and everyone knew it. I pushed open the double doors.

The cafeteria was large, lined with high windows overlooking the foggy hill and the long drop down to the Panhandle. It was cold, gray-carpeted, and crowded full of people at all sizes. I had not expected that. A table in the back was loaded with potluck dishes, all of them protein-based—turkey cold-cuts, mostly, and some cheese and chicken fingers. *Can you get weight loss surgery if you're a vegetarian?* I wondered. *Vegetarians probably aren't fat.*

Groups of people clung together and separated and came back together again, like drops of water. It was like the email list had come to life. They had the odd intimacy that is created when people get to know each other online, plus that sense of unbending friendship and connection that occurs when people have something very, very specific in common—in this case, not just the surgery, though the surgery was the major component, but morbid obesity.

And there was a hierarchy in place: the fat ones wanted to be the skinny ones, the not-yet-skinny ones were so glad that they were no longer the fat ones and were just a breath away from being the skinny ones, and the skinny ones were the ones who had won, who had all the answers, who spoke with great authority and magnanimity, bowing their heads graciously at the compliments, considering the eager questions thoughtfully, handing out bits of advice and encouragement like they were sugar-free hard candies. The skinny ones coated in triumph and wide-eyed optimism. They had reached their goals, and now was a new dawn, a new era.

I wanted to duck away, gallop down the hallway in my pink shoes and escape out the back door and not have the post-operative people look at me with warm-hearted understanding and sympathy in their eyes. I didn't want to be an object of sympathy. I didn't want to develop that same smug look of relief and triumph. This felt so much more complicated than it should have been.

But I had to find the coordinator first, register my presence. Hello, I am here, just give me my appointment with your office. I made a purposeful circuit around the room looking for someone with a clipboard, and I was recognized by my shoes.

"Jen!" she yelled. "Jen!" until I turned around, and there she was, waving at me, nodding her head and flapping her shawl.

"I'm Aimee," she said. "Hi!"

I must have looked confused.

"AzureSky?" Her email address.

"Oh!" I said. "Hi! I'm so glad to see you!" And I was. Aimee was active on the email list, a popular, years-out patient with seniority who spoke and wrote with great authority and confidence. It was warm in the room, but she was wrapped up in a sweater, a scarf, and a shawl wound all the way around her twice and then tucked into her armpits, and she was still tiny instead of bulky.

"I'm freezing!" she told me, when she noticed that I had noticed the way she was dressed. "I'm just cold all the time! It's what happens when you get so skinny, ha ha!" She took my arm. She said, "I'm so glad you made it! Those certainly are pink shoes!"

"Yes," I agreed, and we both examined them for a moment.

"Aimee, hi!" someone shouted, ran up, kissed both her cheeks. "You look so good!"

"I had my tummy tuck!" she said. "This is the first time I'm out of the house in weeks!" She flashed her belly, flinging her scarf out of the way, her sweater flapping open. "Next up is my boobs. I have to save up for that. Can't remortgage the house again," she said, raising her voice. Everyone around us laughed.

She turned back to me and said again in a serious voice, looking very hard into my face, "I'm so glad you made it. We're glad to have you here." She was the voice of the whole surgical practice full of people who had been operated on, the head of the collective body that had lost thousands and thousands of pounds over the past ten or more years. She had a sweet voice, vaguely Southern, and a bright and brittle motherly kind of way about her—she seemed so cliche of the stay-at-home, all-surfaces-disinfected, my-child-eats-apples-for-snacks, knees together, posture upright. She seemed to keep the patience and compassion that flowered inside her for other, flawed human beings carefully at the fore-front of her mind, because otherwise she'd snap and kill us all. Her fingers were cold when they closed around my forearm.

"Where are you, now? I mean, in getting the surgery, honey," she said patiently when I looked around the cafeteria. She looked down at my thighs and back up at my face, smiled sympathetically as if she had just answered her own question.

"Well, this is informational," I said. "I mean, it's the orientation. I have to do this first, and then I make an appointment—"

She ducked as if she was going to headbutt me, and I jerked back a bit. Her voice was very intense, and her eyes flickered back and forth across my face. "Talk to your insurance company. Do it. Do it now. It's the most important thing you're going to do, because they're the ones with the power, they're the ones who are going to try to stop you, believe me I know, I fought for years. For years! But I knew that I needed to do it. It's important to get the ball rolling now, do you know what I mean?"

"So I just call them and say that I want to get weight loss—"

"That's it exactly, oh *hi* Darlene, I know, I can't believe it's only been a month either but I'm up and walking because they are miracle workers, as if we needed any more proof, am I right? Look at this!" She let go of her grip on me, swiveled around, and yanked up her sweater. "Look at that! I haven't had a flat belly since I was *six*! This is Jen, she's just starting out, she's going to be so happy, am I right? I know! Best thing I ever did, don't you think so? The best thing you ever did?"

Everyone agreed that it was the best thing that they ever did. She was the skinniest of all of them, and I realized that there was another layer to the seniority of weight loss surgery patients, and that was your level of success, how thoroughly you managed to eradicate all traces of your previous life as a fat person, how skinny you managed to get. She was so skinny that you couldn't ever imagine her having been fat, though she wouldn't let you forget it—her "before" picture was in her purse, and it was laminated. She pulled it out for me and I reached for it, unable to help myself.

I exclaimed over it. You'd only have known it was her by the blonde hair, vaguely at the same length, in the same shape. She watched my face as I looked at the rumpled photograph and then she plucked it from my fingers.

"I know, huh?" she said. "That was four years ago. Two hundred twenty pounds, gone forever. Hi, honey!" She flapped her photo and inclined her head gracefully at the newcomer who headed toward us, exclaiming at how beautiful Aimee looked.

I realized that that was what I wanted, exactly. She was so happy with her body. She'd had two surgeries, and another one coming, but I did not think of that then. I thought it must be wonderful to be told all the time how beautiful you are, how beautiful. Aimee tucked her photo back into her bag, and I wished I could grab it back.

I learned that almost all of them carried their "before" photos around. They wanted every single ounce of credit available to them for having undergone such a dramatic transition. They never stopped being amazed at their success. They wrote things in their emails like "I wake up every day Grateful and Thankful to have gotten my surgery and to be where I am today. God Bless the Doctors!!"

It was easy to roll my eyes at their effusiveness. But watching them bound around the room with endless energy, their joy in action, their happiness written on their faces as their bodies moved so effortlessly and efficiently, it was like they were saying, *Never mind your pink shoes and your eyebrows and your sense of self-awareness. You want to be like us. You do.*

"Oh!" Aimee said, interrupting her own comparison of the protein counts of various frozen foods from Costco. "They're starting now! Scoot scoot, go! The surgeons are waiting!" Part of the cafeteria had been walled off by a temporary accordion room divider, and the makeshift room was filled to capacity with people who were fat like me.

They weren't actually starting—they were setting up the whiteboard and the screen for the projector, and fat people were sitting awkwardly around tables, looking at each other from the corners of their eyes and trying to figure out who was the fattest in the room. I was the only one with pink shoes. I felt like an asshole as soon as I noticed that, but I smiled at the people around me. The woman across from me said, "What surgery are you going to get?"

"There are so many!" the woman next to her said. They looked like sisters.

"The DS," I said. That's how they referred to it in the email group. Everyone who knew anything about weight loss surgery knew it was *DS*, not duodenal switch, the way San Franciscans know it is never, ever "Frisco." But I was a phony, tossing around acronyms. I elaborated. "The duodenal switch," I said. I stumbled over the word *duodenal.* It's a terrible word. Duo-denul. Doo-ah-dehnal. The DS. "I'm nervous," I said. I was swept up by their expectant faces and something gave inside me and I said, "But I'm excited about the meeting, because it's the first step, you know, and I want to get going with this." That was exactly the feeling.

Wanting to *go*, in so many senses of the word.

"I know," said one of the sisters, the one with sweet face. The smaller of the two. She was wearing a little gold cross that she kept smoothing her thumb over.

The other sister, the one with the bangs, said, "I'm considering the vertical gastrectomy. The restrictive portion of the surgery seems a little excessive."

"It's how it *works*," the smaller, sweet-faced sister said.

"Are you getting the DS?" I said to her, before a fistfight could break out.

"Oh," she said. "I've already done it." She patted her cross down against her neck. There was a pause as I stammered and she rushed to say, "I used to be way more big."

I tried to come up with a way to say "I wasn't trying to suggest that you are fat just that we're all here in the same room so I assumed that we were all here for the same purpose hey have you tried the dip?" that would be polite and clear the air, but I stammered some more instead. "But you're not!" I said. "When I saw you, I was surprised that you're here with us." I flailed my arm around to indicate all the fat people. "But, you know. I thought it would be rude to say 'hey, you're not as fat as we are.'" I laughed weakly, to indicate that that was a hilarious joke.

The sisters both looked at me, and I thought we probably weren't going to be Surgery Buddies, the kind you develop on the email board. We would never get to root for each other's smilestones and give hugs and cheers and smiley faces when we had reached another Ten Pounds Gone Forever. I would never get to compare my progress to theirs and jealously note every .1 of a pound and quarter of an inch by which they were beating my own numbers. We would not call each other for advice, talk each other out of pudding and milkshakes and blending a McDonald's breakfast and drinking it because you *must* have a Sausage McMuffin *or you would die* of Sausage McMuffin–related deficiencies. If I called they would say, "We hope you choke on a biscuit," and set the phone down quietly.

They did not seem broken up by the loss. They leaned their heads in together and pretended I was not there, blushing up to my fancy eyebrows.

The doctors didn't come in time to interrupt the awkwardness and provide a distraction, so I sat with my hands in my lap for a while and tried not to look at them.

Then the lights went down, and the slideshow began.

Weight loss surgery is your only option! You can't lose weight any other way! Things can happen, as things do, but it's surgery, you know. The doctor was very tall and carried a little pointer. He was firm, and his words were polished and warm like antique furniture, and just as valuable. We were all leaning forward. He was real, and so was this surgery. *Go, go, go.*

The lights came back up. On the other side of this divider was a room full of people who had gotten skinny and not experienced any complications. They lined up to tell us how wonderful it was, to hand us packets and folders and flyers. They showed us their "before" pictures, and pictures of their babies, whom they hadn't been able to conceive until they had lost two hundred pounds, and their business cards, because they couldn't get a job before they lost two hundred pounds, and their engagement rings, because they hadn't been able to find love before they lost two hundred pounds, and their friendship bracelets, because they hadn't been able to make friends who knew the real them before they lost two hundred pounds.

Along with these they gave me their compassion and their heartfelt sympathy, their empathy, because there I was, with two hundred pounds to lose. They could help me.

a confession . . . your *intestines*? . . . potsticker calculations . . . the things that have to be done

I got lost in the hospital again on the way out, a folder of important and valuable information cradled in my arms. I held it in my lap on the bus all the way to my neighborhood and carried it to the bar, exhausted and raw, but exhilarated. I had talked to people and been in public and not exploded, though I could at any moment.

Andy was waiting for me. I saw him inside, through the cocked-open door. He was sitting at the bar and had a Maker's neat waiting for me, a beer and a shot in front of him. It was cold and humid, the kind of weather that makes you want to peel the layers away from your skin and encase yourself, somehow, in a bubble of super-heated air. The sky was clear, and stars pinpricked around the corona of floodlights on the bar sign. He watching a baseball game on the television, his chin in his fist. I slid onto the stool and put the folder down in front of me. He grinned and said, "How was your day? You look very fancy today!" He leaned over and kissed me on the cheek.

"I'm sorry," I said. I wanted to say, Thank you for the drink, you are always very thoughtful in small ways that mean a lot but also always seem like apologies. As if with every gesture you're saying *please forgive me*. But I don't want to accept your apology because an apology is not what I want from you.

I was supposed to speak rationally and think of a rational way through this, but instead, on the duct-taped stool of the Mucky Duck, in a bar filled with sports fans who wore carved teeth and gold finger rings, I burst into tears.

Andy plucked the napkin out from under my drink and handed it to me, put his hand on my back and rubbed down my spine. "What's wrong?" he said. "What happened? What's going on?" He kept rubbing my back as tears ran down my face, and he peered at me like he could figure out what was going on from my twisted up mouth and shining cheeks. "Jen?"

"I got this today," I said. I blew my nose. I pushed the folder over to him. He picked it up, still looking at me carefully. I jerked my chin at it, and he opened it, furrowed his brow at the glossy diagram of the stomach, the intestines, that I had become so familiar with. Under it, the doctors' names, the office, the words "Surgery for Weight Loss." A grainy black-and-white picture of a fat person, a sharper photo of a thin one. He looked at me again, and I took a breath and said, "Weight loss surgery."

"What?" he said. "What's going on?"

"It's. That. There's this fairly new procedure, a bariatric procedure—"

"Bariatric?"

"Weight loss surgery."

"Weight loss surgery?"

"A surgical procedure. To lose weight. But it's not like stomach stapling. It's more advanced." I wiped my cheeks with the butt of my hand and took a sip of my drink. I looked at him.

"You don't need to lose weight," he said.

I ignored that, because I didn't want to burst into tears again. "I read about it on the Internet. And I—I went to a seminar thing. To learn more about it. How it works. It's surgery to fix you. When you're fat."

"You don't need to be fixed—"

"They make your stomach smaller," I said. "So you actually, physically have to eat less—and they reroute your intestines—"

"Your *intestines?*"

"Yes. So you malabsorb. It's called malabsorption. You malabsorb calories and fat, you're not taking as much in. And you lose the weight so quickly."

A skeptical look. "That sounds awful."

"No," I said. "No, it's not," I gripped the edge of the bar. My voice was getting louder. "It's the most effective weight loss surgery. There are so many of them, but this kind has the highest rate of success. People lose the most weight, of all the surgeries. And they keep it off! They're keeping it off for years and years. I saw them."

"Weight loss surgery," he said, experimentally, like he'd never heard the words before and didn't want to have to say them ever again. He was frowning.

"I'll show you," I told him. "When we get back to the house. I have these papers. And there's a website, you'll see. I'm just thinking about it. I just wanted to mention it," I lied to him. "As an idea. Because it isn't healthy for me to be so fat. I mean, I've gained so much weight. And it can't be healthy at all. I should take care of myself. And this is a way."

"Okay," he said, and he tapped out a cigarette and went to smoke. I sat at the bar with my hands in my lap and looked at the baseball on the television. I wanted to read my folder and take notes, but I pushed it into my bag. We finished our drinks and walked back slowly, holding hands. I wanted to tell him about the hope that had started to bubble up inside me and made me feel lighter than I had ever felt, in a long time, how hope felt so much better than feeling wretched all the time, and was so much easier than trying to like myself.

As soon as we got back to the house, I pulled out the laptop.

"Look," I told him. I had to have him on my side.

I showed him statistics. I showed him the official home page. I wanted to show him "before" and "after" pictures, but instead I showed him the surgical diagrams. He grimaced. He pointed to the dotted outline of the new stomach.

"You can't fit potstickers in a stomach that size," he said.

"I can fit one potsticker," I said. "I won't want more than one, so it'll be okay."

"That's your *stomach*," he said. "They take away your stomach. That can't be right."

I knew that there could be complications and side effects and possible terrible, unsuccessful outcomes, I told him, but if you took precautions you could minimize your risk and increase your chances of happiness. By happiness I meant a healthy body, of course—I did not at all mean being able to fit into a size 16 instead of practically a size 30. I was logical, practical, knowledgeable, and thoughtful, full of reasonable doubts and a respectable but not suspicious amount of optimism. Trying to get him on my side.

What I really wanted to say was, Don't you realize how much I need this? Don't you understand?

Andy sat on the futon next to me with his hands on his knees, and he looked at me until I petered off. The laptop was hot on my thighs. I set it on the coffee table. I was afraid to look at him.

"We can go on a diet together," he said.

"You don't need to diet." He was quiet. I said, "And diets don't work. They don't."

I couldn't tell him that I was *giddy with relief* that I didn't have to do it the hard way. I couldn't live with it; I couldn't diet it off. This was the only possibility.

Instead I said, "I'm not healthy, you know." I said, "I bet my cholesterol is terrible."

He reached over and tugged on my shoulder, and I leaned over into his side. He smelled like cigarette smoke and laundry detergent, and his jeans were dirty. I wished he did laundry more often, laid in bed watching television and smoking by himself less often. But it wasn't like I didn't understand bone-deep, unshakable depression.

He said, "If it's what you think you need to do."

"I'll send you links," I said, lifting my head. "You can read about it. It's laproscopic but you stay in the hospital for three days and then you have to take a month off work, and I'm going to have to figure out how to do that and whether I want to tell my boss. And you eat only protein shakes at first, and you're pretty weak for a while, but you get stronger and you lose something like twenty pounds in a couple of weeks, a hundred pounds in under a year. Isn't that crazy?"

His arms went around me, but not all the way around me.

"I'm still thinking about it," I lied again. "I have to go to an appointment to see the surgeon. I don't even know if they'll let me do it. If I'm a candidate. Or whether insurance will cover it." I sounded exactly like I knew what I was talking about.

"Okay," he said. "Okay."

"It'll be okay," I said.

a sense of inevitability . . . the appointment
arrives . . . the power of PowerPoints . . .
signing my stomach away

My hands were steady and my nerves were sure and I felt a sense of inevitability that this was going to happen. I just had to wait through this next part—three months until my appointment with the surgeon—in order to get to the good part. It was like I was sitting on the lawn overlooking the Bay, waiting for the sun to go down and the barges to pull out and the fireworks to finally begin.

For three months, I didn't say a word to anyone about it. Andy was the only person I had told, and I avoided the subject even with him. I was afraid someone would talk me out of it. Monique would be disappointed in me, furious even. Hurt. Jen Wade would think it was lazy. My mother would be horrified, and think it was dangerous. Maybe she would be heartbroken, because didn't it mean I was rejecting who we were? Our genetic history? I would be letting everyone down.

Sometimes, I thought maybe I was giving myself away too readily. That I was opening up my hands and offering away something that could not be returned. My stomach, so many feet of intestine, the ability to digest food properly. I was walking away from a normal life, the possibility that I could find a sense of self, worth, strength, beauty, and happiness entirely outside of and having nothing to do with my weight.

I ate while I waited, because it was pretty likely that soon I wouldn't be able to eat at all. Soon, finally, the surgeon would click off the switch that made me eat like someone was going to steal food away from me, like I had a deadline, as if it were my job.

I didn't binge; my overeating was steady, consistent. My hands felt itchy if I didn't have something in them, and my stomach felt hollow even when it was full. I ate quickly and automatically, not even tasting what I was eating half the time. I pushed it all in steadily, to the drumbeat of my heart. I shut myself away entirely. I kept my phone off most of the time. I thought, *My friends hate me.* I thought, *I deserve it.* I told myself it wouldn't be for long. Soon it would be over.

I kept a countdown tumbling in my head: It'll be over in three months, two months, one month, tomorrow morning, in just a few hours. On the day of my appointment, I pushed down the terror that had grown steadily like a mushroom in the dark every time I thought about leaving the house. I put on makeup, smoothed my eyebrows down, chose my outfit carefully from what was left of clothes that fit.

I didn't eat breakfast before my appointment. Why? I was afraid they'd X-ray me, see a breakfast burrito in my stomach and scold me? Because the smell of Lucky Charms misting around me would alert them to the fact that my problem wasn't metabolic or in any way medical? My problem was me, and surgeons only helped those who helped themselves. I was afraid they'd pull my patient forms out of my sweaty hands and push me out the door with a stern, "Have you tried celery?" I'd stand there and wail heartbrokenly in the hospital corridor, completely bereft and out of options. Except for celery.

I knew I was cheating. I hadn't tried Weight Watchers. I hadn't exhausted my options. Everyone knew diets didn't work. Everyone knew that, and I couldn't do it. But they couldn't find out.

The surgeon's office was on top of a hill. If I had known that it was three steep blocks from the N train to the hospital entrance, I would have planned the route more carefully. I would have taken an extra three buses if I had to, or a taxi even. But I got off the N Judah, hungry, terrified that they wouldn't sign me up and terrified that they would, and sure that this was the beginning of something.

I looked up the hill and I thought, *I can do this. I am a brave person who is making a large and important change in her life. Part of this change includes doing challenging things, such as walking three blocks uphill when it feels like it's going to kill me, but it won't. I am brave, and I'm going to start doing the hard things.*

I almost believed myself.

At the end of the three blocks, I was red with patches of white, wheezing and heaving and hurting and unable to draw a full breath. I realized it was fitting that I'd be lurching red-faced and panting into the doctor's office to confess that I was so helplessly obese I required surgical intervention.

In the hallway outside the office I leaned against the wall and peered through the little window in the door, trying to catch my breath. The tiny receptionist caught my eye almost immediately though, and I had to turn the knob and push my way into the office. She looked me up and down, maybe weighing me in her head, performing reconnaissance for the doctor. She handed me a clipboard with an attached pen and a ream of paper—forms to fill out, pages and pages of questions about my quality of life as a fat person. Do you suffer from any of the following obviously obesity-related ailments? it asked. Please mark the boxes to your right, and if you are smart, you'll mark them all, because obesity is a terrible burden and the more terrible burdens you have to carry as an obese person, along with all that fat, the more likely it is that the insurance company will consider your surgery medically necessary!

The form didn't require me to state how often I suffered from these ailments, or how severe the suffering had been. It just asked if there had ever been any suffering, in a general sort of way, or even if family members had perhaps had brushes with these kinds of sufferings. I propped the clipboard on my belly and moved my pen rapidly down the page in the yes column.

Aneurysm

Angina

Atherosclerosis

Back pain

Breast cancer

Breathing difficulties

Buerger's disease

Cancer

Cardiomyopathy

Cardiovascular disease

Carpal tunnel syndrome

Chronic bronchitis

Coronary heart disease

Cystocele

Depression

Eclampsia

Gallbladder disease

Gallstones

Gout

Heart disease

Heart failure

Heartburn

Hernia

High cholesterol

Hirsutism

Hypertension

Infertility

Insulin resistance

Intertrigo

Menstrual irregularity

Metabolic syndrome

Obstructive sleep apnea

Osteoarthritis

Polycystic ovary syndrome

Pregnancy complications

Sleep apnea

Snoring

Social discrimination

Stress incontinence

Stroke

Transient ischemic attack

Type 2 diabetes

Varicose veins

I handed my clipboard to the receptionist in tight pants. She told me that she'd need my non-refundable deposit of three hundred dollars, and that it was time to calculate what percentage of me was made of fat.

I hesitated and she smiled at me sympathetically, a smile that said,

I've seen it all before. Of course you don't want to get weighed. I kicked off my shoes and stood on the scale, my hands down at my sides, behind my back, over my belly, down at my sides while I waited for the keypad to beep and my results to come up. She kept her eyes on the readout, and I choked back my instinct to make hilarious, charming small talk that would defuse the situation, which was that I was fat.

Endless eons later, the machine beeped and choked out a tiny print-out. "Oh," I said, when she handed it to me. I weighed 308 pounds. Fifty-two percent of my mass was made of fat.

For most people, two hundred pounds is an unfathomable number—the number on the front of tabloid magazines, the screaming all-cap headlines. CRISIS! OPRAH WEIGHS OVER 200 POUNDS! No one has any idea what two hundred pounds actually looks like. I remember looking good at two hundred pounds. Right then, I wanted to *be* two hundred pounds. If, after surgery, I weighed two hundred pounds, I would consider that a raging, smashing, unbelievable success. I would cry with happiness.

But in the world, two hundred was grotesque. And three hundred? That was a wash-yourself-with-a-rag-on-a-stick weight. And there I was, 308 pounds and walking around on my own two feet as if I wasn't a freak of nature.

I tucked the slip into my bag and followed the receptionist over to a blank, ecru wall. She opened a drawer and pulled out a giant black digital camera, stepped back to a piece of tape on the carpet, and gestured to me.

"We're going to take your 'before' picture!" she said, dropping the strap around her neck. "Stand right there for me, and smile when I say 'cheese.'"

I ducked my chin and pulled myself up as if from a cord at the top of my head, standing straight and smiling a cocky little smile, as if I were finding it all terribly amusing, how we were documenting my fat.

"Cute!" the receptionist said, when she looked at the camera's display. She sounded a little surprised. Maybe she wasn't used to the kind of fat people who pretended that they could hide all their flaws and all their doubts and all their problems with lipstick.

In the waiting room, I sat surrounded by pictures of all the people who had sat where I had sat and hoped very hard that this was the very first step for them.

They were all over the waiting room, in frames—"before" and "after" pictures posted by the doctors as proof of their successes, of the happiness that could be mine, if only I put my stomach in their hands. They were postcards that read "Wish You Were Here." They were waving and waiting for me to catch up.

It felt as though there was really no other choice from here on out. I did not stop to think *hey, this was supposed to be a preliminary, infor-mation-gathering appointment where I learned about the surgery, where I asked questions and got examined to see if it was really something I should be pursuing.* Everything was supposed to be tentative and hypothetical, but I had already been frozen in the moment by the secretary, her scale, and camera. This is the highest you'll be, this doctor and his team were saying, because this is where your Weight Loss Surgery Journey begins. It was as if they knew that just by walking through that door I was throwing myself at their feet.

It made me uneasy. My sense of glee and positive wonderment over the miracle of science had receded—just the tiniest bit, but noticeably. But I was still looking up at the idea of surgery and weight loss as if from the bottom of a well, straight into a far-too-bright sky. It was the kind of brightness that makes everything look dull and washed out in compari-son, makes it difficult to look at anything straight-on afterwards because nothing is in focus anymore.

I sat in the surgeon's waiting room, and I waited.

The physician's assistant who finally came to lead me to the examina-tion room managed to look bored and harried at once. She was skinny.

I wondered if everyone in the practice had been operated on—was it a condition of employment?

When the physician's assistant sighed, her bangs fluttered. She waited for me to take off my coat and drape it over the chair. She gestured to me to climb onto the table. It was too high up for me to do it smoothly. I looked at the physician's assistant, but she had her back to me as she unhooked the blood pressure cuff from the wall. The big sheet of hygienic paper whuffed and crackled when I steadied myself against the table and stepped up on the foot rest. I winced at the noise. I pulled myself up and tried to catch and choke off the huff of breath when I landed with an enormous crunch. I didn't want her to turn and see a fat bug flipped on its back, its impossibly round limbs frantically flailing in the air. Maybe she didn't want to, either, because she fiddled in the corner for a long time.

I caught my breath and cleared my throat. "You don't need me to undress, or anything . . ." I trailed off hesitantly.

"No," she said. She turned and wrapped the blood pressure cuff around my arm. I expected it to be tight and uncomfortable—blood pressure cuffs had never really fit me—but it was plenty long, with a long tail left flopping over. The physician's assistant pumped the rubber knob, keeping an eye on her watch, an eye on the needle in the dial that whirled around dizzily. She stood with her hip cocked out. She hadn't really looked at me at all. I cleared my throat again.

"How is it?" I asked, and I heard the concern in my voice that wasn't entirely real, because I knew I had good blood pressure. I wanted her to think I cared about my blood pressure and my health, as if they were taking notes about my motives.

"Pretty good," she said.

The physician's assistant tore the cuff apart in a burst of static-y Velcro noise and said, "Just sit tight." The door closed behind her, and I sat there banging my pink shoes against the edge of the table, feeling very far off the ground, and ridiculous and tired. But then the doctor came in, closing the door swiftly behind him as if he knew part of me wanted to sneak out and run away, three hundred dollar deposit and my top land speed be damned.

He was tall, with a rounded nose. His face was a little puffy, and he was balding in patches near his neck. He wore his white jacket like a sports coat, casually rumpled and open, as if he were going yachting after this. He paged through all my paperwork and looked at me in short bursts, scanning my body—across the face, across the boobs, across the width of my hips and the expanse of my thighs. My little pink shoes. I shifted on the table, and the paper crunched and tore. He looked satisfied, as if he could tell I was fat enough, and I could feel myself slump a little.

"This is a good thing you're doing," the doctor said. He had all the conviction in the world behind his words, delivered with a practiced and smooth welling-up of comfort. After seeing hundreds of fat people, he knew exactly what they wanted to hear. He had been the comforting, persuasive voice of reason for any number of fat people whose friends and family were worried about the idea of an operation, a major surgery. People whose families were worried that the surgery had to be some kind of crazy flimflam from an infomercial, something as ridiculous and impossibly foolish to fall for as a seven-day cleanse or a grapefruit diet or cellulite cream or a seaweed wrap or little red pills you take three times a day with milk. Only surgery was more expensive, more dangerous, and Beyoncé had never tried it. The doctor saw fat patients who were worried that maybe their friends and family were right and this really was an awful lot of money to spend when they could just, you know, *diet*.

The doctor understood the people who came through his door. He knew they were scared. And he knew that even the most cynical patients had partially given in to hope, given in to the fantasy of being thin. As he saw it they, we, were the morbidly obese—people for whom even being just-plain-fat seemed a million miles away. We were exactly the people who wanted to believe in the miracle, and his smile told me he knew how to give it to us.

"You'll see," the doctor said, smiling at me. He took me by the shoulder and leaned me back against the table. He flicked open the extension at the bottom of the table, touched my shin. I lifted my legs up, feeling the pull of my stomach muscles.

"Unbutton your pants," he said, and my hand moved down immediately to the zipper.

"Do you need me to—" I didn't know exactly what he wanted me to do. Undress? Pull off my pants? Lie there naked while he inspected me?

"I just need to take a look at your belly," he said, gesturing impatiently at my pants. He turned away to the sink and pulled on latex gloves. The smell was strong, with a powdery underlay. He turned back, and I hastily sucked in and pried the button free, wiggled down the zipper. The lines left behind by the waistband were raw and pink. It is a terrible feeling to be disgusted by the sight of your own skin. I laid my head back on the table and blinked rapidly.

The doctor spread the fabric open and folded down the waistband. He pressed his fingers hard around my belly button, noted the scars from when I had my gallbladder out at nineteen. "That'll make it easy," he said. "Usually we take out the gallbladder anyway when we go in there. Some surgeons leave it in, but it's a useless organ and it can cause complications. While you're in there, you might as well do everything you can to clean up, simplify the situation."

There wasn't anything really I could say to that. I craned my head up to look at my stomach, soft and mounded under his hands. The back of my neck was stretched and painful.

"You have good blood pressure," he said. "An excellent pulse." Tones of mild surprise. He gestured that I could sit up.

I said, "I think my bloodwork will be good, too. I've always been healthy for a fat girl!"

"For a fat—yes." It took him a moment. He blinked. "Not for long," he said, and that was the first time anyone had said it out loud. *Not for long*, I had been thinking involuntarily sometimes—trying on pants that didn't fit, or taking the bus a single stop up the hill, or when people stared at me as if I were too large to be real. But now that he was saying it, it felt true. He didn't have to say anything else but he kept talking, sitting on the chair across from me with the clipboard in his lap. Flipping through the pages. I sat up, flushed and a little dizzy from lying down.

"So," he said. "You experience urinary incontinence, yeah? Yeah, that's common, to experience that. Difficulty sleeping? No? I'm surprised." He went through the health problems checklist, the chafing and the rubbing and the infections and the breathing. He built up an annotated list of all the ways that fat was ruining my life. Then he set the clipboard aside and stood.

"You're the perfect candidate, Jennifer," he said, but his eyes were already distant, as though he were looking through the walls of the exam room at his next morbidly obese candidate, perched uncomfortably on a paper-covered table.

I said, "Thank you." As if he had just complimented me on my eyes or told me I had awesome shoes. And now I just had to fill out some more paperwork, take a look at some important informational material, sign some forms, and talk to their insurance coordinator, "to set things in motion." To get going. To get started. To begin.

They knew their obese patients inside and out. They must have understood what a frisson those words would send through our hardworking hearts.

The doctor nodded at me and was out the door, leaving me to slide off the table and button my pants. I fumbled a little when another knock came and the receptionist was there with a wide smile to lead me to a small tiled-floor library with a television set up on a rolling cart. She sat me down at a round table next to the television and handed me a folder of material. More information. She gave me a PowerPoint presentation to accompany the movie I was about to see, and when I'd finished watching that, I'd fill out this quiz—she tapped a French-manicured fingernail against the sheet. I'd need an 80 percent or better to demonstrate my preparedness, she said, flashing me a smile. "But you shouldn't have a problem," she continued. I thought she probably said that to everyone, but I was still flattered. I had the presence of mind to be embarrassed that I was flattered. I was drowning in this.

She hit play and left me alone with the overhead lights turned off and the flickering of the screen. Previous patients appeared, "before" and "after," and smiled at me very carefully. The clinic's staff, tiny on the screen, smiled at me and walked awkwardly from one point of the room to the other with their arms held stiffly at their sides and their chins at angles.

I followed along in my handout as the screen switched to illustrations that covered each stage of the surgery. The remarkable innocuousness of the line drawings continued to make it easy to pay no attention to what was actually going on. If they really wanted us to be 100 percent informed and thoroughly, unblinkingly aware of what we were signing up for, wouldn't they show us a real, live surgery? Wouldn't they take us through the layers of fat down into the stomach, have us watch as doctors lasered away an entire chunk of muscle and pulled it, bleeding, through the holes that their tools had made, then stitched up the pink and ragged edges of our intestines, our organs? That was the reality we needed; it was the reality it was too easy to distance ourselves from.

I flipped to the quiz and realized it was set up in the order of the video and repeated, verbatim, actual phrases from the movie. I followed along and circled the letters as the answers were pronounced. True, False, A A B A B C C D A. The video ended, my quiz was done, and I sat there in the dark, flipping through the magazines that lined the walls. They were all medical journals dedicated to weight loss surgery: *The Weight Loss Surgery Journal* and *The Journal of Weight Loss Surgery* and *Weight Loss Surgery: A Journal.* All of them looked like real medical journals, with real medical studies full of empirical medical information, but it made me suspicious, as if they were propaganda put together by a medical establishment looking for legitimacy. Maybe they were props stapled together at Office Max by the surgeon's staff. I studied them carefully, looking for the proselytism and evangelism, the hidden signs that I was being brainwashed. I studied myself for a sign that I gave a damn that I was being brainwashed.

I tucked the magazines back on the shelf, because I did not want any more information than they were willing to offer me. I would believe everything they told me.

A smiling older lady entered the room and flipped on the overhead light. There was something about her that made you think she'd bake you some cookies from a tube and brew you a cup of tea from a bag and listen hard to your problems and really mean it from her heart when she said things like, "It'll all be okay." She was carrying her laptop and a handful of cables, but she stopped to shake my hand and tell me that she really was so happy I was there. She made me happy I was there, too. She set everything up, fussing around the television, and then sat down at the table across from me.

"There," she said. She beamed at me, and leaned over the table. "I just have to tell you that you're a beautiful girl." My heart caught in my throat. "I think that you're doing a good thing here. My son is getting weight loss surgery, and I wouldn't let any other surgeon but our doctor here touch him. I trust our doctors, I really do. And you're making the right decision."

They kept talking about "decisions."

"What about," I said. "Have you—" I stammered again.

She paused and then said, "Oh! Oh, me, no. I haven't gotten weight loss surgery. They don't do it for people my size," she said, and laughed. I would not have thought of her as having *size* or being a person of size, having the quality of sizableness. She looked ordinary to me. She was the size I wanted to be.

She smiled at me for a long, uncomfortable moment. In the pink shininess of her lip gloss I could see reflected a better life for myself, a better me, a world full of happiness and possibility. I looked down at my worksheets and handouts and printouts and she said, "Let's start!" She hit a button on her laptop.

The illustrations again. By now, I could perform this operation without any coaching at all, if it wouldn't be so awkward and complicated, particularly from a medical-malpractice standpoint. Stomachs (pink) and large intestines (light purple) and small intestines (dark purple). They were the same pictures, only awkwardly animated. I waited for the knowledge to really hit me, the truth of it: what was actually being incised by the wobbly clip-art scissors, what the arrows whirling around the screen were actually pointing out, where the big portion of the pink stomach, whisked off screen to be donated to a dog food factory, was actually going.

At every step of the way she said, "Do you have any questions?" "Do you have any questions now?" At every step of the way they all said, "Now, how about asking us some questions?" They never seem surprised that I did not have a single one.

I wish I had kept track of the number of times I had almost opened my mouth, almost said yes, please, actually, I want to know something very specific, and that is, what do you do with all those feet of intestines left over? Where does the three-quarters of my stomach get put? Is it thrown out? Is there a steaming pile of organ meat sitting behind the hospital in a dumpster somewhere? I read once about a Beverly Hills plastic surgeon who used the fat he liposuctioned from his patients to fuel his fancy biodiesel car of the future—could my organs be used to repair the organs of children injured in terrible explosions, in war-torn areas? Could my leftover intestines be mulched into dry and overworked soil in drought-ridden third world countries to create, ironically, nourishment and provide a better life for a starving, big-bellied child with large eyes? Was it really possible that I was electing to get surgical intervention because I had a terrible first-world affliction? When I unfocused my mind and refused to think clearly about any of this—from what actually happened on the surgical table to the actual, eventual physical side effects they promised a patient would experience—was I hiding from the reality of *why* I was getting weight loss surgery, and what was *actually* wrong with me? What was wrong with me?

I had no questions.

The program manager handed me my informed-consent paperwork and a pen, and she smiled at me as I bent over the paper and went through each of the statements. Yes, I have been informed of what "weight loss surgery" and "the duodenal switch" actually entails. Yes, I realize that it is not super-powerful wizard magic and may involve complications. No, I do not have any questions (I lied) and yes, I consent to have you kick-start the jams. Let's get this show on the road. Let's get my insurance together! Let's go! Go, go, go, go!

I signed carefully and dated it, and I looked up at her. She flapped her hands down on the table and grinned at me. "You're all set!" she said, and I wanted to look around to see the orderlies coming, the burly men in white who would haul me up and carry me all the way over to the pre-op room to get hosed down and suited up.

"Well, almost," she said.

All I needed was insurance approval. That's it! I just needed their agreement that spending $56,000 on me and my fat was a sound financial investment. So easy, so simple, so close to the finish line.

"Blue Cross won't authorize your surgery with us," the insurance expert said sympathetically, sitting across from me behind a wide Formica-topped desk. She smoothed her hand over the photocopy of my card. "It's a complicated situation—we are not considered a 'Center of Excellence,'" she rolled her eyes and made finger quotes to indicate how ridiculous that was, "so they won't cover it."

"Oh. Okay," I said. I was afraid to move, because I didn't know where I was supposed to go.

She said, "But we can fight it!" She was enthusiastic. "You just need to appeal."

"Appeal?"

"Right. You apply. They're going to turn you down. Then we just fight back!"

Fight back! She made it sound so easy. Of course it should be so easy—this was something that I wanted, right? Something that would utterly and completely transform my life. Those are the kinds of things you chase, teeth bared and spear raised and heart pounding.

But I sat there and started to mourn already. I hated myself for being terrified and lost and already thinking about giving up.

Appealing is a lot of paperwork, the insurance coordinator told me encouragingly. I would need letters from doctors—both my primary care physician and my surgeon—that stated that surgery was medically necessary and really my only hope. I would need a letter from a psychologist. Letters from heart specialists and skin specialists and pulmonary specialists and sleep specialists, all explaining how my fat was ruining my life. And I would have to write my own letter, stating my reasons for choosing weight loss surgery, outlining my current quality of life as a fat person, proving that in the end, it would be more expensive for the insurance company if I didn't get the surgery.

I was to get the letters, notarize them, and then both fax them and send them via registered mail. I would then send follow-up letters and response letters. I would perform all these feats with great enthusiasm and industry and energy, tirelessly working to fight for my cause.

"It's worth it," she told me. "Fighting them is worth it. Though I have to be real honest," she said, leaning forward sympathetically, a faint crease between her eyes, "Blue Cross is a bugger, and I know a gal who is still fighting them, two years later. She just has to have our doctors do her surgery, you see. She knows who the best is."

"Oh," I said.

"It's worth fighting for," she said again. "But if you want to do this sooner rather than later, you can pay out of pocket." She slid an informative handout across the glossy plastic surface of her desk. She took out a pen and ticked down my options, her polished red fingernails flashing down the list. "You can apply for funding here, here, here, and here. Some people skip the funding and consider their other options, such as mortgaging their personal assets—"

"I don't have personal assets," I said.

She raised her eyebrows at me, and glanced down at the informative handout. She tucked it into a folder with the rest of the paperwork—a stack an inch thick now, a twin to the folder I already had at home—and slid it across to me. "Well, let's try the insurance company first. What have we got to lose?" A bright smile, a seeming unawareness of the hilarious joke that she had just made.

So. They would submit my claim. I would just wait to be turned down. Plenty of time to panic over all the administrata I'd have to delve into, everything that seemed too complicated to handle. She handed over her pen, and I signed more forms, scanning down for Xs to scribble next to, flipping pages quickly and trying not to read anything at all on them.

Then I was back out on the street with a list of things I needed to do while I waited for the insurance company to get back to me. It was comforting to know that there were things I could do in the meantime. Plenty of important, busy things to accomplish. I had to quit smoking if I smoked; I had to quit drinking if I drank.

I also had to start losing weight on my own, in order to make my liver smaller and my surgery slightly easier to perform. They would like me to lose twenty pounds in the next three months. It said so there on the sheet. How often did patients wail, "If I could lose twenty pounds in three months, I wouldn't be here!"

Some people go on a liquid diet! they told me.

Why the hell would I do that? I didn't say.

I had to see my regular physician and get a blood test for a baseline measurement of my vitamins, my minerals, and my blood sugars, as well as a pulmonary test and a general checkup to make sure that the chances that I would die horribly under the influence of general anesthesia weren't too high. Fat people tend to die under anesthesia. But I could try to kill myself before then, with a program of cardiovascular exercise designed to strengthen my heart and improve the efficiency of my breathing in order to both kick-start my Journey to Health and to maximize my chances of survival when the anesthesiologist comes at me with a mask full of knock-out gas.

I had to see a psychologist, too, someone who would look deeply into my eyes and hold my hand and tell me, *now, don't lie to me.* Are you really, truly sure you want to do this? Do you really, truly know what it entails? Do you really, truly know what you're doing here? Are you ready, Jennifer? And I would nod and say Oh, yes, doctor. Of course I am, of course. Of course.

I had a folder full of worksheets, a copy of my quiz, which I had passed with flying colors, a brief handout describing a copy of my consent forms, and a little checklist full of to-dos. I had my PowerPoint handout in which I did not actually scribble my secret question, though I wanted to. I had the little printout of my weight and my percentage of fat. The names and numbers of doctors and specialists they recommended. The entirety of what I need to know and do and consider in order to take the Next Steps in My Journey of Weight Loss Surgery So That My Life Could Finally Start Once and For All was in that folder, and I clutched it to my chest all the way back down the hill to the train.

enthusiastic compliance . . . the psychologist
weighs in . . . the right lies to tell

It should have bothered me that they had handed me a pre-printed sheet with a psychologist's name, his number, and his fee. He knows all about the surgery, the program director at the doctor's office had told me. That's why we're sending you to him, because he understands what you're asking for, and he knows what to look for.

She didn't add that he also knew he must not question the fact that all my answers would be perfect. That I knew exactly what to say to get approved: that I was aware of the risks and also the rewards, had realistic expectations and reasonable goals, and I knew I must follow all of my pre- and post-surgical instructions, dietary and otherwise, to the letter.

Everyone at the doctor's office was very enthusiastic about the word *compliant*. They were very enthusiastic about how behaviors and attitudes had to change, and instructions had to be followed, and eating had to be done properly and in the right way, amounts, and fashion. You had to swear up and down that you were going to be The World's Best Weight Loss Surgery Patient.

I swore up and down that that was me. I *was* the best patient they'd ever see. And I believed it when I said it. My track record may have been poor, yes. Others wouldn't have bet on my success, and I wouldn't have blamed them. But they didn't know the secret, which was that I was going to be a whole new person with an improved personality, a responsible person who took care of her health, once I was thin.

I made the appointment first thing after my appointment at the surgeon's office. I wanted to knock these out of the way while I still had momentum, before my fear turned into apathy and my apathy turned me into a lump who had once considered the possibility of weight loss surgery, but gave up because it was too hard.

The psychologist was absurdly tall, with gray curls that sprung up all over his head. His enormous, whirling eyes belonged in the blue felt head of a muppet. I was the first appointment of the day, and we were the only ones in the office, which was almost totally dark. He plowed through the hallways ahead of me, not switching on lights. He called back, "Do you want a bagel? We have bagels!" His voice echoed in the little kitchenette. I stood in the dark hallway and wondered if this was part of my psychological evaluation. I was supposed to say no thank you, right?

"No thank you," I said.

He came out chomping on a bagel, brushing crumbs off the sleeves of his cardigan, and steered me into his bright office. He sat me down on a wobbly swivel chair in front of a CRT monitor and fired up the program that would evaluate me with multiple-choice questions that had absurdly specific answers.

What do I eat? (Carbs; carbs and protein; carbs, protein, vegetables; mostly sugar; mostly fat.) When do I eat it? (At meal times; when I'm hungry; when I'm awake.) How often do I eat? (2x a day; 3x a day; 4x a day; more than 4x.) More importantly, am I willing to change what I eat? (Yes! Possibly! Heck no!) Do I want to change my habits? Do I think I have bad habits? Do I want to change my bad habits? Do I drink? Do I do drugs? Do I drink and then do drugs and then go knock over a candy store? Was I aware that fat was a bad thing and I should probably be ashamed? Did being fat make me sad? How sad? Really sad? Did I think I wouldn't be sad anymore if I weren't fat?

I knew the right answers to all these questions.

When I submitted my answers, the psychologist came back in the room and sat in the big comfy leather chair. He leaned forward, and I noticed that his socks did not match his shoes, and that his shoes were very shiny.

He said, "So. Tell me about yourself. What do you do? Where are you from? What are your plans?" His arms were at least an extra three feet too long, and his wrists thrust out of his burgundy sweater all bony and white.

I hesitated. Did he mean, What do I do, in terms of my fat? What surgeon's office am I coming from? What are my plans after I get weight loss surgery, or maybe after he tells the doctor that I am not psychologically ready for it?

He nodded at me encouragingly. It occurred to me that he was trying to get to know me as a person. That it was entirely possible he thought about things other than weight loss surgery, and he was encouraging me to do the same.

Slowly, hesitantly, I said, "Well, I'm a . . . a writer." I hurried to finish. "I work at a library. And I write." I smiled and twisted my fingers together in my lap. I could feel my face glowing bright and hot. I had no idea why I said that. I wasn't a writer.

"A writer!" the psychologist said. "That's exciting! What do you like to write about?"

I wished I hadn't said anything. He thought I wrote poems about my cats. I probably looked like a person who wrote poems about my cats. "I have my MFA," I said, slightly defensively. "In creative writing."

"How interesting!" His eyes spun around in his skull like dice.

"I published a story," I went on. "Last year. About a man who loses his ex-wife."

The psychologist reared back in his chair as if I had just produced a dove from under my tunic sweater. "Published! That's wonderful! It sounds wonderful."

"Thank you," I said lamely.

"I would love to read it!" he enthused. I was afraid his eyes would pop like yolks in a frying pan. "Will you send it to me? You should send it to me!" He lifted his pelvis up off his chair, the seat tipping dangerously back, and hauled out a cracked leather wallet from his rear pocket. He plucked a card from a sleeve and pointed to his address. "Send it here. Promise you won't forget!" He pressed the card into my hand.

"Oh no," I said, examining the card. "Of course. I wouldn't forget. I'd love for you to read it." I was very confused.

He frowned and sat forward in his chair, with his forearms hanging down between his knees. He stuck his eyes on me, *splat splat,* with a force that was almost physical. "So," he said, very seriously. "Weight loss surgery." He nodded thoughtfully, tapped his chin. He pointed at me. "It's a serious move," he said. "Are you ready for a serious move?"

It took me a moment to fumble for the clutch. I lurched and stuttered and finally managed, "Yes! Of course. I'm very ready. It's a really serious thing."

"I think you are!" he said, and smiled with a glee that was wild and enthusiastic. He clapped his hands on his knees. "You're a smart girl. You've got a good head on your shoulders. I think you know the score." He caught my eye and winked. "It'll be nice to walk down the aisle of a plane and not see that look on your seatmate's face when they realize you're coming, am I right? I'll write you up this recommendation and fax it on over."

He turned to his desk and scribbled on his prescription pad, his head bent low and his elbow bobbing at a blithe angle that made me want to break it.

That was Step One.

definitely not a turning point . . . insurance comes through . . . so close to perfect

And so I spent months talking to strangers about my weight, my size, my girth. By showing up at a support group, a surgeon's office, a psychologist's office, I had been saying, over and over, *I am buying into your characterization of fat as a grotesquerie. You're welcome!* The doctors and the nurses and the psychologists were excited for me. I was going to get weight loss surgery, and then my life could start. No one even hinted at the possibility that maybe I had been living my life all along.

Here is where the turning point in the story should be, where the light ought to have dawned. In a fictional narrative, it would have been during these dark hours, in offices and information sessions, when crystalline clarity should have come about, formed under the great pressure applied by so much adversity. I should have become convinced of my own strength, my dignity, my capacity for change, and my ability to transform. I should have realized that now nothing could keep me—the heroine—down. All I needed was myself—not a physical transformation.

I was supposed to remember that I didn't need these people and their dismissal of who I was right now. I didn't need to be looked through, as if they were focused on the skinny person I was going to become instead of the distastefully fat person in front of them.

Why didn't it occur to me that I had already done so much as a fat girl?

I had moved from Pennsylvania to New York on my own when I was seventeen. I had quit high school, but I went back to college—first community college, then a four-year university, and I graduated summa cum laude. I up and moved to San Francisco, without a job, to go to grad school. I wrote a goddamn book.

I was fat.

This was not the turning point for me. Sometimes, I wish it had been.

When the doctor's office called me at work and said my insurance has been approved, that I just had to come in and fill out some paperwork, have a final consultation, and then they'd schedule me for surgery, my head and my heart exploded. *Relief.*

The receptionist laughed and said she was excited for me. She was. She was so glad I was going to be skinny.

I raced outside with my cell phone in my hand. It was warm, and underage shirtless boys tumbled like puppies across the lawn. Young girls in bikinis sprawled out on the grass pretending to study, and the fog had cleared off so that you could see Twin Peaks and all the way up to Sutro Tower. I was on top of a hill and everything stretched out around me in all directions.

"Listen," I said to Andy when he picked up.

"What's wrong?" I could hear him exhaling, the sound of street traffic. I knew he was outside his office building, squinting off in the middle distance, smoking a cigarette. I had seen him do it time and again. "Are you okay?" I never called him during the day.

The girls in bikinis turned over and swept their hair forward, sunning the napes of their necks and the long brown lines of their backs. I hesitated, squinting off at Cole Valley, which looked like a rainbow of tiny boxes stacked up along the side of a hill. I looked down at my cuticles. I lowered myself down to the concrete wall around the lawn.

"Jen?" A siren wailing in the background. "Goddamnit, hang on."

"I'm going to do it," I said in a rush.

"Are you there?" Andy said.

I had lost my dramatic moment. I cleared my throat. "I'm going to do it," I said loudly.

"Do it?"

"Weight loss surgery." Only traffic noises on his end. Loud voices. I hunched over my knees. I tried to shout in a whisper. "*Weight loss surgery*," I said. I was stunned that he had no idea what I was talking about. Wasn't that what everyone was thinking about, at all hours of the day, all days of the week? Wasn't that what filled up their entire heads and made their lives seem far away, as if their brains had been packed in styrofoam? "My insurance approved my surgery." *My* surgery, I said. I was already possessive about it.

"Oh!" he said. "Oh, wow."

"I know. I just have an appointment, and then they schedule me for surgery, and then I'm done. It's done."

"When?" He sounded far away.

"I am not sure yet," I said. "Soon, I guess." I paused. The sounds of traffic on his side of the phone. I said, "I'm sorry I've been so depressed lately."

"I didn't even notice," he said gallantly.

"Oh, thanks," I said.

"You know that's not what I meant," he said.

"I know."

Silence for a moment. The shirtless boys screamed a victory chant, and the girls in bikinis pushed up on their elbows to look, then put their heads together to laugh. They boys pretended they weren't paying any attention, socking each other in the stomach, slapping each other's backs, where the bumps of their spines stood out in the bright sun. They were so ridiculously young.

"I'm happy for you," Andy said.

"I know," I said. "Me, too."

the harbinger of doom . . . making promises
I can't keep . . . surgery: scheduled! . . . more
things not to talk about

Three months before surgery.

My final appointment with the surgeon's office, before they scheduled my surgery. There was paperwork, a consultation with a nutritionist,
a consultation with the insurance specialist, and an introduction to the
surgeon who would actually be doing my surgery. He wanted to look me
in the eye when he leaned back in his chair, steepled his fingers, and said,
"Well, why do you want weight loss surgery?" His hair was knife-parted
on the side, swept over his forehead. The knot of his tie, under his doctor's
jacket, was substantial and cinched tight.

Andy, sitting next to me, glanced over. I could feel the confusion
creeping over my face, and I knew I must have looked like a monkey
examining the back of a watch.

I didn't say, "Why the hell do you think I want weight loss surgery?"
Hadn't we covered all that by now? Hadn't everyone in his office told
me, in so many ways, that they understood? Suddenly this surgeon was

asking me the hard questions like they mattered. Suddenly there was a gatekeeper where there used to be ushers.

I said, looking him in the eyes, "Because my health is no longer sustainable at this size, and I am starting to experience a degree of discomfort, both physical and psychological, that is no longer tenable."

He nodded. He paged through the papers on his clipboard, short fingers and shiny nails, then he dropped the clipboard down on his desk and I swear to you he said, like a ghost on Christmas Eve, "You know your entire life is going to change, right? You think it's just losing weight, but it's really going to change. Are you prepared for that?"

He was looking at Andy, not me. I had begged Andy to come to this appointment so he could understand what weight loss surgery was all about. I wanted it to be solid and real for him, something we could talk about. In a desperate, visceral way, I wanted him to be my partner in this.

Andy glanced at me. "I figured it would be," he said slowly. "I mean. It's going to be a—a significant change."

I looked at him hopefully.

"Right," the doctor said. "It will affect both of you. You have to be prepared. Have you two talked about that?"

"Yes," I said. I amended it. "A little." We hadn't. We never talked about anything. But this appointment counted, didn't it? I looked over at Andy. "I know it's something we need to consider. But I think it's something I'm prepared for." Andy didn't say anything.

"Okay then," the doctor said, looking from my face to Andy's, and then back again. "And are you prepared to take the steps you need to guard your health at all times? I'm not going to operate on you and send you off to go kill yourself. You have to remember your vitamins, your water. Your protein. Look at this." A photo of a woman in a hospital bed, gaunt and hollowed out, like someone had taken a spoon to the undersides of her eyes and her cheeks and scraped down her neck with a paring knife. "See her? Malnutrition. She stopped taking her vitamins. She stopped coming in for checkups. She was hospitalized for a month, getting intravenous fluids, nutrients. She had been killing herself. If you don't follow our instructions, you're going to end up where she did, or worse. Do you want to end up like her?" He looked at me sternly. His face was made for stern looks. He must have practiced them in the mirror.

"No," I said. "No, I know what I have to do. I've done a lot of research, and I'm aware of the post-surgical requirements—"

"People say that a lot. But you are going to have to be more aware. You are going to have to stay on top, and stay ahead, if you want this surgery. Do you understand that? Exercise. Weight lifting. Vitamins." He looked at me like he knew every single gossamer, idle thought that had flitted into my head and knotted around the meat of my brain. When had I ever thought about the hard, practical realities of weight loss surgery?

My eyes welled up and my mouth trembled. I clutched at Andy's hand. "I know," I said miserably. He wasn't going to let me do it. "I know," I said. "I would never compromise my health. I know how important—I know." I trailed off.

The doctor looked at me for a long moment. I looked back at him as steadily as I could, sat up straighter, and set my feet flat on the ground, one next to the other, lined up toe to heel. I was aware of my breathing, the tightness of my waistband, Andy's hand in mine, a smudge on my glasses, the stickiness of my lip gloss. I wasn't used to wearing lip gloss. I wanted to swipe the back of my hand along my mouth and wipe it away.

"Okay," the doctor said abruptly, standing up. "You need to schedule a meeting with our dietician—"

"I'm talking to her right after this," I said eagerly.

"And once you're done there, she'll pass you along to Brianna, who will be able to schedule your surgery."

"Oh," I said faintly.

"It'll be a few months out. Surgeries are scheduled only twice a week, and we have a number of patients already. And you have Blue Cross, correct? You may end up having to head down to our hospital in San Jose for your procedure."

"Okay," I said.

"San Jose?" Andy said. He opened his mouth, and then closed it again.

The doctor tucked the clipboard under his arm and held out his hand to me. I took it, and he shook it once, firmly. "Call if you have any questions. Good luck," he said. He swept us out of his office, pointed down the hall, and shut the door behind us.

"Oh god," I said. I leapt from my chair.

"Well, that went well," Andy said. I bounced down the hall, and couldn't sit very still in my seat while the dietician spoke very earnestly to me. I wasn't paying very much attention, figuring I'd look at all the handouts later, when I had to. First, I wanted to enjoy the idea that it was going to happen.

When Andy looked at me with his eyebrows raised, I said, "What?"

He pointed at the photocopied DO NOT list that the dietician had just handed us. DO NOT drink carbonated beverages. DO NOT eat sugar. DO NOT eat everything you've ever enjoyed in the whole of your life. I blinked at the list, and then looked up at the tiny dietician.

"You're going to be learning a new style of cooking," she said. She was in a turtleneck and tweed slacks and appeared to subsist only on tap water, plus pellets of fish oil to make her hair so shiny.

"Oh, I love to cook," I said, and I ignored Andy when he snorted.

"You should have been told it's recommended you lose some weight before your surgery is scheduled—approximately twenty pounds. Here's a sheet to follow. It's very simple. You can do anything simple for just a couple of months, right?" Her eyes crinkled up at the corners. Oh, yes, of course I can, I can do anything. Then she was leading me to the billing department, where I would sign some papers and then we'd schedule my surgery date and have me sign my consent forms and get my pre-surgery instructions and I'd be set!

Okay! I said. Okay! They said. A lot of exclamation points all over the room.

We burst out of the hospital with my fresh new folder full of paperwork and diet sheets, the third stack to add to my growing collection. It was cold and damp outside. Andy bent his head over his lighter and cigarette. "Let's walk," I said, bouncing up to my toes. He looked up, surprised. I laughed. "Let's walk down to the 38, okay? Let's just go. I have to lose some weight, if I want this surgery. Oh, I'm excited."

Andy pushed up his glasses and blew a plume of smoke out of the corner of his mouth. "What if you keep losing weight by just going on a diet and exercising? Would you still consider surgery?"

We turned left onto Fillmore. It was packed, and I got shoved apart from him for a moment. I pushed back, took his hand. That was an easy question. "Well. It's a permanent solution," I said. "Diets don't work. You heard them say that. I've told you about that, right, the statistics? But this is, is a permanent thing."

"That sounds like genocide," he said.

"Coffee Bean! Do you want a coffee?"

"Nah," he said, wrinkling his nose. He took another drag.

"Okay," I said. "I am going to look at my worksheet when I get home. To see what they say I should do. What kind of food and everything. You can help me shop, maybe? Pick things out? Maybe teach me how to cook."

"You cook just fine," he said.

"I have to cook better," I said.

We made our way down to Geary, and he changed the subject, or I did, and we didn't talk about surgery, or weight loss, or the doctor's appointment anymore. We never talked about what the surgeon had said, sitting across from us in his tie and jacket and frown. I didn't bring up the subject again, and I knew Andy never would.

Chapter 15

confessions . . . heartfelt expressions of friendship . . . convictions

Our Sunday dinner party, two days after my final doctor's appointment. I hadn't gone grocery shopping yet, or taken notes. There was time for that, plenty of it. Too much time; surgery was still so far away, and I was here right now sitting on the big black couch in Jen Wade's living room. Anxiously twirling my wine glass in my hand, I kept rehearsing what I would tell my friends in my head: *You guys, guess what?* I was filled up like a balloon with the onrushing truth of it.

Monique stretched tall and put her toes on the coffee table. "My wine is broken!" she said. She held up her empty glass.

Jen Wade came padding down the hallway in bare feet with a fresh bottle, and Edith, curled up in the armchair, extended her glass for more white. Her hair was soft and curled tonight. I ate crackers, plucking them out of my palm, one by one, feeding them into my mouth in a steady stream. If my mouth was full, I didn't have to talk.

Jen Wade's mom was going to come visit for a week, and we all wanted to see her. We were fond of Dr. Mrs. Wade. We considered our various mothers.

"You guys will never meet my mom," I said. "I doubt she'll ever come back to San Francisco."

"I've met all your moms!" Monique said.

"I still haven't met Edith's mom," I said.

"Where were you, when they were here?" Edith said. She shrugged and leaned forward for another cracker. "I guess you couldn't find your pants."

I pushed a piece of cheese into my mouth.

"Everything smells so good, Jen Wade," Monique said. She held up her glass to toast Jen, who was perched on the arm of the couch.

"It's almost ready," she said. "Does anyone need more wine?" She pointed to each of us in turn.

I held out my glass. I thought, *When is the next time I'll be able to drink wine, once I get surgery?* I had started collecting those thoughts: *This is the last time; here is the final time; I won't have to worry about this; this won't happen anymore.*

"You guys," I said. They all looked at me. "So. I think I'm going to get weight loss surgery."

There was a sort of silence—not exactly stunned, but close enough.

They looked at each other. They said, "Okay."

Monique looked not bewildered, not quite stunned. She said carefully, "What does that mean, exactly?" Her eyes were very big and her face was serious. She gazed at me steadily.

I went through the schtick, recalling the charts and the graphs and all the colored diagrams. I explained slowly, looking at Jen Wade for approval—she was the scientist. She knew what I meant when I talked about my duodenum, and she could probably draw a reasonable diagram of the digestive system with a pencil on the back of an envelope right now if I asked her to. She was the one who would tell me, maybe, if it was a really stupid idea.

She nodded. Edith and Monique looked at her, too, as if they were double-checking my story. I wanted them to approve of me, and to forgive me.

I was jealous of Jen Wade, for being fit and smart and logical and utterly grown up and together; I was jealous of Mo, for being strong and brave and beautiful and confident; I was jealous of Edith, for being funnier and more charming and smarter than me, and for making me feel like nobody needed me in the group because she never lied about not being able to hang out. I wanted to start over.

"Wow," Monique said. "That's. I didn't know they did that."

"I don't want—diabetes," I said helplessly. "I don't want heart disease. My mother's got diabetes, and high blood pressure, and she's—she's really heavy. And I don't want to be that way. If it runs in my family." Health was so much easier an explanation. *Health* was embarrassing—but less embarrassing than *misery*.

Jen Wade said, "I think dinner's ready," and disappeared into the kitchen. We shifted, stood, picked up our wine glasses, brushed the crumbs from our laps. Someone said that the food smelled good, and someone else said she was hungry, and we crowded around the dinner table, pulling up chairs and exclaiming about the dishes and the candles. We flapped open napkins and passed around bowls and loaded up our plates and picked up our forks. I thought that maybe we were done, and I was grateful. But we weren't done. They had questions for me. They were interested. Cared. When did I hear about weight loss surgery, they asked, and how did I hear about it, and how did I make that decision? What made me think it was a good idea, and when was it going to happen, and how long had I been thinking about it, and why?

We were all very hesitant, stiff, and a little formal, talking about it. I was trying to sell it to them, I realized. I said, "You can lose the weight within a year. A hundred pounds in a year." I glanced around the table, and everyone seemed a little stunned. I twisted my napkin in my lap. I said, "So it'll be only a year before my life is totally perfect! Isn't that great?"

Quiet for a moment.

"You'll need to get new, perfect friends," Monique said, pushing her fork through her salad, dragging it back. "You'll need a whole new set of friends for your new life. Thin friends!"

"Friends who hate fat people," Jen Wade said. "Because you're going to be so skinny, you're going to have to hate fat people. It's a moral obligation."

"Do you want us to get out of your way now, or should we do a gradual fade to black?" Edith said.

"I'll let you guys know," I said. "I have to see what my new and improved friends say," I said. "It will be nice to have friends who love me for my physical appearance."

No more of that bullshit acceptance for who you are, we agreed.

We all helped clear the table, and Edith went to make a phone call and Jen Wade was at the sink. Monique went back into the living room. I followed her.

She curled up on the couch, and I hunkered down on the cushion next to her. I leaned forward to see her face, turned away from me, and I said, "Monique. Monique, is this okay?" Her mouth was tight and she was looking at her glass, the lipstick smudge at the rim.

I rested my forehead gently on her shoulder. I wanted to tell her that I was sorry. To explain that I wasn't ashamed of her, or us, or our peculiar, weirdly beautiful sisterhood being fat, riding fatty carts. I wanted to tell her how I had no controls, no checks, no balances, no boundaries. There's being fat, and there's being on a runaway train. I had to get the surgery. And I was so sorry.

All of that loaded into three words—*is this okay?* Hoping she understood.

"Monique?" I said.

"It's going to be weird," she said slowly. I sat up. She looked so sad. My heart jerked. "I'm sorry," I said miserably.

"I don't know how I'm going to feel," she said. She rubbed at the knee of her jeans. She said, "It's so strange, because you're just you. I can't picture you skinny. I can't even picture it. I have no idea how it could happen."

"You'll talk to me, though?" I clutched her arm. "I mean, we'll talk about it. Always. Any time you think it's weird, we have to talk about it. We have to sit down and figure out how to make it okay." I threw my arms around her. "I don't want things to change!" I wailed.

"You'll have all-new skinny friends who will hate me because I'm fat," she said, and she had tears in her eyes, and I did too, and then we were both giggling and sobbing.

I put my head on her bosom. "I don't want to lose my tits," I said mournfully.

"Sacrifices," she said wisely, taking off her glasses and wiping her cheeks, and then we were laughing again.

That night I wobbled out of the taxi at my front door. It was the kind of cold and clear evening that San Francisco only rarely gets, especially in the Inner Sunset. I tipped my head back, looking up at the stars that were visible from my quiet little side street. I sucked in a damp, icy breath, and another, and then broke into a run up the driveway, collapsed against my front door breathing heavily, fumbling at the lock until Andy opened the door for me and laughed because I was red-cheeked, glassy-eyed. I threw my arms around his neck and kissed him. He pulled my arms away and led me by my elbow to the couch, tucked my afghan around me, and handed me a glass of Diet Pepsi.

"Somebody's drunky," he said.

"Oh yes!" I said happily. "There was a lot of wine!"

"I can tell!" He caught my soda glass as I tried to put it down on the coffee table, and I grabbed his arm.

"Oh my god," I said. "Oh my god, I told them, and it's going to be okay."

"That's a good thing," he said carefully.

"It is," I said. "It's all good."

"I'm glad," he said. "I'm really glad."

I closed my eyes. I was dizzy, a little too warm. I pushed off the afghan. "I know you are," I said. "It'll all work out."

six thousand up front . . . outing myself . . .
stockpiling protein . . . the possibility of a
horrible death

Two months before surgery.

The doctor's office called me at work on Tuesday. The office coordinator, in a voice that was sweet and brisk like iced tea, said on the phone, "We're ready to schedule you for the next available date. You just need to pay us six thousand dollars up front. Surgeon's fee. Covers follow-up visits. Once you pay us, we can confirm your date."

"Oh!" I said. Of course! Surgeon's fee! Whatever! I didn't even question it or why it wasn't covered by insurance. "Do you take credit cards? Can you take more than one card?" I was pulling out my wallet before she finished her sentence. And I forgot to ask what exactly the six thousand dollars covered. Follow-up visits? How many follow-up visits would I need? I lined up all the cards in a row and carefully read off their numbers: debit card, and then my Visa card, and then my American Express. I repeated the information back. She put me on hold for a moment, and I sat there staring off into space.

She came back on the line and said, "How does November third sound to you?"

"That's my father's birthday!"

"Oh!" she said.

"It works just fine, thank you. November third. This year, right?"

She laughed. She must have heard that before. "Right," she said. "November third, 2006. Just two months away. A little less than that?"

"That seems far away," I said.

"It'll be here before you know it."

When I hung up, I was crying quietly, and a student had come up to the counter. "Excuse me," she said. "This is a quiet study area, and I can hear you on the phone. Could you please keep it down?"

I tried to compose myself, swiping my cheeks dry, sniffing into a roll of industrial brown paper towels. I had a date. *A date with destiny*, I could make that joke now, and it was the most hilarious thing I had ever thought up. I wanted to talk about it. I wanted to see people's faces when I told them what was going on. It was a breathless, reckless, impatient feeling.

When my boss came in that afternoon, I tapped on her doorframe as she was putting her bag down. I was afraid that if I didn't talk to her immediately I would lose my courage and have to quit my job in order to get surgery.

"I'm having weight loss surgery," I said. "In November."

Her forehead crinkled. "What?"

I explained. She looked at me steadily.

"Wow," she finally said.

"I know," I said.

"Is it dangerous?" she said.

"Like any surgery, it involves risks," I said.

"Could you do something—else?" she said.

"I think this is my only option," I said.

"Wow," she said, leaning back in her chair and looking at me thoughtfully.

I looked carefully at her, afraid to see judgment on her face.

Debbie said, "Wow," again, and "okay." And, "When are you doing it? What do we need to do here?" and I was mostly relieved. I could tell anyone. I would tell everyone. This was an exciting thing, and people would be happy for me—everyone seems to be happy when someone loses weight. Everyone loves to say, "You look so good!" There is so much delight, with everyone rejoicing in your triumph, your good fortune, your skills. Everyone would be so happy for me, along with me, besides me.

Debbie listened carefully as I explained that I would need to be out for at least a month, and that I'd have a couple of appointments in the meantime. I'd do whatever was necessary to make sure that things ran smoothly between now and then and in my absence. She said, "Thank you for telling me."

"Thank *you*," I said. I bounced out of my chair. I paused, with my hand on the door to her office, and I looked behind me to make sure the library floor was still quiet. Very quietly I said, "This is really weird." She looked a little startled, and I ducked out of the office.

I called HR immediately to have them messenger me over the forms I'd need to fill out. At the next Reference staff meeting, Debbie announced changes in the Periodicals Desk schedule: The desk would need to be closed for some hours while I was out on medical disability. Everyone's heads swung around and they looked at me.

"I'm okay!" I said. "It's—weight loss surgery." My whole head flushed. I persevered. "It'll take a while to recover."

They all nodded. When the meeting finished I fled back to my desk before anyone could corner me, ask quiet, circumspect questions full of honest concern and burning curiosity. The library was like that— all of us had worked there for years, some of us in the double-digits; all of us expected to be working there until we were forcibly ejected. We settled in amongst each other, wriggling down like chickens packed onto one shelf in a coop.

Coworkers appeared at my desk slowly over the next weeks, and the news slowly spread to the rest of the staff, but no one really talked about it. After a while, everyone knew everything, whether I had told them or not. In the break room the staff and I microwaved our plastic-covered lunches and spoke about when I'd get back as if we had already discussed the fact that I would be gone. They were all librarians, officially and unofficially; they could research both the pros and the cons. They could find the diagrams and the discussions and the medical articles that discussed the surgery's efficacy in treating morbid obesity and the potential risks and drawbacks. They probably knew more than I did.

An entire library of people, six floors of us from basement to rooftop, knew that I was fat, and now they knew that I knew I was fat. It felt like I had finally gotten a long-overdue apology off my chest.

Two months crept by. Two months flew by. At my house, Andy and I talked about my appointment, but only the small details, the background plans, the to-do lists. I got samples of protein shakes that we both tried. We mixed them up in the blender and took careful sips.

"Good god," Andy said, sputtering. "You have to live off this shit for how long?"

"Jus uh fir monh," I said, hanging my tongue out of my mouth as if the fresh air would sterilize it, remove the slightly metallic, chalky taste from my tongue.

"I wouldn't last half that first month," he said.

We talked protein sources, stocked up on measuring cups and small containers and water bottles and a water filter. We talked about clearing out the fridge and making a walking schedule, and all the logistics of what I'd need to have and do after I came home. But we still didn't talk about what I was coming home from.

"I'm going to take a week off work," Andy said. "The first week is going to be hard."

"I'll probably just be sleeping a lot. Maybe you can work from home?"

"Maybe," he said.

"You'll stay here?"

"Of course I will. I will be here the whole time."

"You can pack a suitcase! Or I'll empty you a drawer, if you want?"

He looked startled. "No, I'll just pop home to get my stuff occasionally. Change, shower."

"Okay," I said. I struggled for a moment, and then said, "You can also refill my Percocet."

He didn't ask me if I had gone grocery shopping yet for the things on my dietician's list, so that I could start losing weight before they sliced into my guts. We ordered dinner in every night, and I didn't go to the gym at all. There would be time to worry about that later.

The months crept by, and the months were flying by, and I was slowly telling everyone but my mother about the surgery. I even told the guy at the coffee shop, who looked at me confusedly. When I told my brother, he said, "That's crazy. Have you told Mom?" But I still wasn't ready.

I had two final doctor's appointments, though I didn't really understand what more they needed from me—one more at the surgeon's office, one more at my primary physician's office.

At the surgeon's office, they set me afloat on a raft of paperwork. I was the most well-documented fat person on earth. In a small room on a wide chair, I flipped open the folder. It was filled with a stack of paper as wide as my thumb.

I read quickly, leaping from word to word. Initial each paragraph as you go through, the assistant said. Indicate that you've read and understand the possible risks and complications.

The doctor has explained to me that there are risks and possible undesirable consequences associated with any surgery, as well as risks and possible undesirable consequences associated with the duodenal switch, and these include, but are not limited to:

death **JL**

gastric perforation (a tear in the stomach wall) during or after the procedure that might lead to the need for another surgery **JL**

hospitalization and/or reoperation **JL**

nausea/vomiting **JL**

gastroesophageal reflux (regurgitation) **JL**

spleen or liver damage (sometimes requiring spleen removal) **JL**

damage to major blood vessels, lung problems, thrombosis (blood clots), including pulmonary embolus (blood clots migrating to the heart and lungs) and deep vein thrombosis (blood clots in the legs and/or arms) **JL**

rupture of the wound and perforation of the stomach or esophagus during surgery **JL**

gastritis (inflammation of the stomach) **JL**

hiatal hernia incisional hernia infection redundant skin dehydration diarrhea abnormal stools constipation dyspepsia eructation (belching) cardiospasm (an obstruction of passage of food through the bottom of the esophagus) hematemesis (vomiting of blood) asthenia (fatigue) fever chest pain edema (swelling) paresthesia (abnormal sensation of burning, prickling, or tingling) dysmenorrhea (difficult periods) cholecystitis (gallstones) esophageal ulcer (soreness) wound infection ulceration heartburn gas bloating dehydration regaining of weight anemia vitamin deficiencies and malnutrition atelectasis bile leak bowel obstruction congestive heart failure dehiscence or evisceration depression encephalopathy motility disorders gout incisional and internal hernias intestinal leak kidney failure kidney stones loss of bodily function (including from stroke, heart attack, or limb loss) myocardial infarction (heart attack) organ failure perforations (leaks) of the stomach or intestine causing peritonitis subphrenic abscess or enteroenteric or enterocutaneous fistulas pleural effusions (fluid around the lungs) pneumonia pulmonary edema sepsis or peritonitis stoma stenosis Systemic Inflammatory Response Syndrome (SIRS) ulcer formation urinary tract infections protein mineral deficiencies neuro psychiatric disorders and nerve damage depression low blood sugar vomiting intertriginous dermatitis malodorous gas alopecia **JL JL**

As fast as I could.

Everything I had been avoiding all these months, in all my reading, all in one packet. I skimmed, flipping the pages.

JL, JL, JL.

They weighed me.

"You were—303 when we saw you last. Now you're 313." The doctor looked up from his clipboard.

"I. Oh."

"You need to lose weight before we operate. I can't emphasize that enough. Your liver is fatty, and it makes it difficult for us to see. To maneuver. Taking off some weight will make that so much easier. Exponentially easier. Do you understand?"

I nodded. He slipped his pen into the breast pocket of his lab coat.

I said, "If I don't lose the weight, can you still operate?" and the look he fixed me with was deadly.

"Yes," he said finally.

"I'm going to lose it!" I said, before he could lash me bloody with his disgust and disappointment. "I was just—curious."

He didn't seem to believe me. But he just said, "Have you been exercising?"

"There's a gym at work," I said, perfectly truthfully.

"Good. It's good to get into those habits now. It'll make your life so much easier down the line, believe me."

JL, JL, JL.

I'm very good at not thinking about the things that upset me. I'm very good at pretending everything is going to be a-okay.

Everything was moving so quickly.

the skepticism of Dr. Sartz . . . death's cold
and ominous grip . . . the possibility of regret

A week before surgery.

I had to see my primary care physician. I put it off for as long as
possible. Apparently I was supposed to get baseline stats from him, a general checkup, and bill of good-enough health—a thumbs up that I was
healthy enough for surgery.

I had never seen Dr. Sartz before. He was filling in for the doctor
who was recommended to me by the weight loss surgery forums, someone who was familiar with weight loss surgery, an advocate for it. There
weren't very many doctors who spontaneously suggested weight loss surgery as an option for their patients. According to the weight loss surgery
forums, the doctor that Doctor Sartz was filling in for was the one who
would have cheerfully rubber-stamped my clean bill of health if I looked
reasonably upright and like I was breathing fairly regularly.

Dr. Sartz, however, didn't seem to have a rubber stamp anywhere
on him. He was tall, and ironed flat, and neutral all over—beige from
his hair to his oxfords. Nudging the door shut behind him, he looked me
up and down. I was wearing two gowns, one forward and one backward,

because a single gown didn't fit all the way around me. My feet seemed very white and far away, as if I were dangling them underwater by the edge of a pond. I was just a week away from surgery, and I hadn't lost any weight. I was just a week away. I handed him the form he was supposed to sign and initial (JL, JL, JL). He threw it onto the counter next to him and took a seat with his hands on his knees, looking up at me.

"So," he said. "Weight loss surgery." His tone of voice said, "So! You're kind of an idiot." His flat eyes skated over my bare feet, up to my knees, across the width of my hips, hanging over each side of the examination table. He opened the cover of my medical records folder instead of meeting my eyes.

"Yes," I said, and my stomach clenched.

"Why are you doing this?" he said. He slapped my folder closed. I was annoyed he hadn't even read anything in there. He looked at me.

My jaw flapped. This again. "I—I think. I need to do it. I think it's a good tool. I think." The paper was crinkling under my butt.

He picked up the form and scanned it. "How are you feeling about this decision?" He looked up at me over his glasses, and our eyes finally met.

An endless moment, while the question rocked through me.

I shocked myself with the flood of tears that soaked my eyelashes and spilled onto my hands in my lap. "Scared," I said. My mouth was moving before I knew what was coming. "I'm so scared." My shoulders hunched, my entire body sagged down on that paper-lined table. "I need to do it. I think. But what if I die?" More surprise. When had I ever thought about that? When had I been anything but fully and completely focused on an imaginary me so far in the future that she looked tiny from all the way back here? I bit down on a sob. "It's so selfish," I said, amazed by the unexpected revelation pouring out of me, "if I die during surgery because I wanted to lose weight." I was whispering at the end and the doctor was leaning forward, looking at me. He stood, paced to the sink, paced back. His heel squeaked.

"You don't have to do it," he said abruptly. "If you have any doubts, you shouldn't do it."

Doubts? These weren't doubts. I didn't have doubts. I couldn't be more sure of anything. I was just worried. I nodded.

"Put it off for a year," he said. "Take your time. It's not going anywhere."

I looked up at him, and he was regarding me with a sort of skeptical forbearance.

He was supposed to be soothing me. Petting me. Telling me everything was going to be okay and I would be just fine and surgery was perfectly safe. My stomach twisted and I shifted, the paper tearing.

"I want to do it," I said. Full stop.

He sighed.

"I want to do it," I said again.

"Have you tried dieting? How much do you weigh?" He flipped through my chart.

I didn't say anything. I kept my chin down, and there were my feet, all the way down at the end of my legs.

He blew more air out of his nose and pulled the blood pressure cuff off of the wall, strapped it around my arm and pumped, laid me back and probed my stomach. I was too wide for the table. My arms hung down on either side of me. I stared up at the acoustic tile of the ceiling, counting the black holes while he pushed his fingers into my flesh. He watched me haul myself back up and then he examined my glands, looked into my ears and my throat and my eyes. He tested my reflexes and listened to my heart. He scribbled down notes.

"You're healthy," he said, tossing his pen down on the counter behind him.

"The form that I brought in? I need to have that signed."

He turned back to the counter and shuffled through the paper in my folder. "You think about this hard," he said over his shoulder. He turned and jabbed at me. "You don't need to do this," he said. "But if you do, come back in a couple of months. I want to see how you're doing. Okay?"

I nodded.

He was gone, and I was left alone in the examining room to struggle out of my two hospital gowns and back into my pants. I had a sudden and fixed feeling that at some point—two months from now, or six months, or a year or two or five—I would out-of-the-blue remember this precise moment in time, this gray-walled examination room, the feel of cold tile on the soles of my feet, the zipper of my pants scraping hard across the soft flesh of my belly, the smell of rubbing alcohol, the release paper folded up in my bag, the moment that had just passed. The instant where I could have opened my mouth and said *hold on*, or *wait up*, or *is this really what I want?*

The moment where I shook my head and instead said, "No. I want to do it."

Standing in that examining room, half-dressed and damp-cheeked and hot-eyed under the flickering lights, I wondered if this would be the moment I would always regret.

Chapter 18

like a meatloaf in a pan . . . lies I tell my
mother . . . cleaning out my system . . . going
under the knife

Three hours before surgery.

On the morning of my stomach amputation, the alarm went off at
4:00 AM. I sat on the edge of the bed and scuffed my feet along the hotel
carpet. It was flat and rough and slightly sticky. I was in the closest hotel
to Good Samaritan Hospital in San Jose, and the cheapest.

Weight loss surgery was an hour away. My hands were shaking.
Andy was still asleep with his face smashed into the pillow, his hair a silvery poof. I shuffled over to the bathroom, ducking my head against the
sharp halo of the overhead light, and twisted on the water in the tub.

I thought, *This is the last time I will turn on a tap as a person with a
whole digestive system.* I snorted and flicked on the shower.

I lowered myself slowly, painfully, carefully to the floor of the tub. I
was wedged, I thought, just like a meatloaf in a pan. My hips and thighs
filled up the tub from side to side, trapping the water behind me. Folded
in half as best I could, the heaps of my stomach mounding up and getting

in the way, I stretched down to work my disposable razor carefully around the fleshy parts of my ankles, the divots of my knees, one leg and then the other leg. I shaved carefully, as if everything relied on the perfect silky smoothness of skin my surgeon wasn't going to go anywhere near. But there might be a shin emergency, or an ankle crisis. Someone might see my legs. Someone might care. I cared.

This is the last time I'll shave my legs with an entire stomach. Who needed an entire stomach? I obviously didn't do very well with the one I had for thirty-two years.

I heard the door open, and then there was a rush of air that rattled the shower curtain. "You're up so early," Andy said around a yawn, his voice echoing in the bathroom. "Are you okay?"

"Don't open the curtain," I said quickly.

"I won't," he said. I heard the toilet lid flip up.

"They said to shower," I said. "I needed a shower. I feel like I smell like—like horrible things."

"You don't smell like horrible things," he said. Toilet seat back down. He didn't flush.

"I've been pooping," I said. For three days, twenty-four hours each day, I had been drinking milk of magnesia, pooping, drinking water, drinking milk of magnesia, and then sitting on the toilet again to poop.

"Oh honey. Well. You're all clean inside then, right?"

That was pretty much how it felt. On the outside I was sweaty and grubby, but inside, I had been taken by the head and the ankles, stretched flat and then scrubbed down hard, until I was clean and hollow and practically sterile. You could eat a last meal off of my insides, before you carved out a slice of my stomach and whacked out half my intestines. And I wasn't sure if that feeling in my so-empty stomach was terror or hunger. Maybe that had been my problem all along?

My heart lurched. I hung on to my disposable razor. The water was getting cold.

"Are you sure this is what you want to do?" Andy said.

We were both very still for the longest moment, each of us on either side of the curtain. The sound of the shower.

He had never asked me that before. He had always said, every time, *Okay*. And, *I support you*, and, *If this is what you want to do*. Even, *I'm nervous, but if you think it's the right choice*. But he had never said, *Maybe this isn't a good idea*.

"Yes," I finally said.

"Okay."

"I'll be out in a minute," I said. "Do you need to shower?"

"If you want to change your mind, we'll get right back on Caltrain," he said.

I clutched my legs, sitting at the bottom of the tub. Maybe I was wedged more like a muffin in a tin. I liked muffins better. "No," I managed. "I'm okay."

The door swung shut, and a rush of cold air plastered the curtain to my skin. I waited for a moment, then hauled myself up off the floor of the tub. In a rush, all the water that had built up behind me poured around my legs, filled the tub, swirled down the drain. I scrubbed myself clean with hotel soap, a tiny bar that smelled like perfume tastes in the back of your throat when someone's wearing too much. I ran the tiny little bar over the slope of my shoulders, the expanse of my belly. The soap was miniature, and I was a giant.

I wondered when I'd be allowed to shower again, and I wondered how soon it would be before I was different, and soaping up an entirely alien body. And oh, hey. *This will be the last time I shower with my entire stomach.* I started giggling and inhaled a noseful of water.

"When do we have to leave?" Andy called.

"Five," I said, choking. "Five!"

"Okay. We have to leave soon," he said, and I could hear him pacing back and forth in front of the door. "I'm going to go have a cigarette," he said abruptly. The door to the room closed behind him with a steel-reinforced thud.

The towel didn't fit around my hips. I rubbed my hair dry—it was flat and orange. On Halloween, it had been spiky and red. I swiped the water off my arms and wondered if the surgeon cared if I moisturized. If anyone would care if I moisturized.

Andy came back in when was I elbow-deep in the little roll-on suitcase, wearing stretchy pants and an oversized sweater, some of the last clothes I had left that fit.

"I have my nightgown," I said as the door closed behind him, "and baby wipes and face wipes for my face. I don't need a comb. Here are my slippers. Maybe I should have brought more books, but I can get some from the gift store. They always have books at the gift store."

"You'll be on so much morphine you won't even know what a book is," he said. He smiled at me with his sweet smile. He smelled like cigarette smoke, even from across the room. He must have smoked more than one. His glasses were a little crooked. He said, "You're going to be okay." He looked less certain than he sounded.

"Of course I am!" I said. "Did I forget anything?"

He came and sat on the bed next to me. "Did you bring your pillow?"

"It wouldn't fit."

"That's so sad."

"I know!"

"I have everyone's number," he said. "I have your mom's number."

I stuffed everything back into my suitcase and zippered it quickly. It would be the last time I zippered a suitcase as a person with a whole digestive system. Andy put his arm around my shoulder and I stopped and sighed.

"You don't have to call my mom."

"Jen."

"It'll be fine."

"You still haven't told her!"

"I didn't know what to say!"

"Jen. You have to tell her. You have to call her right now."

"It's too early!"

"It's 7:30 in New Jersey. It's not too early."

"I can't," I burst out. I sprung from the bed and flew across the room. I leaned against the big, heavy curtains that covered the window, and I looked at him plaintively. "I can't. Please don't make me call her." I was dizzy from not eating, from evacuating everything from my body, from standing up too quickly, from rushing. Everything was so ridiculously delicate. I couldn't talk to her.

Andy stood across from me in his jacket. He frowned, and I hated to see him frowning. He said, "I am not going to call her and say, 'Oh, hello Mrs. Larsen! I'm fine, how are you, yeah, your daughter died on the operating table this morning.'"

"You won't have to!"

"Please?"

"I'll email her," I said in a rush. "I'll email her right now." I rushed to the desk and yanked his work laptop out of his bag. He looked down at me as I crammed myself into the narrow armchair. "It's too early to call. What should I say?"

"That you're getting weight loss surgery this morning?" He sounded as close to peeved as he ever got. He never got angry at me.

I didn't answer him. I typed, "Dear Mom, I'm just writing to let you know." I backspaced all the way to "Mom." I closed the laptop. He laughed. He reached over and flipped it back open.

"Come on, now," he said.

I typed. I pressed send, and closed the laptop with a snap. "There."

"Thank you."

"I told her I have diverticulitis."

He snorted. "Oh my god."

"I'm sorry!"

"What did you say?"

I opened the laptop up again, and let him lean over my shoulder to read.

He read, "I am heading into the hospital this morning. It's routine intestinal surgery for a condition called diverticulitis. I'll be just fine. Please don't worry. I'm sorry I didn't tell you earlier. Andy will call you when I'm out and will let you know that everything went fine. I'll have my phone off. I love you very much."

He put his hand on the top of my head. He started laughing. "Do you even know what diverticulitis is?"

"Not really?"

"She's going to kill me when I call her."

"I'm sorry," I said. I pushed the chair back and collapsed onto the bed. I folded up with my face in the pillow. Andy lay down next to me and rubbed my back. I sniffed, and sniffed again. "It's so stupid. I know. I'm just afraid of what she'll say."

Getting weight loss surgery, after thirty years of being my mother's daughter, was like I was saying I didn't want to look like my mother. It was like I was saying, *I don't want to be your daughter. I don't want to be you.*

"I'll tell her later," I said into the pillow.

"Don't you dare die on the operating table," Andy said. "I don't want to be the one to tell her."

"Do you think I'm going to die?" I rolled over and clutched at him. Those reams and reams of paper I had skimmed—*You may die, you may die, you may die. Okay,* I had said. *Okay, okay, okay. JL, JL, JL.*

"No," he said. "Don't be silly." He kissed my forehead. "Let's go, okay? Let's get this over with."

I sat in the bathroom outside the surgery prep room to go just once more before I changed into my hospital gown. Andy paced the hallway outside the door, up and down. He had been hovering close to my elbow, as if afraid I was going to faint. As if I was going to ask him to sweep me away, saying *quick, let's go,* and he had to be ready at a moment's notice. Alone in the bathroom, I didn't cry, though I had expected to.

I made him turn around when I changed into my surgical gown. When they slipped the IV into my hand, I caught my breath, and Andy squeezed my other hand. He looked sleepy and dazed and a little unbelieving that we were in the hospital, between two curtained walls. Up and down the row, people on either side of me were being swabbed, fitted with IVs and caps and gowns, and signing the same kinds of forms I was signing, getting ready for their own surgeries scheduled for seven in the morning, an hour and a half from now, which was not that far away at all.

Andy hadn't said much. He followed me into the waiting room, and then down the hall, obediently turning away when the nurse whisked the curtain closed and waited for me to change into my gown. He sat patiently through the paperwork and the signing and the questions they had for me. He told me it would be okay.

"You can come all the way up to the operating wing," the nurse said kindly to Andy as she capped off my IV and strung the tube up on the pole. "She's going to be just fine," she said, and patted his hand.

"She better be!" he said, and fake-angrily shook his fist. "Or I'll give her what-for!"

"I'll be okay," I told him. What I wanted to say was, *I'm so sorry I have to do this.*

I hadn't told him about my breakdown in the doctor's office, or the doctor's suggestion that I put this off or even forget it. I had gone home and eaten Chinese food with him.

Did I think it was worth it, to risk my life for this operation? I thought it was. I thought I was being brave.

But I think the truth, the absolute and unvarnished truth that I didn't let myself consider—that I didn't even recognize right then—was that I really didn't expect to be risking my life. I was afraid that something would go wrong, but there was an iron-solid core of me that was utterly convinced that nothing could go wrong. I wanted it so badly, and complications were rare, and nothing *could* happen when I was so focused on everything going correctly, emerging triumphantly, dropping all the weight easily, and moving smoothly into a fresh new life. I wanted the surgery, I would get the surgery, and it would be just fine. Statistics for complications, injuries, death, things gone horribly wrong—I looked at them complacently. I wouldn't be among the point zero one. I couldn't be.

But I was still afraid, because surgery is terrifying, and the needle in my hand was terrifying, and the plastic hat covering my head and my surgeon coming in and glancing at my chart and glancing at me and saying some words—I didn't even know what it was he said, and he was gone, and the next time I'd see him was at the end of a knife. It was terrifying.

Sitting up in the hospital bed, my whole body trembled and jerked. Terror was filling the empty space the laxatives had left behind. The nurse noticed and slid a warmed blanket on top of me, then another one. Another nurse came and fitted me with inflatable cuffs that covered my legs from ankle to knee. They pulsed slowly, pushing the blood through me, discouraging clots. They were disconcerting.

"What are you going to do while I'm in surgery?" I said to Andy. His knee was bouncing up and down.

"Go find a bar," he said, and laughed, and I laughed too.

"No, really," he said. "I'm sure there's got to be one around here somewhere."

"You should," I said. "I'm going to be okay, though."

"I know," he said. "But a drink will help me believe it."

"Do you need to go smoke, or anything? You should go if you need to."

"I want to wait," he said grimly, and I said thank you. I didn't feel like I was close to crying, but I thought he might be, and I said, "I'm sorry." He shook his head, and I said it again, and put my head on his shoulder. We stayed like that for just a few minutes, and then the nurse was there, clunking down bars and twisting knobs and pulling down the side rails and asking me if I was ready to go.

"We want to have you walk in," she said. "Maximize the amount of time you have your full circulation. We think it's best this way."

"Oh, that's kind of cool!" I said, and looked at Andy, who didn't look like he thought it was very cool at all. I swung my legs over awkwardly, and the nurse rushed over to unhook my leg compression sleeves. She handed me a second robe, one that snapped at the shoulder, and helped me into it to make sure my back was covered.

"There!" she said. "You're all set! They're waiting for you."

I took Andy's hand and looked at the nurse. "Can he come? He can come into the operating room, right? Hang out and watch, make sure everything goes okay?"

She laughed. "He can go up to the doors of the operating wing," she said. She handed my bag of personal effects to Andy. I tucked myself into his side and took small steps, the nurse pushing the bed behind us slowly.

"Listen," I said. "If I wake up after this and I say anything like, 'What the hell did I just do to myself?' I want you to hit me, okay?"

"I'll just tell them to save all your guts. In a bowl! So they can put them back," he said.

"Oh," I said. "No! Oh, I won't want them back. Remind me that I won't want them back, okay, please?"

"Okay," he said.

We went through some double doors and then down the hallway to the next set of doors. The nurse stopped us.

"Here's where he gets off," she said, and smiled at both of us.

"Okay," I said. "I'll see you in a few hours, all right? Be careful. Have a good afternoon. Don't worry so much. I'll be okay. You just take care of yourself, too?" I put my hands on either side of his face. The scruff of his beard was soft on my palms. "Don't do that," I said, running my thumb under his eye, across his cheek.

"You take care," he said. "You be careful. I'll be here when you get out." He took my glasses and tucked them into his pocket, and everything went Impressionistic. He kissed me. I clung to him for a moment, and then he let me go and turned. The nurse pushed open the doors in front of us, and when I glanced behind us, he was a blur halfway down the hall, and the doors were swinging shut behind us, and I was about to have weight loss surgery.

The room was bright and huge. A tall table covered with fabric or paper stood in the center, ringed by equipment radiating out to the corners of the room. There were machines and tables draped with cloth, tubes running from one station to the next. The fixture overhead looked like the lights of a spaceship descending, and made me squint. "You could tan in here," I said, and the nurse grinned.

"We have to," she said. "We work a lot. Now you're going to need to take off your robe and hop on the table. Can you do that?"

"No," I said. "Oh, no, I can't do that. No." Rushing, blurry adrenaline panic. I was shaking again. I took hold of the surgical table, padded with what looked like sheets. I couldn't possibly move. My knees were numb and my heart had gone missing entirely, and I could not stop the sobs that had started to roll up out of that empty space. "No, I can't, please." I held my robe tight against me, and the needle in my hand pulled at my skin.

"It's okay, honey. You jump up here and just take off just one robe now. Then we'll get you covered with these blankets here, see? And you'll wiggle out of the second one nice and easy. Okay?"

Everything was dark around the edges. The nurse taking me by the elbow, her voice firm. "Hop up now, honey, there you go." The nurse gently tugged on the snaps at my shoulder, pulling away the gown. The rush of cold air, her hand tugging my other gown closed as far as it could go. "Now lie back and we'll put these blankets on you. A couple more, there, you'll stop shivering soon. They're heated." I lay there pinned underneath the warmth and weight and nodded frantically to let her know I was just fine. She busied herself next to the table with a brisk purposefulness that was comforting. I stared up at the enormous disk of light above my head. My mouth shook when I tried to form words. My tears were still streaming down my face, into my ears.

The nurse appeared at my head, leaning down to look into my face. I saw the pores in her nose, her kind smile. Around her head was a corona of light. The edges of the room were far away and seemed dark. The blankets were heavy and warm on top of me. I breathed in and out.

The nurse said, "Now, can you wiggle out of that second robe for me? Just like that. That's right, honey, now shh. It's okay." I breathed in, and breathed out again. "We're going to put this mask on you now, okay? It's just oxygen, just breathe deep. Can you do that for me?" The mask over my nose smelled of sterilized rubber, of strange gases. "That's good. Now, here's the anesthesiologist who is going to give you something to relax. It's going to feel like your veins are very warm, isn't that right?"

The anesthesiologist's face appeared above mine. His eyes were crinkled above his mask. He looked like a medical ninja. He said, "Hello, Ms. Jennifer. Is Jennifer okay?" I nodded, my head rocking on the table. Of course I was okay. Calling me Jennifer, that was okay, too. I wasn't sure what he meant, and I wanted to ask him.

"Just keep breathing for me. Let me get that." He dabbed my cheeks quickly with a folded up cloth, turned, and started to fiddle with my IV. "We're going to get you settled down now. This is going to feel nice and easy. We're going to ask you some questions, just a few questions, and you just need to be patient with us, and relax, and breathe, and then you'll go to sleep and when you wake up, it'll be a whole brand-new day, won't it?" Literally, figuratively. I nodded again, formed my lips around answers, clutched at the blankets on top of me, closed my eyes against the bright light that shone down hard. The room was huge, and I was almost small on the table, under the mound of heavy blankets.

"It's time. Count back from ten for me now, Jennifer."

"Ten," I said. I breathed in deeply, closed my eyes. "Nine," I said. "Eight."

Surgery.

When you come out of anesthesia, it feels like you've got your eyes closed even when they're open, because everything is vague and dark and far away. Voices faded in, and then out, and I heard someone talking to me, and then talking about me, and then talking near me. A laugh—Andy's laugh, oh, that was him, he was here, and I was here, too. I was here! I had made it. I was alive. I moved my arm, which was only coincidentally attached to the end of my shoulder. It seemed to respond, far away in the dark. I tried to lift it, to touch my stomach, feel the wounds that had been punched into me, but I couldn't control something that was so distant and alien.

Andy said, "Is she awake?" and I felt him come closer and I opened my eyes wider, but I still couldn't really see anything. I said, "Hi. Hello, I'm here," and he laughed again, that laugh that meant he was right there with me, and his hand was on my wrist. On the other side of the bed, a woman's voice asking me questions about nausea, and dizziness, and how was I feeling, and could I take a deep breath for her and then cough? I tried, but nothing happened, and I said, "Oh, look at me and all the things I can do, what?" Andy laughed, and the woman said, "She'll be out of it for a while."

Then we were moving, the bed swaying and doors opening. Vague impressions of bright lights overhead and darker corridors, and then my room. I lifted my head and opened my eyes as far as they could go and I saw Andy, in his baseball cap with his grizzled beard, and he said, "You're awake!"

"Thank you for waiting," I said. The fog was clearing up all around the corners and things were brighter. "My glasses? Can I wear my glasses?"

I put them on and he came into focus. He looked exhausted. The nurse bustled around and said things to me about my catheter, and how I could manage my pain by pressing a button to access a bucket full of morphine, and how to call a nurse, and how they were going to have me up and walking just as soon as they cleared all my vitals.

"Morphine!" Andy said in tones of wonder.

"Excited about morphine," I mumbled. My throat was so raw. My voice sounded crumpled and discarded. The nurse had told me about the breathing tube, but I couldn't imagine a tube threaded down through my throat. I couldn't imagine surgery. I couldn't imagine that such a huge chunk of my insides was gone.

The nurse left, and Andy sat next to me, dropped his forehead down briefly to my hand.

"Are you okay?" I said. "Are you doing okay?"

"I should be asking you that," he said. "It took five hours. They told me it was only supposed to take max, three."

"I'm sorry!" I said.

He laughed. "I blame the doctor," he said. "The nurses got sick of me. I kept coming up, asking for news. They said they didn't know anything. I thought I was going to have to sneak back and find you. Demand to know what was going on. I was going to give them some what-for."

It hurt my stomach to laugh, a deep-down pulling that made me cough unexpectedly. I put my hand to my stomach, touched the bumps of surgical tape, five punctures sealed back over. It hurt, a faraway ache. Everything was wrecked and sore and uncomfortable.

"I made it," I said.

"I know," he said, and took my hand again.

"I'm sorry," I said.

This time he said, "I know."

"Did you call my mom?"

He grimaced. "Yes. She's so mad at you. She wanted to fly out here right away. I had to talk her down."

I laid my head back and closed my eyes. "She'll get over it."

He sighed. "Are you going to tell her?"

"No," I said.

He jumped up. "Do you mind if I go have a cigarette?"

"Yes! Go, go. M'okay. I have drugs." It felt like thumbs were pushing behind my eyeballs, and I just wanted to lie back and close my eyes and drift off in the haze that was still hanging around me.

He flicked on the television for me and kissed my forehead, set the remote by my hand. I rested my palms on my stomach, which was enormous and inflated—for laproscopic surgery, I had been informed, they pump your cavity full of gas to make everything easy to see. My surgery had happened, and I had passed my leak test—that's what the nurse said, that I was just fine and sealed tight, after all those incisions—my stomach cut down and hemmed up the side with neat stitches. My intestines ripped from their moors and reattached in brand-new places. All my Frankensteined guts were neat and tight in their new homes, and nothing was going anywhere.

The television was turned to CNN. While I was sleeping, the Democrats had taken over the House. Scrolling letters at the bottom of the screen—Democratic majority, Democratic majority, Democratic majority. That is what I had woken up to, and I laughed at the wonderfulness of it. The Democrats had stormed the House, and my god, I had gotten weight loss surgery.

I lay there with my eyes closed, CNN commentators jabbering in the background, my hands on my stomach. I carefully examined how I felt. Enormous; inflated, yes. Tired. Sore. Aching. Strange. Lighter? Empty? Like I had been scraped out with an ice cream scooper. Like I had been shaken loose of my moorings and could drift away.

I wondered how much weight I had lost already, how much muscle and intestine had been dragged out of my body and discarded. I wondered when it would start. It was about to start. It was starting. It had started.

part two:
the imaginary after

I have chosen surgical weight loss for the improvement of my health, my well-being, and the course of my life.

* I realize that surgical weight loss is just a tool in the process of losing weight.

* I realize that I must learn to use this tool to my best advantage.

* In learning to use this tool for changing my life and my lifestyle I must commit to participating in my own education and applied learning.

* I realize that success will depend on my choices in changing my life, my habits, my attitude, and my behaviors regarding food and the part food plays in my life.

* I will actively participate in my own recovery.

* I will attend a minimum of twelve support group meetings a year.

* I will notice what is happening to my body and emotions over the course of my recovery and subsequent weight loss.

* I promise myself that I will do everything within my scope to make the changes necessary for optimum success, using surgical weight loss surgery as a tool for change.

Signed_____

Date_____

Chapter 19

the secret post-surgery handbook . . . hot,
half-digested protein . . . my body as an alien
from hell

The first month.

They said it was going to be pretty rough, recovery from surgery.
The packet they sent home with me to add to my collection of packets,
made it clear that I would be tired, but that I needed to exercise, drink
my protein shakes and as much water as I could handle in slow sips all
day, and keep my incisions squeaky clean. And that sounded reasonable
to me. Easy, even. Recovery from surgery would be like a month-long spa
vacation from work, during which I'd lay back on a pile of pillows and
watch myself reduce in size in a very satisfactory manner. Lots of naps,
lots of leisurely sitting around, lots of being smug and getting skinny.

But soon—ten minutes in, ten hours in, two days later, one week
later—I wanted to take a thick black permanent marker and cross out the
misleading paragraphs, scrawl all over that packet of after-surgery information in big block letters:

"Hey! You with the weight loss surgery. What we actually *meant* to say, when we said you'd be 'tired,' was this: You will be *exhausted*. You will feel like you've been beaten from head to shoulder with a sock stuffed full of stale Ding Dongs. You will walk to the kitchen and want to lie down. You will walk back to the futon and want to take a nap. You will be fussy, and cranky, and tired, and you will find yourself napping like the whiny toddler you've become.

"You will experience heavy-limbed, body-lugging misery. You will feel twice as big as you did before you ever went into surgery: enormous, lumbering, ponderous. Dragging your weight around will feel like an impossible task, but it's something that must be done to prevent embolisms and clots and other horrible things that could destroy you in an instant. 'Oh god,' you will say. 'I don't want to go for a walk. Please don't make me walk to the corner and back.' And you will cry, because everything feels insurmountable, but you will have to drag yourself out the door anyway, and probably in your nightgown, because the idea of lifting your arms over your head will be laughable. So you will walk out of the door in your nightgown and all the way to the corner and a part of you will feel like nothing at all has changed. And then you will stand there and you will cry, because your house is so far away. But you will turn around and shuffle back in your flip-flops, aching all over and keeping your head down because it will be too difficult to lift your chin.

"And when you get back to your house you will crawl into your bed and pile the pillows around you as best you can (it will still hurt to stretch, to turn, to lift even a folded blanket) and you will fall into as deep a sleep as you ever have. You will wake up four hours later with a silver trail of drool dried down your chin and wish you could go back to sleep, but it will be time to get up again and drink a vile protein shake that makes you nauseous.

"But then, everything will make you nauseous: the smell of food will be wretched, but that will be okay, because you may only drink those protein shakes anyway. You thought they tasted pretty terrible before surgery? Somehow after surgery they become chalkier, thinner, more gritty, and they leave a film in your mouth that will make you need to brush your teeth immediately. If you aren't too tired to brush your teeth.

"After drinking a shake made with fat-free milk, you will feel full to the point of vomiting, and you'll feel nauseated for hours. If you make your shake with water, it will take on the consistency of a gruel that will coat the back of your throat and make it hard to swallow. The fruit-flavored protein shakes will taste like Kool-Aid that is trying to kill you, and they will make you gag.

"You will have to drink a lot of water, too. Warm water will be vile and too thick; cold water will make your new tiny little belly spasm. A gulp will fill you all the way up. Another gulp on top of that will threaten to make your stomach overflow and send everything rocketing back up your throat and out of your face.

"Nothing will taste right, and it will seem entirely possible that nothing will ever taste right ever again. Worse, the smell of the hospital will cling to you for days, a thick, sticky organic smell that will seem to linger inside your nose and taint everything. You'll remember that smell for years after you leave the hospital; scent memory is the strongest kind of memory there is, you know.

"You will have to poop a lot. Are you surprised? It will seem surprising, since you'll be consuming so little. What little goes into you comes right back through you, and it will be uncomfortable. It will remind you of being sick, that sensation of looseness in your bowels. You don't want to turn and look at what just happened there, but you do. You will look into the toilet, and the word you will think is 'pile.' The color will ruin for you your favorite sweater, the pretty beige one.

"The fact that poop and its consistency is something that occupies any portion of your brain will drive you a little bit nuts, but you'll be too tired to care much. You'll hurt too much to care, and the liquid Vicodin will only help so much. Mostly it will make you even crankier about being so achy.

"You'll flush, light the candle again—you really ought to just leave it burning all day, because when you're not pooping, you'll be farting and when you're not farting, you'll be pooping, and then it will be time for your walk again.

"Your chest will hurt and your wounds will be red and irritated, even though you will keep them clean and dry them thoroughly and wear loose clothes. You'll have pains in your shoulder and neck that the doctor will assure you are simply the gas they used in the operation making its way out of your body, and you'll be trying to figure out what these noises are in your stomach and your intestines, these cramps and rumbles and sounds. Your body will be alien to you.

"You won't know when you're full. That feeling of hot, half-digested protein shakes pooling in your stomach, sloshing into your esophagus and flooding your mouth, that is a feeling you would do anything to avoid, but it will take time to figure out how. What is enough? When is enough? It will seem to change every time you open your mouth. Sometimes it's a sip and sometimes it's two sips and sometimes it's three sips. You will get tired of being sick.

"You won't be getting enough protein, and you'll be frantic about it, about getting enough water in you, enough sustenance, all your vitamins, all the pills you're supposed to be taking. It won't be enough. It will feel too hard.

"That's just too bad.

"Now go for your walk, and then come back and make a protein shake and stop your bitching. This first week, you've already lost thirteen pounds. Next week you'll lose twelve more. Eventually you'll see it in your face, when you look at yourself in the mirror, in the fit of your shirt, in that feeling you get when you know you're just a little bit lighter. You'll take another walk and then take another nap and you'll keep doing that, over and over, because that's what you've got to do, and it won't be forever.

"Soon you'll be able to focus on something outside the immediate demands and exhaustions of your body, your stomach, your new set of guts.

"Soon your focus will widen and swing out and you'll be a reasonable human being again—probably. Hopefully.

"Drink your protein shake."

more lies I tell my mother . . . things are looking up . . . pants return

I was home. Edith had rented a car and driven all the way down to San Jose to pick Andy and me up and drive us back to San Francisco. I dozed upright in the back of the car, swaying gently as we took the curves of the highway, and then I was home. There was a gorgeous bouquet of flowers slowly wilting on my dining room table, sent by my friends. They were unaccountably glad I was alive. I was glad, too.

From the hospital I had taken a signed contract from the nutritional counselor (*I realize that surgical weight loss is just a tool*) and Barry the Bariatric bear, a stuffed animal who was both for hugging to minimize my abdominal pain when I coughed and for reminding me that someone was always watching me, with beady button eyes, to make sure I followed the rules.

These were strange weeks. I slept, and time jumped forward in fits and starts, but nothing seemed to change. I'd wake up, gag on my protein shake, fuss that I didn't want to take a walk, go take a walk anyway, come home, take a swig of my liquid Vicodin, and take another nap.

My mother had called Andy a dozen times when I was in the

hospital, and was still calling for regular updates. Andy had been picking up the phone and telling her I was tired. This afternoon, on my two-week surgery anniversary, he stood over me in the bedroom, holding the phone to me. "It's your mom," he said pointedly. He stood there and looked at me. He had always yielded, given way, let me slide by. This time, he stood there and held the phone out.

"Tell her just one second," I said, and hauled myself up. All the muscles in my abdomen were clenched and aching—it felt like they were pulled taut, and would snap if I made too sudden a move. It was hard to turn over, to lift myself into a standing position, to stand for very long. But once I was upright it was hard to want to go through the rigmarole of letting myself back down into a sitting position. Andy tried to help, but I waved him off. I took a deep breath and took the phone from Andy. My mother's voice was weepy and thin.

"I'm just fine," I told her. "Mom, I'm okay. You know, it's major surgery. So I'm going to be out of it for a while," I said. "Just sore. But the doctor says I'm going to be completely okay. Diverticulitis is easy to treat. It's just that any abdominal surgery is going to be complex, you know." I was still out of breath from sitting up, and I didn't believe myself, either. I couldn't think of anything else to say about diverticulitis.

My aunt said she knew loads and loads about it and had told my mother I was certain to die a terrible, septic death if I was not careful, and my mother believed her, because my mother is a good sister and because my mother believes that terrible things can happen all the time. My mother believes in the helplessness of the individual and the loving capriciousness of a god who knows what is best but doesn't want to tell us what that is.

I said, "My friend Jen Wade, who is a scientist—she is a *biologist*—says I will be just fine. Truly, Mom. I swear."

Andy sat at the dining room table in the wake of the shedding floral arrangement, in front of his work laptop. He put his chin on his fist, listening to my side of the conversation. He shook his head at me and I glared.

"Andy is taking good care of me," I said, glaring back at him. I eased onto the futon, wincing. "I'm okay," I said to my mother. "You don't need to come out. But thanks, Mom." I had to get off the phone before I got impatient, angry, said something rude. Eventually, surely, I'd be happy and not a cranky, aching brat. I would be more patient. I'd be able to talk to her. Maybe I'd even be able to tell her the truth. Maybe she'd forgive me when I surprised her with how much had changed, and how happy I was.

Right then it didn't feel like anything had changed for the better. Or that any of this achiness or soreness or tiredness had any real cause. Sometimes, when I lay down for a nap, I stayed very still and concentrated on my insides, tried to *feel* my stomach, its size and proportions. Trace my intestines, figure out if I could tell that something had been altered inside me. I wondered if people who donated a lobe of their lung, or had their appendixes removed, or woke up in a bathtub of ice with a note taped to their chest that said "call the hospital," could tell that there was a missing space inside them. I wondered what rushed in to fill that hole that was left behind. I stacked my hands on top of my stomach and closed my eyes and didn't feel much different.

A month later, I thought I could stand the idea of pants. Our walks around the block had gotten a little longer. Andy said, "We're not turning here?" when we reached the corner, and I said, "No! One more block!" and I marched on as if I could walk to the end of the earth. We got home and I fell into bed immediately. But time had snapped back into shape, and I was feeling more alert, less irritable. More like myself. Things did not smell so much like the hospital, anymore—as if I had shed that layer of skin that had absorbed the stink of anesthesia and sickness and sterilization and all the fluids that were put into me, came out of me.

"I can do this!" I told Andy when I woke up one morning at a reasonable hour, rolled over gingerly, slowly, and found myself resting on my side without that terrible, hollow ache that I imagined was caused by my organs swinging loose in the vast, empty cavity of my midsection, stretching out and banging into one another.

"Good!" Andy said. "Go take your vitamins."

"In a minute," I said, pushing my face into the pillow and enjoying the sensation of being almost like a normal person who could move her body in normal ways. My bulk felt as unwieldy as ever, the size of me and the weight even harder to maneuver and navigate with the fatigue that seemed to follow me around. But I got up and I took my vitamins the way I always took my vitamins. I looked deep into the heart of the silky vat of protein powder and thought about just putting it up my nose but I mixed a shake anyway. I went and took my walk around the block, and it was almost like my life had assembled itself into a normal shape. Jen Wade emailed that afternoon, as if she knew I was turning a corner, and wrote, "How are you? Would you like to meet up?" I said, "Yes," and I meant it, the way I always did, but this time I followed up on my desire with action. I put my pants on.

"Are you sure you're okay? Can you walk that far by yourself? Do you want money for a cab? Or I can walk down with you. Are you sure you want to go out? You can just tell her you're feeling tired. I mean, it's about your bedtime soon, anyway," Andy said as I carefully and with great deliberation wedged my feet into a pair of flat shoes.

It was almost 7:00 PM. I made a face at him. "I'm okay. I want to go. It'll be good for me, right?" I was looking forward to being alone, and being outside and awake after dark. I felt like I was kneeling over a rabbit hole, thrusting my arm in deep and hauling back out yet another piece of my life that had squirmed away from me. I was already different. I was drinking water; the idea of Diet Pepsi nauseated me. The idea of Chinese food was a strange and foreign one. The idea of staying home on the futon and ignoring my phone was shameful. Such tiny things, such elation.

I set out a full half hour early, to make sure my shuffling would get me over the five blocks with enough time to spare. I walked slowly and with deliberate steps in the cold night air. I got there a little bit before Jen

Wade, which made me feel like I had accomplished something responsible and thoughtful and so unlike me. Already I was taking the first steps toward being a better me.

The coffee shop was brilliantly lit, almost a warehouse-sized space, ceilings two stories high and hung with enormous orange cranes that glazed the light, made it buttery and rich. One wall was glass, facing the park across the street; the rest were covered in local art. There were couches on which kids with sharp hair and skinny jeans tapped on their MacBooks. And it was cold, and loud, and echoing, and music played and people hunched over working and talking and laughing and making wide, sweeping gestures. Standing by the front door, peering around for Jen Wade, I felt like I was grinning like a fool, little apple cheeks all wound up and pink, because I was there and looking around and walking and in the world.

I wasn't supposed to have coffee—something about acids, and caffeine, and too harsh on my new little belly. It was something I didn't need anyway. But tea was utterly foreign to me. Tea was something that healthy people drank. It was something I should be drinking now, as a healthy person who cared about her health. It had antioxidants and minerals, or something like that. It was a terrific alternative to water. I was a tea-drinking kind of person now.

At the counter was a sign listing all the teas they had to offer from all over the world. I had given up caffeine, too, so I needed something herbal. Jasmine. Jasmine sounded fancy, and fragrant, and it came in a pot. It smelled like leaves and steam. Balancing my pot and my cup and my saucer, I bumped my way through a maze of tables, trying to hold myself in. People caught their cups and rolling pens when I bumped a thigh against the table or my ass swept across the surface. "I'm sorry, I'm sorry, I'm sorry," I muttered, holding my tea steady, wishing I could say, "I've done something, don't worry, I know." I'd wish that for a long time, that I had medical documentation to explain that this—all of me—was really, truly only temporary. I snagged a table near the window and set up my implements, wondering how long I would have to wait for my tea to steep, and whether I should go get more packets of Equal because I had given up sugar, too. Maybe I didn't need artificial sweeteners, because tea-drinking people didn't generally use them. They simply enjoyed the essence of the tea itself, naked and pure.

I poured a cup. The tea was a clear, pale, yellowish color. I breathed in the steam, choked down a sip, then another. I poured in a packet of Equal, and then another, furtively.

I had brought a book in the pocket of my jacket, but instead I sat and looked around, enjoying the novelty of society and breathing and talking and people and noise. And then Jen Wade was pulling out her chair, her cheeks pink and her flyaway hair and her eyes bright.

"Hello!" she said, and I leapt up and cried, "Jen Wade!" I nudged my way around the table and leaned forward to hug her, hard, and she hugged back hard, too. Jen Wade was not a big hugger—she was more of a firm arm around your shoulder, and a pat, and the pull-away, but she let me hang on to her for a moment, and she held tight, and let me go. She undid her scarf and took off her coat and said, "You look good!" and nodded. She pointed at the counter. "I'm going to go get something to drink."

"What did you get?" I said, when she came back and put her pot down.

"Jasmine tea," she said, pouring a cup.

"That's what I got, too!" I cried.

She laughed at me. "Oh good," she said. "How are you feeling?" she said. "You look tired."

"I'm okay," I said. "It's getting better. I haven't gone looking yet for my new friends who will only like me because I'm thin."

"You've lost weight," she said. She nodded at my torso.

I looked down. I was wearing my favorite black sweater. I had always believed that it made me look thin. It was almost baggy now. There was room in it. "I have!" I said. "I must have."

"Do you have a scale?"

"I'm afraid to get a scale," I said. "I'm going to order one tonight, though." Because how had it been possible that I hadn't noticed? I looked at my wrists and my forearms, snuck glances down at my stomach, my thighs. In the restroom I was grateful for a chance in front of the mirror for a moment. I backed away, and then came close, looking at my neck, my shoulders. I met my own eyes, and there was a shine there. I bounced a little on my toes. I had been poured in concrete, but now I had broken loose, and a firm hand between my shoulder blades had pushed me sharply ahead. I was taking a few stumbling steps, and I would take a few more, and soon I would be sprinting. But right then I was so tired, and I had to go home.

"I'm sorry," I told Jen, and she shook her head at me.

"It's fine," she said. "I walked, or I would give you a ride."

"No," I said, "I want to walk home."

Jen walked briskly, with her coat buttoned up around her chin. She was all slender legs and bulky wool and silky blonde hair. At my corner, she hugged me, her arm patting swiftly at my back, and then she hurried away up the hill toward UCSF, the hill I used to take the bus over.

I took a deep breath and carried myself the opposite way down the block, deeper into the Sunset, past the convenience store where I used to buy large-sized Kit Kats, past the Bikram Yoga studio. When it was dark and the studio was lit up, you could see the rows of people on their mats, only a breath away from each other, each of them glistening beneath the long lights overhead. Their faces were crumpled and serious, making yoga look more like a complicated logical problem that needed unknotting and less like physical exertion. I took a brochure from the clear plastic box on the door and held it under the streetlamp, looking at the available times. I'd be back at work in a week, and it could be part of my new routine—I'd hop up in the morning at 5:30, run over to the studio just a block away, and twist myself into complex theoretical equations. Then I'd run home, glowing in the dawn, brighter than the sun coming up over the Bay. Blood pumping hard and fresh through my veins, filling up my head to bursting. I wouldn't care that people on the street, getting off the N Judah, could stop and stare through the window at me, look at the expression on my face and wonder what exactly I was doing to look so strained, so serious, and so seriously in pain. Yoga would be hard at first, but then it would become simple and simpler, until it was the simplest thing I had ever done. Just like everything else. Learning how I liked my tea. Going out to meet a friend.

When I burst through the front door of my building I saw Andy in the backyard smoking, the door to the hallway half-closed. I pulled it open gently, startling him. The backyard was a tiny, overgrown shared space, with just a concrete path and a patch of weeds separating the main house from the in-law studio across from my living room windows. Andy was sitting on the rickety unpainted steps that led down to the backyard. The light was streaming through my living room window, making bright circles on the dead grass.

"How was your coffee?" Andy said, putting his arm around my hips. I settled down on the step above him and put my cheek on his head.

"Tea," I said. "I can't drink coffee. Coffee sounds terrible." My stomach was full and uncomfortable from the pot of tea I had drunk too quickly.

"How was your tea?" He leaned forward and stubbed out his cigarette on the concrete walkway.

"It tasted like leaves," I said.

"Did you have fun?"

"She says I've lost weight. That you can tell."

"You have," he said. "I told you that." His face was half-bright, half-shadowed, and the silver in his beard, the silvery reflection in his glasses were the clearest things I could see.

"You did?" I said. "I'm sorry."

Inside we moved through the rooms, turning lights on and pouring glasses of water and settling ourselves in for the night. I changed into my nightgown. The neckline seemed wider, and the gown seemed longer. I was getting smaller inside it. I was changing and I hadn't noticed. I had been locked up inside my head, letting *tired* win out over *hopeful*.

But I was already wishing that I could go from being big to being small without having to worry about all these intervening steps. I wanted to know, right now, exactly how skinny I was going to be. I didn't want to wait through these tiny, incremental changes.

Andy turned off the light in the living room and stretched out on the couch in front of the television. I stood in the doorway, looking at him. His face had gotten so lined. We talked about me. We talked about protein. We talked about my life. I would say, "Andy?" and he would say, "I'm fine. Don't worry about me. I'm more worried about you," but somehow that was worse.

"Andy?" I said.

He looked up at me and smiled.

"Really, is everything okay with you? At work? Everything?"

"I'm fine," he said. "I'm a little worried about bills, but you know how that is."

"Can I help you?" I perched on the edge of the futon and plucked at my nightgown hem. "Do you need to borrow any money? Can I do anything?"

"I'm not going to borrow any money from you," he said. "Don't be silly. It's not a big deal. I just have to look at my account book."

"Okay," I said. I sat there for another moment, looking at him seriously in the flickering light. He looked back at me for a moment, and then he reached his arm up, hugged me awkwardly. "You go on to bed! You must be so tired! Do you want me to tuck you in?"

"No," I said. "I'm okay."

I stood up and my nightgown dropped around my ankles. I took a breath.

"Do you love me?"

"I do," he said. He sat up.

"No, lie down. Good night. Thank you for everything." I leaned down to kiss him.

I climbed into bed and lay there. The volume on the television dropped slightly. I closed my eyes tightly, then opened them again. Me and my body in bed. I considered it. I tried, again, to feel if anything was different inside me. I put my hands on my stomach and tried to see if I could feel the difference that other people saw, but I couldn't. Drifting off to sleep, I couldn't find anything new.

Chapter 21

forty pounds gone . . . the leave of absence
ends . . . "so good, with so much less weight!"

The second month.

Hormones—they're stored in fat. And when you lose fat incredibly quickly, it's like flushing your hormones, too, just like they've been flushed directly into your bloodstream.

I had thought things were going slowly, but in cold, hard numbers, forty pounds were gone. Two months. It wasn't anything like I had expected. The constant, nagging exhaustion had dialed back, but craziness began to creep in—an anxiety that wrapped itself around my head and clung heavily like a wet towel. A feeling that I had done something wrong, was doing something wrong, was about to do the worst thing wrong ever, as I tried to figure out what I was actually supposed to be doing. I was still figuring out this new and weird body and its new weird-body demands. What were those sounds in my stomach? Was that echoing, audible rumble just random gas pains, or was I hungry, or were my overtaxed intestines about to shake apart and collapse into a puddle of Jell-O inside my crosshatched gut? Was that shooting pain across the mound of my stomach, up along my side, in my back, also gas, or was I about to explode? Would I ever stop cramping up and then pooping my life away? Would I stop farting as if I were trying to deplete the ozone layer? No, the Internet reminded me. I tried not to think about how that hadn't seemed important when it was just one more item on a bulleted list I had skimmed over.

My month's leave of absence was up. I had to go back to work exactly the way I was, frazzled, still stopping mid-stride to stare off into the distance and carefully consider my insides and wonder helplessly what they wanted from me this time. I had to go back into the world, and I wasn't ready, not yet. It didn't seem real enough yet.

The library was a hike from the bus stop. I walked down the sidewalk across from the chapel and the law school, then cut through the side entrance where the trees arced high and then arched down toward the concrete. I stepped across the path of stones that led to the back of the chapel. I remembered every crack in the pavement past short and squat Fromm Hall, the flagstones that were broken and lifted, the paved ramp that hugged the lawn in front of the library. The building was a concrete block on one side, a soaring green glass atrium on the other.

I stopped at the fountain outside the atrium and sat down on the low wall to catch my breath and try to stop sweating a little. This was where I had been sitting when I called Andy to tell him what I was going to do. It felt like that happened a hundred years ago. It was December, sunny, a little chilly, and a little humid. Someday I'd stop sweating like this, stop feeling the soft sheen that broke out and clung to my face and neck like steam on the bathroom mirror.

The people standing behind the Circulation desk could probably see me sitting there, panting. My coworkers. Maybe they wouldn't recognize me. My hair was a little longer, but it seemed thinner. That happens, it said in my weight loss surgery handbook. Your hair will start to get thin for the first few months, and that is because you'll be struggling to get all the protein you need. It probably wasn't as thin as I thought it was. Nothing about me was anything like I thought it was.

I didn't want to move from the sun and into the library. The atmosphere of the library was always a little dim, despite all the windows. But I pushed my way through the turnstile, and everyone behind the Circulation desk looked up, and all the patrons turned around, and the security guard perked up, and everything was perfectly quiet as everyone took a moment to investigate: the entire science class there to learn about looking up double-blind studies, all the student assistants who did the alphabetical shelving but didn't know the alphabet, the old neighborhood women who came to walk slowly through the library's gallery, bent forward with their hands clasped behind their backs, the old neighborhood men who came in to spend hours folding the newspapers carefully into thirds and reading every word on every page.

The entire library stopped and held its breath when I walked in the door. The entire library made mental calculations. The entire library looked at my body, and it was like I was back in gym class in middle school, wearing shorts. I ducked my head and tried to move quickly. I wanted to wait for the elevator, but it was in the lobby across from the Circulation desk and just a half a room away from the Reference desk. I didn't want to stand there and make eye contact with anyone.

The place smelled exactly the same, like conditioned air and books and rubber-backed carpets, with whiffs of the musk of twenty-four-year-old boys. Everything was gray and orange and brown and expensive and expansive, but it always felt stuffy. It was like I had been away for only a weekend, and I was about to head upstairs, sit in my chair, and just sink back down to the bottom of my job and stay there in the dark, drifting quietly in the gentle, invisible current.

At the top of the stairs I had to stop and rest on the bench. Something enormous and invisible was pressing my lungs between their meaty palms. I looked over the railing and down at the front door. The security guard had her chin against her chest, and I would have guessed that she was sleeping, but her head snapped up when a student in little shorts and a giant sweatshirt swiped her student ID card and it beeped at her, not letting her through. The security guard motioned her over to the gate, and the student set down her enormous soda cup and started going through her backpack. Someone at the Circulation desk called over—"You can't bring that drink inside," and the student started to argue with both of them. Nothing at all had changed, and students were the same and the rules were still the same.

I stood and wiped my hands down the legs of my pants—pants I hadn't fit into in a very long time, made of the same space-aged fabric that so many fat girl pants from Lane Bryant came in. I wondered if I was wearing the same button-down shirt I had during interview here. I wondered if it was too late to extend my medical leave.

My boss's office light was on, and I had to go in. I headed across the floor, through the rows of file cabinets full of microfiche, to the desk that hadn't changed at all.

My student assistant glanced up at me as I came toward the counter, and then looked at me again when I walked around the desk and pushed through the low swinging door. The floor was mostly empty at this time of the morning, and I was grateful.

"Jen!" Grace said, dropping her pencil. "You look so different! You have lost much weight!"

"Yes!" I said. "I have!" and I did not know what to say after that. *It's true! I agree with you!* That was the strictly polite and noncommittal thing to say, but I wanted to say, "Thank you!" as if her noticing my weight change was a gift, and I suppose it was the outside validation that I had been hoping for. I wanted to chirp, "Forty pounds!" but it sounded like bragging.

"You look great!" she said. "So good, with so much less weight!" My neck and the back of my ears flushed. Part of me wanted to tell her to dump the drink and go shelve something, and part of me was stammeringly grateful. All of me didn't like this evidence that you are never as invisible as you think you are and wish you could be. I wasn't sure if she knew I had gotten weight loss surgery. I wasn't sure if I wanted her to know.

Before she could ask any questions, my boss was coming out of her office, smiling at me.

"Welcome back," she said. "Wow! Look at you!" Debbie, usually so reserved and formal, put her arm around my shoulders, leaned forward, squeezed once, sharply. "You're just wasting away, aren't you! You've already lost so much. Is that usual? Is that normal? Put your bag down there, yes, we haven't moved your desk, put your coat, there, come into my office, sit down, let me close the door, let me look at you! You look terrific. How do you feel?"

I sat down, noticing that I did not have to pop my butt into the chair by pushing against the initial resistance of the arms because I was slightly too wide to fit. I was chair-sized now. I reached from arm to arm, but I wasn't overflowing. This was me in the real world.

I wrapped my hands around the armrests and looked at Debbie, twinkling at me from across the desk.

I said, "Thank you so much! It's pretty exciting!"

"You look a little tired," Debbie said sympathetically.

"I'm okay," I said. "It's a lot to recover from."

"How much have you lost? If I may ask?"

"About forty pounds!" I said, glad I got to say it. I didn't say: I became the person I am because I grew up fat; my personality, my quirks, and the good things about me were as much shaped by my size and my weight and my complicated relationship with food and my body as the bad things were.

"Wow," she said. "That's great. So quickly!"

"I know! I still have a way to go. But I'm getting there." I didn't say: Getting weight loss surgery was like setting off in a full-out sprint, away from all the terribleness inside me that had clearly developed as a result of my weight. But in my flight, I also carried away all the good things, the things that had been untouched by my size, that had nothing to do with my weight or my self-image. You see, I wouldn't so much be changing as *revealing* these things that had been obscured for so long.

"You really do look good," Debbie said. "It must be a relief."

"It is," I said. "It's weird, too." I didn't say: I thought that those things, the good and the bad, were clearly delineated, easily separated, and it would simply be a matter of picking out the good and discarding the bad. That the bad would disappear as quickly as the weight. That the bad *was* the weight, literally, figuratively.

"That's terrific," Debbie said. "You look fantastic."

"Thank you," I said, and I beamed. I didn't say: But every time I lose a pound, it feels as if I am taking a step away from the person I used to be. I am deliberately disassociating myself from the body I had given myself and the life I had led all the way up to my highest weight. I am abandoning the person I was, negating all my previous accomplishments, my entire life. Debbie was complimenting me on not being that person anymore. I soaked it up.

crossing my legs . . . becoming obsessed . . .
the pleasure of resentment . . . nothing ever
changes

Three months went by. I got smaller, and smaller, and smaller. Almost seventy pounds down.

I was shrinking—it felt exactly like that. Like I was contracting and leaving my clothes hanging on my body. I was shrinking back inside the acceptable boundary a body was supposed to have, feeling less and less like I was taking up an outsized, overgenerous portion of space, coming into proportion with the rest of the world. I was narrowing down to a point, indistinguishable from all the other points on the chart—not an outlier anymore, but getting closer and closer to the top and center of that lovely arc the bell curve made.

Finally, I started to become aware of how quickly my body was changing, but small things still startled me. At work, a circulation assistant came upstairs and tucked herself into the chair with me, right next to me. Both of us, side by side, in the seat. We fit. We sat looking at WorldCat and talking about shelving issues. Inside, I was squealing. My butt was demonstrably less wide.

It was the end of March, and I was still losing a pound a week, two pounds, sometimes three or five. I was moving steadily downward, despite my constant, nagging sense that I wasn't doing this right. I sat down on the futon one night at Jen Wade's house and looked down at my knees. I lifted one leg, hooked one knee over the other. There I was, sitting with my legs crossed.

"You guys!" I said. "You guys, you guys!" I was hysterical, shrill. "You guys!"

"What? What?" Monique said. They all looked over at me, but I hesitated. I didn't know what my *rights* were. I was rejoicing in these physical changes that let me walk a block, two, three, more, that meant the raging yeast infections in my thighs were settling down, that meant energy, hope, a sense of lightness. What was I allowed to say about having been fat? What was I allowed to say about being less fat now?

They looked at me expectantly and I gestured at my legs. "Do you see?"

"Your legs," Jen Wade observed.

"No," I said. "Yes. I'm crossing them. I've never done that! I never have crossed my legs ever in the history of the world," I said excitedly.

"That's awesome. But I'm sure there must have been a point in the past where you managed it," Edith said.

"Well." I considered. "Maybe. I don't know. I don't remember ever doing it, is all." I was blushing. "I'm sorry," I said. "I just got excited."

"Clearly," Monique said. "That's so good, though!"

"It is!" I said.

I became preoccupied, *obsessed* with my physical changes. How many inches smaller was I, and were they inches that were visible to the naked eye? How much more like a normal, ordinary person was I? I wanted to stop people and ask how I looked. I wanted to be looked at. I wanted, almost more than anything, to strip down and beg someone to describe my body to me, because I couldn't be trusted when it came to the size and the shape of who I was. When it came to how I appeared to the outside world, what people thought of me as opposed to what I believed about myself.

The world's opinions shouldn't have mattered, of course, but I wanted to be sure. I didn't want to embarrass myself by just *assuming* I was okay.

I really felt okay.

And it was wonderful, and it was terrifying. It was the best thing that ever happened to me, and it was awful. If I didn't want to leave the house, I had no excuses left. My clothes were hanging off me, but clothes shopping was overwhelming now. How was I supposed to go into a store with four stories full of clothing that I could fit into? All my previous shopping experiences had taken place within in the confines of a sixteen-by-sixteen-foot store with limited selection and very particular ideas about what a fat girl should look like. In the wider world, I could be whomever I wanted.

It was an idea that filled me with panic. I shoved it away, because I couldn't think about that, not yet. It was too soon. I wasn't done yet. I was losing weight so that I could start my life, finally—but that meant soon, too soon, sooner than I could handle, I actually had to *start my life*. Every pound down was like another short drop closer to free fall.

And the pounds kept coming off, despite the fact that I hadn't changed at all. That was both the beauty of the first years of weight loss surgery, and also the most terrible thing about them.

Because, see, surgery had meant that I would be *done*. I would be skinny, and I would never have anything to worry about, ever again. My body would not be something constantly, consistently on my mind, something that occupied far too many of my waking thoughts and my unconscious thoughts and my weird dreams. My body wouldn't be an enemy. It would be me, and I would be it.

But most importantly, I wouldn't worry about food, ever again, because I was a skinny person, and that's how skinny people were. So surgery would cure me of food. Being told that post-surgical patients can't eat candy—that translated to me as I *could not eat candy*. That it would be physically impossible to want candy, to put it in my mouth, chew, swallow, digest.

I'm not saying it was rational. It wasn't even a truly conscious thought.

What I had done, essentially, was look for a way out of my eating disorder without ever acknowledging that I had an eating disorder, a— let's call it a *troubled* relationship with food.

There are a lot of reasons that fat people are in the world—and it's not because fat people can't control themselves around cake and ham. I hated the cliché of the fat person who was helpless in the face of bacon cheeseburgers. I hated being told, "Just put down the fork," by assholes who had *no idea* what any fat person's situation was, who were ignorant and smugly superior.

And I hated myself for actually being a fat person who sometimes just couldn't control herself and her fork around cake.

I lay back and closed my eyes and let my surgeon pull out my disordered parts along with my guts so that I'd never have to face the fact that it didn't matter if I was a cliché. Surgery was an end-run around all of the hard parts.

However, of course, it turned out that I still had to eat after I got weight loss surgery. As it happens, I had to think a lot about food after surgery. It turned out life was still about food and what I could eat and what I couldn't eat and what I wanted to eat, which was usually the same thing as what I couldn't eat.

Portion control wasn't automatic, and that came as a shock. I only had so much room to work with, now that I had a tiny stomach—how could I possibly struggle with portion control?

The problem was that I also still had the urge to eat and keep eating until I was full, sick-full. And sick-full after surgery meant nausea, lightheadedness, chills, and weeping self-pity. The cutoff point was different at every meal. I could finish that chicken breast and be fine, or the next bite could be the one that sent me over the edge. I spent a lot of time on the floor in the last stall of the bathroom with my head on my knees, wishing I could amputate everything from the neck down.

I was supposed to be done with my body, but my body wouldn't go away. It changed under my hands in the shower, my topography shifting and moving like an earthquake was rumbling. It kept demanding food, and as I recovered from surgery, I felt my old urges, my hungriness reemerge, that sense of need, that sense if I did not eat now, right this second, I would be missing something, losing something that could never be recovered.

I tried to follow a grim and unrelenting schedule, terrified to do anything else.

A protein shake before work. I wanted pancakes.

A single-portion tuna can, mashed up with mayo until soft, in the break room. I wanted an enormous burrito.

A protein shake, shaken up in a little plastic container, lukewarm and grainy, in the break room. I wanted Cheez Doodles, a Hershey's with Almonds, and a Diet Pepsi.

A spoonful of sugar-free plain yogurt at my desk. I wanted cake.

A protein shake, blended at home while the cat meowed at my feet. I wanted *two* cakes.

A single-portion can of chicken, mashed up with mayo until soft, eaten while sitting on the futon and watching television with grim and unrelenting determination and resentful focus.

"Have you had enough protein today?" Andy said, coming through the door after my show was over. I didn't want to get up and wash the blender.

"How was your day?" I said.

"Fine," he said. "Did you have your last protein shake yet?"

I sullenly drank a protein shake, standing in the kitchen.

"I hate it," I said, stomping into the living room where he was sitting on the couch watching the World Series of Poker. "This isn't what I signed up for," I said, kicking the coffee table and clunking down my big Tupperware glass full of gritty protein. Tantrum, tantrum, tantrum.

"Well," Andy said.

"Don't say it. Don't. Don't you say it."

"Can't you eat different things yet? I thought you could start eating more things. Add more stuff into your diet. Here, where's the booklet?" He got up to rummage across my desk and around my dining table, where all of my important papers collected and sank slowly into an undifferentiated pile of mulch. "Is this it?" he said, holding up a folder.

"I think so," I said. "Probably. I don't care."

Maybe I could blend a steak. A cheeseburger. A ham and a pie? An entire Thanksgiving dinner! Could I make a milkshake with big chunks of Kit Kat if I smooshed them up really, really well? Could I open up a Taco Bell burrito and suck out all the filling? Could I eat a pizza if I ate it very, very slowly, or just maybe licked all the cheese and kind of nuzzled the pepperoni and found my way underneath the toppings to cover my face with tomato sauce and just sort of cuddle with the crust?

"Okay," Andy said. He stood at the table and flipped through the post-surgery handbook quickly, past the pages of diagrams and warnings. "Okay, here. Diet progression." He made a *hmm* noise. "Says here that eggs are almost always acceptable, and tofu is a good and very tolerated source of protein."

"I do not want eggs," I said, flopping around on the futon. I flung my arms out and rested my head on the seat. "I do not want *tofu*." I could hear the petulance in my voice. I could barely stand myself; I didn't know how Andy could stand there, tolerating me like I was tofu.

"What do you want?" He looked at me, baffled.

"I don't know," I wailed, and fell over. I put my face in the couch pillow.

"Maybe you could look at this list, here, and get yourself some things on it. Chicken breasts, see? You can have chicken, real chicken. You could broil it, maybe. Can you have cheese? Let me see."

I jumped up and snatched the book from him. "Can I have hot dogs? Bacon? Ice cream cones? Cotton candy? Cookies?" I threw it down and kicked it under the coffee table. I flopped back down and put my head back in the cushion.

"Are you feeling fussy again?" he said, sitting down next to me and putting his hand on my head.

"No," I said into the cushion. I could feel my face drawing down into a miserable pout.

He started laughing. "Fussy Jen, I am putting you down for a nap."

"I don't want to," I said, still into the cushion.

No answer, which meant he was laughing at me.

I sat up and put my forehead against his arm. "I'm sorry," I said. "I am rotten."

"You're still recovering," he said. "Do you want to take a nap? Work still tires you out?"

"It's fine," I said. I paused. "Oh, god I hate it. When did it start to suck so much?"

"You've always hated your job."

"No I didn't. I love my job. It's so easy. I will never be fired. I don't have much to do. I can be on the Internet all day." I sighed. "I am so tired of the Internet."

"It'll get better when you get more energy back," he said. He leaned back against the couch and I swung my legs around, lying full-length with my legs in his lap.

"I'm just going to close my eyes. Put a blanket on me and I won't bother you anymore."

He reached over and snatched the throw off the carpet, lifted my feet and tucked it under my heels. "There," he said. I didn't answer because I was halfway asleep.

Andy left the house hours before I was up, off to work on the weekend again. He left the nutrition guide behind, and I bounced over to the couch to page through it. I felt like I did on the dawn of every new diet—anticipation, hope, that sense that I would never do anything wrong ever again. This time, I would only do everything right.

I made my way slowly down to the grocery store, and came back with a sack full of real food that was also nutritious. I sat down for an hour. I stood up when I thought that maybe my stomach was telling me I needed food, or maybe it was gas.

I beat an egg in a small dish. The sound of the clinking fork against the ceramic was pleasant and satisfying and adult. I poured a bowl of breadcrumbs out and seasoned it with salt and pepper. I poured a quarter-inch of oil into a pan, and let it heat until it sizzled. I dunked a chicken breast into a dish of milk, rolled it in the breadcrumbs, laid it carefully in the pan. The kitchen filled up with the smell of frying, that heavy gold smell that is rich and deep and sinks right into your pores. The smell of real food. I took another piece of chicken out of the package, dunked it, slid it into the pan, and another, and another. I stood over the stove and watched my pan carefully, hunched over slightly, intent, focused.

The entire pan was covered with an entire package of chicken breasts. I could eat these for days. A week. Another week after that. I could slice them up and eat them cold, or warm them up and eat them with a little mustard on the side. It was real food, that I had cooked. I hated cooking, but there was something immensely satisfying about this moment in front of the stove, sliding each breast, a toasty golden-brown, onto the plate lined with a paper towel. I piled them all up on the plate and poured the oil off into the sink. *I should clean up,* I thought. Put away the milk, the eggs, pile the dishes in the sink, run soapy water into the oily pan, and let it soak away the crunchy bits at the bottom. I was tired from standing.

Instead, I speared one of the glittering breasts from the top of the pile—still pan-hot, still sizzling just a tiny bit—and took a bite, right off the end of my fork. It was perfectly done, crunchy on the outside and juicy in the middle. I should put it on a plate, portion it down to the appropriate size and wrap up the rest, sit down at the table with a napkin on my lap and eat it like a normal person, with a fork and a knife. I pictured every step of the way, from the kitchen over to the table. But instead I stood there leaning over the plate on the stove and I took a bite, and then another, and another, eating around the fork, spinning the breast in a circle. I ate away the thinner, crunchier perimeter and worked my way toward the juicier center.

I was eating something healthy and good for me. It was what I was supposed to be doing. I held the fork up to my face and kept eating. Bite after bite after bite, standing in my kitchen and not really thinking about anything except chicken, and moving my jaw and swallowing. The chicken breast was gone and my stomach was full, more than full, over-full, backed up to the bottom of my throat.

I swallowed, and swallowed again, and the nausea subsided slowly, the feeling of fullness seemed to recede, and I realized I was still hungry. Like there was extra room in my stomach that needed to be filled. The whole house still smelled like chicken. I picked up another chicken breast and put it on a plate, grabbed a fork and a knife, but I didn't need the knife. I started cutting up the chicken with the side of my fork before I had even left the kitchen. By the time I was parked on the futon, half of the breast was gone and the plate was greasy with fried breadcrumbs, and I was so full, packed full, feeling sick. I pressed a finger to the crumbs and licked them off, thinking of my mother, the pound cake, my grand-mother's kitchen table. I speared the rest of my chicken and ate it off my fork again. I pulled the last bite off with my fingers and pushed it into my mouth. I was full, I thought, and it hurt. It hurt, but I was back in the kitchen again, a few minutes later, a half an hour later, an hour, all afternoon, feeling sick and full and unstoppable. I picked at the chicken, pulling it apart, letting the crumbs drop all over the plate and the floor and my pajama bottoms. I licked my fingers clean, wiped them down my thighs. I could see the bottom of the plate now.

I fumbled at the roll of paper towels and crumpled one up in my face, scrubbed my face with it, scrubbed my mouth. My eyes were heavy. I was full. Really, truly full this time. I hoped. I went into the bedroom. I was exhausted. My throat was thick and blocked up, the nausea bub-bling up and the taste of chicken backing up to the bottom of my tongue.

I could feel it, thick and fried and pasty, and I couldn't swallow it away. I was swallowing and swallowing saliva. I laid down and was afraid I'd choke, but suddenly it was completely dark out and I was sweaty, my face pasted to the pillowcase. I kicked the blankets off. I didn't know how long I had been sleeping, how quickly the sun had set. I took my dirty plate into the kitchen and slipped it into the sink, picked up a cold chicken breast almost idly, thoughtlessly, wandered back into the living room to turn the lights on and open my laptop and check my email. I left greasy fingerprints on the keys, stuffed the last bit of chicken into my mouth as I clicked reply to respond to an email, and then I was choking because it was too much, entirely too much. I heard terrible noises and gurgling in my belly and felt my gorge filling up the entire column of my throat.

I dumped my laptop on the coffee table and buried my face in the futon cushion. I tried to breathe. I sat up because I couldn't get enough air, settled back against the couch, squirmed again, trying to find a position where I wouldn't feel like someone had tried to punch through my stomach, leaving stretched-out, bruised knuckle prints behind. I was crying. A package of chicken. I staggered, ran to the bathroom, and cradled the front of the toilet. The seat bounced against the wall, fell against the back of my head. Huge chunks of chicken that barely looked chewed were falling out of my mouth and I was heaving and heaving and heaving, my stomach spasming and twisting, my throat closing up around the taste of bile, chicken chunks coming out of my nose with snot and bile and blood. Crying, the sobs strangling my chest and my breath entirely gone, nothing left but the taste of bile.

It was getting late, and Andy was going to be coming soon. I flung open the windows in the kitchen, and they swung out hard and banged back into their frames. I pushed them back out, shook out the kitchen curtains. Everything smelled like grease and oil and frying. Everything smelled terrible. I smelled terrible. I dunked all the pans and plates and dishes and forks in the sink, poured dish soap over them, ran the hot water until the sink almost overflowed. With a rag I scrubbed down the stove, the splatters on the walls, the floor. I hurried into the living room and opened the window in there, opened the front door and the door out into the backyard, opened the window in my bedroom. You could smell it in my bedroom. I straightened out my sheets and turned the pillow over. It was chilly and damp out, smelling like fog, the beach, San Francisco. I smelled damp grass in the backyard, wet wood, and salty, sandy dirt.

The bathroom. I hurried into the bathroom, flushed the toilet, and then again, and then scrubbed it with lemon-scented cleanser, scoured the floor around the toilet, wiped down the sink. I stood and swayed a moment, tilted forward, and pressed my forehead against the chilly mirror. I wanted to bang my head against the mirror again and again. The veins in my eyes had broken and spread, making them pink and watery. My cheeks were blotchy.

I splashed cold water on my face, and then thought that in this lemon- and Inner Sunset–smelling house, I smelled like fried chicken and oil and breadcrumbs and vomit. My stomach was still full and clenching up. It hurt, and I was so stupid. I opened the window in the bathroom, leaning hard to push it up—it always stuck tight. I undressed quickly, goosebumped all over. I ran the shower hot, sinking down to the bottom of the tub and letting the water fall on me. I noticed that I fit—I wasn't squished in against the sides of the tub. I kept taking deep breaths, then deeper, then deeper still. I was still sitting there when Andy let himself in, poked his head through the door. "Hello?" he said. "What are you doing taking a shower at this time of night?"

I leaned out, wrapping the curtain around my neck. "I was just trying to get warm," I said. "I am trying to raise my core temperature."

He looked at me for a moment. "Maybe it would help if you closed all the windows," he said.

I flicked the curtain closed. "Could you do that for me, please? I'm almost done."

I heard the bathroom window clunk shut, hard enough that it probably would never open again. He closed the door behind him and I assumed he was moving around the house, shutting all the windows. He wouldn't notice the pans and dishes, or if he did he wouldn't say anything.

I hauled myself out of the shower and wrapped a towel around my head, and one around my body. The bath towel was fitting better—it closed down the front when I tucked it under my arms, instead of leaving a wide gap over my hips. The house was freezing cold, but it didn't smell like food anymore.

Andy said, "Have you had your protein today?" and I said, "Yes."

"Good job!" he said. He held up his hand and I smacked it lightly. High five for me.

"How was your day?" I said.

"Fine," he said. "But I'm more interested in how you're doing." He had dark circles, and was sleeping poorly and smoking more and drinking every night, and he hated his job. His hands shook in the morning and his hair was silver all the way through, as if it had never been brown.

"What's going on?" I said suddenly, desperately.

He said, "Nothing."

"Are you sure nothing?"

"I'm sure."

"Andy?"

"I'm just fine." His voice was conciliatory, soothing. He took me by the shoulders. "Work is just busy. You know." He wrapped his arms around me. "Are you okay?"

I stood inside his arms for a moment, let myself lean into him. They still didn't fit all the way around me. I pushed back. "I'm going to go to bed," I said.

I left the door to the hallway open, a little, for the light, for the sound of the television in the next room and Andy sitting quietly on the futon. I fell asleep listening to the wrenching, gurgling sounds my stomach made.

secret Oreos! . . . running away . . . waiting for an epiphany

I did not learn. I lost weight that week, and if you opened my fridge you'd see take-out containers and ice cream.

It was almost as if I hadn't been filled with a bright white light that seared away all the awful, flabby bits of my soul and left behind only my purified red-hot essential core. I was supposed to be leaving behind my old life the way I was leaving behind my old pants. But every day was the same, the same, the same. I ate whatever I could fit inside me, and suffered for it, and lost weight anyway. In that way I was rewarded, every day and every week.

Every day and every week did not seem different than any day or week before it. I got up when the alarm went off and then spent an hour puttering around when I should have been getting ready if I wanted to be at work on time. Eventually, reluctantly, I made my way to work, usually an hour late.

I sat at my desk, and I finished my work in an hour. Or I ignored my work and looked at the Internet, the same pages over and over. I went to lunch. I poked my fork in my tuna and thought about the vending machine. I sighed. I got candy out of the vending machine. I ate it furtively and too quickly while I paged through the *San Francisco Chronicle*. I sat with my empty container and wrapper and sticky candy crumbs in front of me and looked at the comics again, looked at the clock. I was supposed to be back already. I should be sitting at my desk for three more hours, with breaks to hit the vending machine, and then going home, and then thinking about having a protein shake but eating a couple of Oreos instead. Andy and I would sit on the couch and eat take-out and watch television, and I would go to bed before Andy did, and he would finally come in late and I would snuggle back against him and he would turn over and I would count on my fingers how long it had been and how long it might be and if I would feel okay if we immediately started having sex again when I hit a certain number on the scale.

I didn't look at the clock, and wondered what they'd do to me if I came back late from lunch. If I took an hour-and-a-half lunch. A two-hour lunch. If I went home and didn't come back. That sizzling, reckless feeling, that what-if, that sense that I could push out of the break room and swing left instead of right, push out the side doors that were for emergencies and let the alarm blare behind me while I stalked down the hill onto Haight Street and went—somewhere from there. Home to weigh myself again, drink a protein shake, crack open a can of tuna, and look at the same websites I'd been looking at all day.

I could do anything. Except I didn't know what I wanted to do. There was too much to change, and it was so easy to say I wasn't ready yet. I hadn't lost *all* of the weight. I hadn't had any kind of epiphany yet. Surely that was on its way. I just had to be patient and wait for the kind of happiness that stuck around for more than a moment after brief flashes of joy—*I fit in the chair! I can walk up a hill!* It just hadn't happened yet. It would, though, because it had to.

Chapter 24

the bridesmaid's dress . . . a confession at last
. . . feelings suck

My brother called me in April, when I was almost exactly one hundred pounds down.

"Carrie wants to know when you can get your measurements taken for your bridesmaid's dress," he said. "Please."

"Soon," I said, lowering my voice. "Hang on," I said. "Hang on a second." I got up from my desk, piled with a backlog of work I was supposed to be doing and somehow just never got around to—and walked away from it, out into the stacks, all the way over to the far windows in the corner. I stood with my back to the wall, found myself leaning onto it, sliding down. "When do they need to be done? I'm still losing weight, you know." I really was. "I'm going to keep losing weight really fast, so the measurements won't even mean anything." I really would be. I let myself think about that for a moment.

"I don't know," he said. He sounded distracted and there were clanging noises in the background. He worked as the head chef at a busy restaurant, which usually overloaded his multitasking circuits on the phone. "Look, Jen-Jen, I have to go-go. Just get your measurements done and send them to Carrie, okay? Mom's on my case about it too, though I don't know why."

"You haven't told her," I said, straightening up. "Have you?"

"Told her what?" he sounded impatient. "Hey, I need those over there!"

"What?"

"Nothing. Told her what? About your surgery? No. I haven't brought it up. Why haven't you told her yet? She's going to know. You think you're going to come to town what, a hundred pounds lighter?"

"I don't know. A bit. Around there. Maybe. You can't really predict—"

"She's going to know that something is up. Our mother is not stupid. She's a little dopey sometimes, but she's not dumb."

"Diverticulitis makes you lose weight! I have to eat a special diet!"

His laugh was more of a bark—we both made the same, startled-sounding noise when we were caught off guard by something funny. "Oh, oh, right, of course. That makes total sense. Just tell her, Jennifer. I don't want to accidentally say something and get you pissed at me."

"I don't want to tell her! It's complicated!"

"You say, 'Mother, I got weight loss surgery.'"

"And when she says, 'Why didn't you tell me a year ago?' and 'Why did you lie to me?' what am I supposed to say?'"

"I don't care," he said. "You're being stupid."

"Don't call me stupid!"

"I didn't call you stupid, I said this was stupid."

"You're stupid."

"Get that out of there now!"

"What?"

"I have to go. I love you too. Get your measurements. Call our mother."

The phone clicked and he was gone and I was close to tears in the corner of the library. Oh, shit. I would have to tell my mother. I could have gone for the rest of my life without ever telling her. I could have said, *lean protein!* and *long walks!* and felt shitty forever. I was used to carrying around that low-grade sense of having done something wrong.

Or I could tell her. I leaned against the wall and slid down. *Mom, I could say, I lied to you because I was afraid of what you would say to me. I was afraid of what you would think of me. I was embarrassed to tell you I was getting weight loss surgery. I'm sorry, Mom.* I would even have to confess that I wasn't very good at it, this post-surgery thing, and that things didn't seem to have changed very much.

And she would say—what? I had no idea. I would be red-hot with shame for having lied, for lying every time she called to ask me how I was doing. Fine, fine, I told her. I'm doing just fine, I would say, vibrating with the fear that she knew and was trying to dig it out of me. I didn't want to have hurt her.

I hate the phone. I didn't call her that day, or the next day, or the day after that.

She called me when I was on the bus, on the way to work, four days and a weekend later. The bus was rattling down Parnassus Avenue, about to swing left onto Cole. It was almost empty, because it was late morning and most people had already gotten to work on time. I was sliding around on my seat as we bumped down into potholes and up over moguls of rumpled asphalt, staring off into space, watching the shoulder-to-shoulder houses shuffle by. I heard the phone ringing in my bag, and I pulled it out and flipped it open before I could think about it clearly.

"Mom," I said. I found myself hunching forward, my forehead drifting down toward my knees.

"Hello, my dear," she said. "How are you? How are you feeling? Are you doing okay? I haven't talked to you in a while. I figure you're busy with work and everything. Are you feeling okay? I know about being busy with work, let me tell you, when school is back in session—whoa!" she said. She chuckled. "Father Smith says it's the biggest enrollment we've had in a long time, and I said to him—"

"Mom?" I interrupted. I stared at my pink sneakers. They were scuffed at the toe. I wondered if I were going to say it even as I said, "Mom, I have to tell you something." I kept my voice very low and hoped no one would hear me.

I shouldn't have paused for breath, because she panicked, and I did too. "What is it? What? Are you okay?"

"I got weight loss surgery," I said.

There was a long, long silence. We turned off Haight Street onto Masonic, and someone pulled the cord for the next stop. I heard a gusty sigh, and then my mother's careful, considered tone of voice.

"I know," she said. There was hurt behind her voice, and the sense that she was trying very hard to be reasonable, to not let me know she was hurt. I paused for a moment, sat up. The bus flew by my stop, past the Starbucks and the grocery store and started up the hill.

"Shit!" I said. I jumped up and yanked the cord and swung myself over to the back door. "Hang on. I'm sorry. What? How did you know? Did Kenny tell you?"

"Kenny knows?" Andy always said you could hear the Brooklyn in my mother's voice, but she always just sounded like my mother to me— except when she talked in that tone of voice.

The bus shuddered to a halt, and I climbed down the stairs.

"I told him," I said. Standing on the sidewalk in front of the athletic field, I squinted up the hill toward the campus entrance, so far away. The street was tree-lined, forested along the border of the campus, and rows of convex-windowed houses with plant balconies lined the other side. I closed my eyes. "I'm sorry. Mom, I'm sorry. I wanted to tell you, I really did. But I was afraid to."

"Why?" she said. "I wouldn't have said anything. I would have been worried, sure. But I would have understood."

"I'm sorry, Mom." I wanted to sit down. "How did you know?"

"I thought it was a little strange. That you were going into the hospital. And you didn't tell me about it. And you had weight loss surgery books on your Amazon wish list."

"Oh," I said. "Well, that was stupid."

"It was a *little* dumb," she said, and she laughed her belly laugh. I could picture her little apple cheeks, and her eyes.

"I'm sorry," I said.

"How much weight have you lost?" she said. "How much do you weigh now?"

"I was 318 pounds. I've lost about 100 pounds."

"Wow," she said. "That's a lot a weight."

"Right," I said. I had to go. I had to walk up the hill, and I didn't want to pant on the phone.

"Will you send me pictures?"

"Sure," I said. "I haven't taken any pictures yet." I bounced on my toes. I was starting to move away from that rare and surprisingly comfortable place of sincere regret and love for my mother, who accepted me and valued me and did not judge my actions—how could I have thought she ever would? Guilt had briefly buoyed me up into being a better person, but I was sinking back down into that place where I became a sullen teenager, reluctant to share anything at all with my mother, resentful of all her attempts at trying to connect with me. I hated it when I could feel it happening.

"How could you not?" my mother went on. "What size are you? What does Andy think? Andy knows you've gotten weight loss surgery, right?"

"Mom, could you do me a favor and not tell anyone else in the family? Please don't tell Betty or Evelyn. I don't know what they'd say."

"Okay," she said, sounding bemused. "I don't think they'd think it was a bad thing. They'd be proud of you."

"I guess," I said. "I don't know. I just feel stupid about it."

"You don't have to feel stupid about it! You made a choice, and that choice was all about what you thought was best. My daughter is very smart, and she knows what's best for her. Oh, honey—"

"You know, you're a—candidate," I said abruptly, carefully. "I could tell you about it, if you wanted?"

"Oh, no," she said almost immediately. "I'm okay. Did I tell you,

Evelyn has me on a new medication that's good for my blood pressure? It's supposed to be good for appetite suppressing too. It's supposed to make you less hungry, and you lose the weight that way. Though I'm tired of all the pills, I gotta tell you. It's a lot of pills."

"Aren't you taking too many? Is that right?"

"Evelyn's keeping an eye on me. I'll just lose the weight, slow and steady. Slow and steady wins the race. I've been trying to walk. And I'm going back to water aerobics. You know how much your mother loves the water!"

"I do," I said. "I'm proud of you, Mom." I was. She was doing it the normal way. I kind of wished she'd do it the way I had, so I wouldn't be the only one.

"I'm proud of my daughter," she said. "My kids, they're such good kids. I brag about you all the time. My son's a chef and my daughter's a writer—"

"Sort of," I said. "Mom," I said quickly. "I have to go. I'm sorry."

"Oh, no problem," she said cheerily. "I love you," she said, and she was so sincere. My eyes burned. "I love you so much," she said.

She did. I didn't know why I always forgot it.

I trudged up the hill slowly, trying to breathe in and out instead of holding my breath like I was afraid I'd get punched. It was still hard to get up the hill, and that didn't seem fair. I should have felt like I could sprint. I should have felt like I could run a marathon. Once I lost it all (How much was *all*? Where would I stop?), I would be capable of winning the Tour de France. And my mother would tell everyone, "My daughter writes *and* knows Lance Armstrong *and* lost 180 pounds!"

I had forgotten that when people love you, they forgive you. That is what they give you along with their love. My mother and friends loved me unconditionally, but I had to set a new condition for myself: I had to stop disappearing into a dark hole, pretending like no one gave a shit. I was supposed to be honest and true about my feelings, not hide them.

Honesty sucked. My feelings sucked. I climbed the hill to the library, panting hard.

Chapter 25

drinking again . . . rejection . . .
light as a feather

"I talked to my mother," I told Andy after work. We hadn't met for drinks since my surgery, and it felt comfortable, familiar. It felt good. I was going to have a drink for the first time since November. We were at Finnegan's Wake, just a few blocks from his apartment.

"Why would you do something like that?" He lifted his shot glass and tossed the whiskey back neatly, in a single swoop.

I took a sip of my whiskey, gently, and it burned down my throat. I wasn't sure that it was the best idea. I sat still for a moment, considering my stomach, my intestines, imagining that I could feel the whiskey pulsing through my rearranged organs. I was warm. It tasted so nice. *I can do this,* I thought. I touched my lips to the rim of the glass, let it touch the tip of my tongue. It was warm and so was I. I took a larger sip, and put my glass down, and sighed, slumping in my stool.

"Are you sure you can drink that?" Andy said.

"Oh, I'm sure," I said.

"Is it so delicious?" Andy asked, looking amused.

"It is so delicious," I said. We were sitting at the corner of the bar, next to the door, and I was chilly. I had been getting colder, and my skin felt drier, like it would crack and flake and peel.

"I missed drinking. Does that make me an alcoholic? Probably. Did you know that weight loss surgery patients often become crazy alcoholics?"

"Really?" he took a sip of his Miller High Life. ("One champagne of beers, my good man!" he had said when he ordered it.)

"They need to replace food in their life. They need something to fill the terrible, gaping void. Like alcohol!" I lifted my glass and raised it to him. He clinked with me, tapped the bottom of his bottle against the bar, and we drank again, he tipping his head back, his throat bobbing, me sipping delicately, quickly, tiny sips over and over because I didn't want to stop.

"I'm going to have another one after this," I told him. "I need another drink. I told my mother about my surgery."

He grabbed my arm. "Oh no. What did she say? Was she furious?"

"No, she was really nice about it, actually. She was even really interested."

"She didn't castigate you? Try to make you feel guilty?"

"No," I said. "I'm the only one making me feel guilty. Like whatsherface. Eleanor Roosevelt. That's what she said."

"Right," he said. A moment of silence. I sipped at my drink again. "So," he said, "you're glad you told her?"

"Probably. I think. I guess I am. I should have told her a long time ago. Clearly I need to drink more so I stop feeling so—so icky and strange and unhappy about it. The whole thing just—I don't know."

"I'll buy you a drink," he said. "Just finish that one."

I lifted it to him, and then swallowed it whole and gasped. A punch in the gut.

"Whoa! Don't hurt yourself."

"That hurt a little bit. I'm okay! I'm okay. I want another."

"Are you sure?" He looked carefully at me.

"Yes, yes, I'm definitely sure. I'm a-okay. I would like *two* more. I would like a dozen more. I would like all the whiskeys that they have. Maybe also a Manhattan. Yes, that is what I want next! I want a nice Manhattan."

"You're drunk already," Andy said. He peered into my face. I was sure he couldn't see my face, silhouetted against the window. I squinted back at him, affected a mean look. "You are!" he said. "You're already drunk. Man, you're a lightweight!"

"I am not," I said hotly. "I've only lost one hundred pounds, and I have, like a hundred and million to go or something. At least." I slapped my hand down on the bar. "I am just *happy*. To be *alive*. And I would like that drink now please," I finished with great dignity.

"You're totally drunk," he said, and he gestured to the bartender and ordered me a Manhattan.

"I am!" I said happily. "I'm a cheap drunk! I think it is because I am metabolizing things in a faster amount. It has something to do with absorption," I said, making an arcane swirling gesture around my stomach, indicating my rearranged insides. I shifted on my bar stool, back and forth. I was uncomfortable with the way my ass still hung over the sides, still wondered what I looked like from the back. There was nothing worse than a fat person riding a bicycle, a guy had said to me once in high school. He wasn't being intentionally cruel, but that is the kind of cruelty that is the most breathtaking. I resettled, and said, "How about you? Are you drunk?"

"No, I'm not drunk," he said absently, pulling out his wallet. He shuffled through his money. He didn't have much cash on him, and he frowned, gazed into space for a moment, and then looked at me. "I'm going to run out to the ATM."

"No, no," I said. "It's on me. You don't have to do that! I want to buy the drinks."

"You're as broke as I am," he said.

"How broke are you?" I said, frowning. "You didn't tell me that you were broke."

"Oh, you know. It's just old bills. I'm still paying it all down from when I took care of my father."

"But, the raise didn't help?"

"Not really," he said, shrugging. "It's fine."

I caught his arm. "Can I lend you some money? Let me give you some money. I can help you."

"You have hospital bills to pay!" he said. "I'm just fine. Wait right here, drunky."

He dashed outside and I slumped on my stool. The bartender set my drink in front of me. It was pinker than it ought to have been, and it had a sword in it. A cherry was impaled at the end. The liquid brimmed all the way to the lip of the glass. I leaned forward to take a sip, ended up slurping when the surface tension broke and whiskey came pouring over the rim. The glass and my chin and the bar got sticky. I dabbed at it all with Andy's napkin, thought about how nice it was to be drunk. I hadn't been drunk in a very long time. This was a pleasant sensation, dreamy and warm, a place where everything was okay and everyone was kind to me. I smiled down the bar at the young, skinny kid with the spikes of hair, and he moved his mouth up at the corners, glanced down at his beer. I wasn't skinny enough yet. That seemed hilarious to me. I wanted to tell him it was okay. I understood, really.

Andy slid onto his stool, tucking twenties into his wallet. "How's your drink?"

"It's so good!" I said. I leaned down to take another sip. The bartender came over, and asked if we were doing okay. "We're just fine!" I said brightly. "This is delicious."

"Good," he said. Andy ordered another beer and shot.

"How was your day other than your mother?" he said after he knocked back his drink.

"Well, I walked up the big hill by campus, and I *almost* didn't want to die when I got to work. I didn't even have to sit down for a minute when I got to the library."

"Woo hoo!" he said, and carefully clicked his glass against my still very full one, sitting on the bar.

"And I applied for jobs." Something about my whole family

probably finding out I had gotten weight loss surgery had made me panic, decide that I had to fix things immediately. It was like uploading my resume directly into the hole that anxiety had punched into my chest. It had worked, a little bit. I meant to tell him that, but instead I said, "And why didn't you tell me that you were having problems?" I was afraid to look at him.

"It's not a big deal," he said. "I'm okay, I promise." He said it soothingly, in a dismissive kind of way. He was good at that tone of voice.

"I'm sure you are!" I said. "I know you'll be fine, but—but aren't you supposed to tell me about things?"

"You have so much going on. I didn't want to worry you."

"But that's what I'm supposed to do, right? Because I'm your girlfriend."

"You're the best girlfriend ever," he said, now in his playful, subject-changing voice. He put his arm around my shoulders and squeezed, pulling me against him. My head was close to his, and I looked up at him from the corner of my eye.

"Maybe we could—have you thought of moving in together? I mean, we've only been dating over four years, I don't want to rush you or anything." My heart was beating crazily. I sat up. "It would be so much cheaper," I went on, a little too quickly, and he looked down at his beer. "My apartment, split between the two of us? It would save so much money."

"Your apartment's so tiny!" he said, looking up. "You can barely fit Fang in there!"

"He is not fat."

"He is the fattest cat in the land."

"But it could work! I know it's just one bedroom but we could put your desk in the walk-in closet in the living room, and my desk could go in the bedroom, and I would go out all the time, to coffee shops or whatever, so you'd have plenty of time to yourself. It's not huge, but we could totally make it work."

"It's not much bigger than a studio," he said. "And besides, wouldn't I get cooties all over your stuff?"

"You already have, right?" I was tugging on the sleeve of his shirt. "It's such a good idea. Tell me what a good idea it is."

"It's a very good idea," he said. "I'll definitely think about it. Do you need another drink yet? Don't forget your cherry! It looks very delicious."

I looked at my cherry, impaled on its sword. "No you won't," I said suddenly. "You won't think about it. We'll never talk about it again and you know it. You say, 'I'll think about it,' and then it'll never come up and it'll be another four years before we—whatever." Tears. I took a long sip of my drink so I wouldn't have to look at him. I lifted the glass and drank until the cherry floated up and bumped into my lip. My body had iced up all the way into my chest, but now I was warm again.

"Oh honey. No."

I shrugged.

"I'm sorry," he said. A moment. He looked so unhappy. "I just haven't lived by myself, ever. I've always had roommates. I like having my own space. I need that for a while."

"But you've had it for a while, haven't you? Two years?"

"I need a little more time," he said. He sounded unhappy.

"Forever?" It came out sounding so tiny and pathetic.

"No!" he said, sounding incredulous. "Of course not forever."

"Okay," I said.

"So do you want another Manhattan? Maker's Mark, with a cherry for dessert?"

I nodded.

"Do you need anything else? Can you have pretzels? Or chips? How about peanuts? We could go next door and get sushi, if you want? That has lots of protein. You love sushi."

I shook my head. "I'm okay," I said.

"But sushi!" He sounded outraged.

"Maybe sushi next time?"

"Okay," he said. "Next time."

"Thank you. You are so nice."

"Anything for you," he said. "You know that."

We raced to the train stop. It was dark and quiet at the intersection where the train came rushing out of the ground, though there were people milling up and down the sidewalk in front of the burger joint. Some people sprawled on the curb, their legs hanging out over onto the tracks that crisscrossed the asphalt street.

"I want to sit," I said, flailing my arms around. "I want to sit on this pipe," I said, gesturing fitfully at the tall concrete pylon that stood incongruously on the corner. "I can't get up." I tried to haul myself up, but it was too tall and my arms were too weak to heave myself around.

"Here," Andy said, and he was in front of me, had my elbows in his hands, was lifting me without effort—without a grunt or an exhalation of breath, and I was flying up off the ground. A shriek startled out of me, a wild laugh, and then I was sitting on top of the concrete pole, balanced with one hand on his shoulder and I was babbling, "Oh my god, oh my god."

"There you go."

I lifted my hands from his shoulder slowly, carefully. I held myself still, balanced. "I'm doing it!" I said. I couldn't find words for what I was doing right then—balancing. Not stumbling, or falling. I was light. Light enough to lift, light enough to maybe never come down. When he boosted me up, I was weightless, and I had never felt like that before, and hadn't known it was possible. I couldn't imagine feeling any other way, ever again.

"Do you want to get down?" Andy said. He held out his arm to me.

"No, no, no," I said. "I'm good. I'm okay." I was light as a feather, perched like a bird up high, and everything was perfect.

grand metaphors! . . . sweeping pronouncements! . . . cleaning out the closets . . . digging up the dead past

In April I picked up my phone and a voice on the other end said, "We'd like to have you come in for a job interview."

I didn't stammer. I said, "I'd be delighted!" I wrote down the time and the date. I had an interview.

I was 115 pounds down. I was almost under 200 pounds for the first time in—I didn't remember the last time I had been under 200 pounds. And I had told my mother about my weight loss surgery, and I had a job interview, and I was losing more weight—it had slowed down to just a pound or two every week, but it was consistent, steady, a drumbeat. Down and down and down.

I was lighter, and I had a spring fever kind of feeling, like I needed to fling my arms out and explode the world. I needed to upturn everything in my life, drag myself kicking and screaming into—I didn't know what, yet. Or how, exactly. But, it was a time for grand metaphors and sweeping pronouncements and striding bravely into my new world.

It wasn't a sunny and bright afternoon, though. The fog was dark, as if the ocean had been lit on fire and filled the city with smoke, and it was cold and miserable outside. The weather did not match my mood and my energetic will, my vast and sprawling intentions. I bundled up for a trip to the grocery store. I hauled home an enormous box of big black garbage bags, the industrial kind. I bought lemon-scented cleaner and Pledge surface wipes. I bought cans of tuna, because I was going to get back on track with my diet. I stood in the meat aisle of Andronico's, where my friend Heather had once seen Daniel Handler, and I decided that I was having an epiphany. I decided that everything had just become different. I decided that right there and then, I was dividing my life into a "before" and an "after." This turning point should have come back in November, back when I woke up from surgery, but I had never been a quick learner.

It was time to become the person I wanted to be.

Tuna, I thought. I would start with tuna fish.

I dropped all my packages in the living room when I got home, and without pulling off my coat I strode into the kitchen and opened all the cabinets. I pulled out a regular-sized garbage bag from under the counter. Into it went Oreos, Milanos, and dark chocolate chips. Rocky road ice cream. A bottle of soda I'd stored in the back of the fridge, as if pushing it back there would make me forget that I had bought it. I threw away things I'd convinced myself were high in protein, like fish sticks and chicken fingers that were actually breadcrumb-coated faux foods loaded with trans fats. I tossed in the container of thick slices of Oscar Mayer bologna. I'd brought these items into the house because I thought they'd be occasional treats, but I kept finding them in my mouth. I'd mindlessly drift into the kitchen and find a handful of chocolate chip cookies halfway finished before I even considered what I was doing, before I even left the kitchen.

I swept everything out of my cabinets and the fridge and into my garbage sack. It was too heavy to lift. Corners and edges of containers punctured the plastic, and when I bounced the bag behind me on the steps down into the garage, I was afraid it was going to burst open, and then I'd be crawling over the cement, chasing after runaway Ding Dongs and smashed boxes of pierogies. I couldn't stand that much unintentional significance. I couldn't stand the idea that I might change my mind on my knees on the concrete floor of the garage and lunge at a bag of Double Stufs to have just one last cookie.

I hauled the bag desperately, begging it not to break, and lifted it up and into the can. When I slammed the lid shut, it felt sudden, final, irrevocable.

I was tired of letting things happen to me instead of making things happen. I was tired of being sad because there was nothing I could do, being weighed down by junk food and a closet overstuffed with clothes that didn't fit me.

I elbowed open my front door and kicked it closed, and scrubbed my hands. I took another big black sack and opened up the window in my bedroom to clear the air, to make it cold and refreshing. A flash in my memory: the stink of pan-fried chicken, the sensation of kneeling in front of the toilet. I waded into the closet. I pulled all the hangers off the bars. I pulled down everything that was folded on the shelf. I tossed armfuls of clothes onto the bed, mounding them up. I pulled armfuls of clothes off the floor of the closet. The pile was almost up to my neck when I stood by the side of my bed. I thought, *Why stop there?* I emptied out all the bags of clothes I'd been saving for the brand-new me. I kicked them into the center of the bedroom, dresses flying up into the air, tangling around my ankles. I viciously kicked them again. I pulled open all the drawers of my dresser and emptied them out, one by one. All my socks, underpants, bras, T-shirts, sweaters, pants, skirts, nightclothes. I raced around the apartment, grabbing sweaters from the hook in the living room and the back of the chair by my desk, a shirt kicked aside in the bathroom, a nightgown hanging up next to the towels. I scoured my house clean. Everything I owned was a tottering pile on the bed, spilling down onto the floor. Now it reached almost higher than my head.

I had collected clothes, saved clothes that fit me at every size I'd been over the years. I kept all the clothes that used to fit me, even the ugly ones. Even the stained clothes, the ripped clothes, the terrible clothes in which I'd always looked awful. Because someday I was going to fit into them again. Having those clothes there waiting for me was like an insurance policy, a guarantee that the ever-growing body below my neck wouldn't be mine forever. That this was not real life, me at this weight.

And when I lost weight, and fit into smaller clothes—including some of the clothes I'd been hoarding—I still didn't throw away the larger clothes. Because what if this was temporary? What if this was a mistake, an aberration, and one day I'd wake up and find myself ten or twenty or fifty or a hundred pounds fatter? I saved them. They were a warning, a fear made manifest.

I sat down hard. On the bed I faced—I couldn't even begin to guess how many years of useless accumulation. It made me tired. I had an overwhelming urge to get a bottle of lighter fluid and a match and torch the mess.

I left it there, closed the door behind me, reopened the door to let the cat out, and closed it again. I wrote Monique an email: I'm getting rid of all the clothes I've ever owned. Do you want any of it? Most of it won't fit you because it's stuff from when I was my highest weight, but there's a lot of stuff you might like. Let me know.

A lot of backspacing and careful wording and rewording, terrified of implying, "I am too skinny for this stuff, but you're still fat so you can wear it!" I was always walking on eggshells. I didn't want to forget the person I used to be. I didn't want to be a person people thought I wasn't allowed to be, either. I had tuna fish for dinner.

Monique drove from the East Bay so that she could stuff her whole car full of clothing. She went through the pile while I ate my way through the cheese I had bought for both of us. Special occasion cheese. No harm in eating it. I drank all the wine, too. I thrust another handful of clothes at Mo and disappeared into the bathroom to lean over the sink and rest my head against the cold mirror. That familiar feeling, my stomach packed full, backing up, nausea overwhelming. I wanted to crawl into the pile of clothes on the bed and nest until my stomach emptied out and my intestines cramped and my body was ready for me to deposit everything in a pile in the toilet. When had my life become so biological? So disgusting? Funny how I thought the same thing every time I ate too quickly. I always ate too quickly.

"Are you okay?" Monique was standing outside the door.

"I'm okay!" I said. "I'll be right out!" I knew I'd be back in the bathroom within the hour, though. I hoped she'd be gone before then.

There were still piles of clothes left around the house after we finished loading up Monique's car. I left the cheese on the table—Monique hadn't wanted to take it home, even though I had pressed urgently. I was afraid to say, *please, I can't eat it,* because that might imply that I thought she could, or would. I was afraid there was an insult in that idea. My stomach was still packed and stretched, expanding into the bottom of my chest, up into my throat.

I should throw out the cheese, I thought. I put a paper towel over the plate and walked away. I turned back and grabbed the plate and stuck the whole thing in the fridge. It would get hard and moldy, and I would be absolved of the actual act of having to throw it away, wasting it.

I sat on the futon, and tucked my feet under me, and drank the last of the bottle of wine. I wondered how much money, how many resources, how much energy had gone into all those clothes that I had bought at all my different sizes. I wondered if I would miss any of it. If someday I would think of a particular sweater with a pang of regret.

I stumbled to the bathroom. When I was drunk, the need to take a bath always overcame me. I stripped down quickly and splashed into the tub, ducking my head under the water. I still fit, there was still room from side to side no matter how I felt. I floated there in the dark, the water a roar in my ears. I drifted. I might have slept. I imagined myself as a primeval creature. I imagined myself as something strange and new, evolving violently and silently in the dark. I imagined that you could see the whole history of my body stretching behind me in a series of line drawings, from chubby baby to skinny kid to fat prepubescent, the lines becoming curved and further and further apart. I saw the long unbroken chain of my life, all the sizes I had ever been, and I knew I wouldn't be anywhere now without having been who I was. I was drunk in the bathtub, and falling asleep.

I stumbled out of the bathroom wrapped in a towel and went into my bedroom. I couldn't stand the idea of going to bed alone. Cold sheets, fluffed pillows. I dragged the quilt off the bed and into the living room. I dropped the towel. I wondered what my body looked like in the flickering of the television. The fat was leaving, but the skin was staying behind, folds of pale, rumpled linen draped over my bones. My belly sagged, my thighs spilled down over my knees. I looked soft, as if I could be pulled apart like warm taffy. I didn't have an intact body anymore; I was melting fat and unfastened skin and bones rising up to the surface. All over I was pockmarked with divots of rumpled, cheesecloth flesh and blemishes.

This was what I looked like underneath everything. And I was okay with that, because this was the person I had made. This was the cumulative effect of all those years of being who I was. This was important. I tried to remember it. I wondered what it would feel like when I wasn't drunk.

the morning after . . . yet more lying . . . trying not to think about it

When I woke up, my mouth felt dry and sticky, and the wine bottle was knocked over and empty. There were dried red blotches on the wood floor, perilously close to the white area rug. My phone was ringing in my bag on the table, and I staggered over and answered it without looking at my caller ID.

"I saw a show on weight loss surgery," my mother was saying, as I fell back onto the futon. I wasn't hungover, not hurting, but there was a heaviness to everything, all my movements, all my thoughts, as if I had gained the weight back while I slept. "They were talking about malnutrition, and malsorbing—"

"Malabsorption?" I said. I stretched out on the couch and covered my face with a throw pillow, tucking the phone in under my chin. I kept my eyes open, and the dimness was soothing. "That's the point of the surgery, Mom. They want that to happen. You absorb fewer calories, less fat. It's what helps you lose the weight." I was always an expert.

"Well, they were talking about how dangerous it is, because some vitamins can only be absorbed in the intestines, and people get sick and some of them die. Your Aunt Evelyn was talking about a patient of hers who had to be hospitalized and get shots every day. They put her on a line, a lifeline. And now she has to get shots every day for the rest of her life, and she said it happens all the time, that it's going to happen to you with the kind of surgery you got."

"Aunt Evelyn is ridiculous. She doesn't know what surgery I got."

"The switch, right? That's what I told her."

I sat up. "You weren't supposed to tell her. Why did you tell her?"

"I was worried about you," she said defensively. I could hear her chin coming down and her eyebrows going up—the face she made when she was mad, and afraid of getting me mad, too. "I asked her questions about it."

"Mom!" I said. "Mom, I asked you not to. You could have asked me. I told you that. I would have told you anything."

"I'm sorry," she said, but it was a defensive apology.

"It's fine," I said sullenly, reluctantly. "But she doesn't know anything about it. I mean, it could happen if you're stupid. If you're not careful." I got up off the futon, paced the stuffed living room. "I'm not stupid. I take vitamins every day." Almost every day. Often. When I remembered. When I could bring myself to chew the horrible things, and gird my loins for the terrible metallic aftertaste they left. "I'm fine, Mom."

"Okay," she said, sounding a little distracted. And then her voice brightened. "How much weight have you lost? Are you a skinny little thing yet? You'll always have your booty. Even when I was a skinny minny, I had a booty, and your father loved it."

"Mom!" I said, though I wasn't really outraged. That was what I was supposed to say.

"Well, he did!" she said. "I guess you'll see. How much do you have to lose? Do you stop soon?"

"I don't know," I said. "I don't get to decide."

"Send me pictures," she said, and I agreed that of course I would, just as soon as I took them, any day now, I should be keeping track of my progress and I'd get right on that pretty soon, and then we hung up. I put my head down on the futon, and then tucked my legs up under me. I could do that, I could almost double over before my stomach got in the way. I could make a small ball on the couch and push my face into the pillow and rock back and forth with my eyes closed, letting the dark and the rush of blood inside my head settle me, letting my agitation recede, letting my mind, everything settle back into calm-water stillness.

Chapter 28

intestinal incidents and the official death of
dignity . . . job interview! . . . inside my head
and inside my gut

In the bathroom of the ad agency, right before my first job interview in
five years, I scrubbed my tights out in the sink with hand soap. My heart
was pounding, and if someone came through the swinging door I would
know that the world was a more unfair place that I had ever imagined. I
had already mopped myself clean with a handful of paper towels. I was
crying so quietly that I was startled when the tears dripped off my chin
onto my hands.

I blasted the faucet again and again over the crotch of my tights,
watching the suds boil up and change colors and the water finally run
clear. The tile floor was cold under my bare feet, and I wondered what
kind of germs were crawling through my pores. My stomach was still
cramping and roiling and I tasted bile. It wasn't my fault, it wasn't.
I hadn't eaten anything worse than usual—I hadn't eaten anything
that day, I hadn't. As if I was pleading with my body, a force that was

stronger than the universe or a god who plucks sparrows out of the sky. What had I done? I hadn't done anything. I had a latte for protein. Hot, to kill the butterflies in my stomach. I imagined them boiling alive, being flushed down through my new system that I still didn't understand, that seemed as much an enemy to me now as the old system that kept me fat.

This one, though—it felt cruel, it felt capricious, and it kept me skinny, getting skinnier. Sometimes there were mornings when I couldn't leave the house because I had to go take a crap again and again. Cramp after cramp sent me running back down the hallway and fumbling with the front door key and racing to the bathroom before an accident happened. Mornings like that, I tried not to think about.

Mornings like this one. I showed up early for an interview to be a proofreader at a fancy (*internationally known!* I shrieked in a panic inside my head) advertising agency. But the latte combined with my panic and anxiety overcame me and my stomach. A searing, incredible cramp doubled me over. My bowels just—let loose, hot and wet. I hadn't imagined this could be even be possible.

Standing frozen there in the lobby, hunched over, afraid to move, I wondered what I looked like. One moment I had been waiting for my interview in the lobby and casually but professionally inspecting the entire wall full of trophies, hoping that my cool-but-classy business casual outfit was being broadcast over secret monitors that the agency partners all gathered around, to inspect the latest crop of freshest meat. The next moment, I made an incoherent, involuntary grunt like I had been punched in the chest. I lurched. For one long and utterly still moment, a look of wide-eyed realization and quick-moving terror spread across my face. Then, the agency partners would have seen my rapid, inexplicable, stiff-armed waddling, away from the imaginary camera.

I went to my interview with the department head, took the proofreading test, talked to the other proofreaders, and spoke to HR while wearing wet tights and with my knees clenched. I hoped—*breathe in*—hoped—*breathe out*—hoped to god I wouldn't have to choke off mid-rapture over *The Chicago Manual of Style* and my endless pursuit of textual perfection in order to excuse myself in a flail of limbs, leaving my interviewer with lingering doubts about me, and a lingering odor.

I don't remember what I talked about. My legs were clammy. I was afraid I smelled strange. I shook hands and smiled wide, and I pretended that everything was perfect and I was exactly where I needed to be and had everything I needed. That was what I was good at. That was what I *excelled* at.

I held it together until I could flee, and I then headed straight home instead of going back to work at the library. I emailed my boss to tell her I was sick, that I was lying down, that things were very difficult and please don't question me. Hunched over on the N train, letting the rhythm of the track rock me side to side, I thought that if I wanted to, I could go into a store—almost any store in the mall, or up and down Grant Street—and just pluck a new skirt off the rack, buy a new package of tights. I wouldn't do it today, but I could do that. I turned over that idea in my mind. The thought was bright and shiny. It was the other side of the coin, the opposite of my wet tights and clenching gut and itchy, damp eyes. I was skinny.

Sometimes, when I noticed I fit through the Muni turnstiles without having to slide sideways, the side effects meant even less than they did pre-surgery, back when I had skipped so facilely over the bullet points. Sometimes I could pretend nothing had actually happened: no obesity, no surgery, no recovery—that this was just how I was, a normal-sized person who sometimes had stomach problems that mattered very little. Someone who was not secretly impressed by the feat of fitting into a seat on the train without overlapping onto other passengers.

I could get away with it. No one looked at me sideways. No one knew anything about me except what they saw. And what they saw—an ordinary-sized person, maybe even skinny—had changed so radically from what they used to see, what my body used to say about me—*hello,*

I am fat—that it still felt a little impossible. How could you not tell I used to be fat? How could you not tell what I had gone through to not be fat anymore, to never be fat again? How was it possible no one knew my secrets—the weight loss surgery, the soft skin left behind? My still-damp tights?

In some ways, being skinny was the same thing as keeping secrets better. I did not have my fat to give me away, to tell anyone who looked at me exactly what kind of person I was.

Sometimes I wondered what the fuck I had done, and inside my head I heard the ringing cries of horrified people, both fat and skinny, asking, *Why anyone would do something like that to themselves? How could you even consider doing something so radical, so clinical, so brutal to your own body? Was being fat really that bad? Was making your stomach your enemy really the solution?*

It didn't matter anymore. It was the solution I had chosen, and I was sitting on the train on the way home from a job interview, for a position I would never have applied for when I was fat, to work in a huge and beautiful building perched on a hill in Chinatown and filled with floor after floor of ridiculously beautiful people, and I could almost, almost imagine myself there. A feeling of hope with jagged edges was huge in my chest.

The train ground up out of the tunnel and into the light. I pulled my phone out of my pocket. I wanted to tell—someone. Andy. My mother, Monique, my brother. I wanted to tell someone about my interview. I had done so well. But more than that, I wanted to tell someone what had happened, for the shared horror of it. *I crapped myself ten minutes before a job interview, and it's a direct side effect of a decision I made.* I wanted absolution, for someone to say, *It's not so bad, and you shouldn't be ashamed, and it could happen to anyone. In fact, let me tell you a great story about the time I shit myself on a bobsled during the Olympics.*

I wanted to make it funny, and make it meaningless, and make it nothing. I didn't want regrets. Regrets belonged only to the person I used to be. I wanted nothing to matter except the benefits I was enjoying, the new life I was only starting to understand was opening up for me.

It didn't matter if my insides—inside my head and inside my gut— were fucked up. No one could tell, and now I could be just anyone. I could do anything, and that felt like the real and final truth.

portentous portents . . . fitting in a chair . . . waiting for something

Almost a year.

"Let's go to Chicago," I said to Andy on a Sunday morning, as I tore open packets of Equal to stir into my tea. We were sitting at the coffee shop in his neighborhood, and the sunlight was bright in the backyard. I was sitting in a seat that had used to be too tight, a plastic chair that my butt used to spill out of on all sides, squeezing through the cracks in the back and the space under the armrests. I shifted experimentally. I had room in the chair. A lot of room. I could fit a palm on either side of my butt. It was the same as all the other chairs scattered across the little garden, lining the path up to the deck, overlooking the tiny tinkling stream.

We were nestled down into a bright crevice carved into the heart of Cole Valley, a place lined with paving stones and tiny-leafed bushes that could only be called shrubberies. We heard water and wind and the N train screaming out of the tunnel and stopping right in front of the restaurant next door. The tables were clustered close to one another, but it wasn't crowded yet. Andy lit another cigarette and squinted at me.

"Why do you want to go to Chicago?" he said. He was leaning back in his chair with his long legs crossed elegantly at the knee. "Isn't it windy there? There's nothing in Chicago." His hands were trembling again, the way they did every morning, and he had waved off my concern the way he did every morning. The cup shook at his mouth.

"Wendy's having her birthday there. She wants people to come out for the weekend. We will do exciting things like go to fancy restaurants and bars. Dance or something, I think."

He made a face. "Nah," he said. He caught the expression on mine, when he looked up from the ashtray. "You should go, though!" he said. "You should go have fun! Have a weekend! Do the dancing and the business." He made a sharp little dance move in his seat, twisting his torso, pumping his arms. He approximated the noise of a bass thump—"Umph, umph, umph, umph. Oh yeah. Oh yeah."

"I dance much better than that," I said, indignantly. My tea was way too sweet.

"You do," he said. "But you should go on. Go to Chicago."

"I don't want to go without you," I said. "We should go together! It'll be fun! You could use the break!" I could feel my voice lifting up at every exclamation point, every new plea. "When have we ever gone away together? We have never even been on a plane at the same time! Have you ever even been on a plane?"

"Only to *Germany*," he said, gesturing imperiously.

"Oh! Right! They let you smoke in the back of the plane! That's so cool. You are distracting me. I just—" I looked at him and stopped. He looked at me steadily, and his eyes were very brown, and he looked sad. "I'm sorry," I said. "I know this is not your kind of thing. I didn't mean to make you feel guilty, I really didn't."

"I know," he said. "Go to Chicago. You're going to have a great time. You won't want to come home, I bet."

"I will always want to come home," I said, making a face into my tea. It was too cold.

I don't know whether to be grateful to have saved a snapshot of that morning in my memory: the coffee shop, the garden, Andy's face, the baseball cap he was wearing to tame his hair, which sprung wildly from his head, silver and coarse. The torn packets of Equal lying on the table, the cigarette butts in the ashtray, him sitting across from me and telling me to go. Me sitting across from him, surreptitiously sneaking my hands down to the seat of the chair to measure out, by the width of my fingers, exactly how much room I had in this chair, side to side, exactly how wide I was. I should have been leaning over the table, taking his shoulders, and shaking him and screaming, *What the fuck is wrong with us? Why isn't this working?*

He had said, over and over, *it's not you, it's me.* And I had never said, *then what are you doing about it?* And I had been afraid to say, *then what is there to be done?* It had never occurred to me that maybe it wasn't him, and maybe it wasn't me—maybe it was us. For so long, I had been so scared to say anything, to make any sudden moves, to have what we had built come tumbling down, leaving the bare, cracked, and crumbling walls of our foundation naked and exposed. I couldn't imagine us not being the most important people in each other's lives, but I couldn't imagine us being frozen like this forever. I had waited four years. We hadn't had sex in four years. We had been dating almost five years. I had been waiting. I had been waiting for him. For him to get better. For him to tell me what was wrong. For him to tell me things would never change, to chase me away. For me to get better, and figure out how to fix things.

I had thought I could wait forever. I had always been sure that things would be okay if I just waited. I cleaned out my closets and my fridge and watched my body change and bought all new clothes and tried to be a new person, one who was exactly the same as I used to be, only better. But I was still waiting.

On that bright, gray San Francisco morning, I was chilled, and my scarf was triple tucked around my neck, and my tea was cold and too sweet, and he was sitting across the table, telling me to go. He loved me and I loved him, and that's what I remember.

sex in the Sears Tower ... super-secret
relationship secrets ... the possibility of
happiness

"Oh my god," Monique said. "You're going to split a room with Ben? You're going to love him. When I met him last year, the first thing I thought was 'he is totally Jen's type.'"

We were having dinner after work in the Ferry Building, at Hog Island Oyster Company. The place was packed, but we were oblivious to the crowd as we hunkered down on the tall chairs and slathered our crusty rolls with butter and drank champagne.

We gossiped about the Chicago trip we were both going on—me without Andy. Friends from all over the country were going to be there, and friends of friends. I was going to share a hotel room with Ben, someone I had never met. Hotel rooms are expensive things. It made sense for us to split the cost of a room.

"Oooh," I said, waggling my eyebrows. The waitress came over with a stand and a huge ice-covered tray, set them down in front of us. She went over the varieties of oysters and where they came from. I nodded and smiled, but was mostly waiting for her to stop so I could start eating. I picked up my little fork, selected an oyster, and stopped with it halfway to my mouth. "Hey, wait, so what does that mean?" I asked.

She waved her oyster fork in the air. "You know. He's tall. A big guy. Linebacker type. Funny, loud, outgoing. He's, like, an alpha male."

"And I like alpha males, is what you're saying?" I selected an oyster and heaped relish on it, squeezed a lemon carefully over the top. "I like to be mastered!" I tipped the shell over my bottom lip, threw my head back. "Oh, god, that's so good. And I can eat like, all of these." They didn't seem to fill up my stomach at all. I could eat every one of them and never be full. The mineral taste of the oysters was rich and oceany. The Bay Bridge broke from one side of the huge wall of windows to the other, the widest and largest thing I could see. "Big manly men?" I closed my eyes for a moment. "Mm. Okay. You got me."

"Seriously, that's the first thing Wendy and I said."

"Maybe we will have a torrid Chicago affair," I said. "Maybe we will make love in a—Chicago landmark. The Sears Tower? Maybe we will do it in the Sears Tower. I'm skinny enough to have an affair, right? There's a weight class. For girls like me, I mean." I snapped my mouth shut before she realized that I had said that, so I didn't have to explain that I didn't mean it that way, I didn't. But it seemed easier to make skinny jokes nowadays than fat jokes—I wasn't even sure I was allowed to make fat jokes, when I was almost less than two hundred pounds. But there was no one who found my skinny jokes funny, or wanted to feel my new hip bones instead of my fat rolls. "I mean," I said, and I could feel the stuttering coming on, and I ground to a halt. Maybe it was too loud for her to hear me, because she lifted her glass and said, "To doing it in the Sears Tower!" I raised mine, and we clinked them.

I let the bubbles in my throat slip down into my belly, plucked another oyster from the tray. "Seriously, though," I said casually. "What if he really is cute? Maybe I am in trouble."

She looked at me oddly. I shrugged. I swallowed my oyster quickly, wiped the tips of my fingers on my napkin. I had hardly tasted it.

"Well," I said. "You know." I waved my hand around, grabbed another hunk of bread, and swirled it around in the butter dish. "What if I develop a terrible crush on him? That would be embarrassing." I pushed the bread into my mouth and was buttering the next piece. My stomach had started to feel full.

Monique and I had never, in the five years I had been dating Andy, talked about my problems with him. She didn't know how long it had been since we had had sex. I lied.

"Well," Monique said. "What if he develops a crush on you?" She winked saucily, tipping her oyster at me.

"That is unlikely!" I thought for a moment, looking at my third hunk of bread. "It would be kind of cool, though, right? I've always wanted to be a femme fatale."

"We'll have a signal. I'll ask you a question, and your answer will be indicative of whether I should leap in and save you!"

"Okay, once I meet him, I'll say, 'Hey, Monique, what time is it in San Francisco right now?' if I want you to save me. Or if it turns out that he's totally my type and I am overwhelmed with lust, I'll say, 'I love Chicago!' That's really meaningful."

"It's a plan," she said, and we both giggled. We raised our champagne glasses again, and I was as fizzy as the alcohol, as light as the bubbles racing upwards and exploding at the surface. A little dangerous, a little reckless.

the mysterious Ben . . . letting myself pretend . . . reveling in the moment . . . when guilt is not enough

Wendy was staying at the fancy hotel, a few blocks away from my hotel on East Ontario. I stood at the window of my room, looking down at the river and over at the amazing tower of parking right across from us. Everyone below looked very far away and impossibly small. On the phone Wendy said, "We're hanging out at the hotel. Do you want to come over now?"

"Who?" I asked.

"Jake is here, and Ben, and me. And we've got cocktails!" I heard shouting in the background, a big booming laugh like a freight train, and the sound of glasses and bottles.

"I just have to—" A war whoop in the background, and Wendy was far away saying something and everything was muffled and loud. She came back on the line.

"Sorry! Sorry. The boys are getting a little rowdy. Do you want to come over?"

"Come over!" I heard in the background.

"They want you to come over," Wendy said.

"I have to change," I said. "I'm all grimy from the plane." I promised to be there soon.

Monique and Ian hadn't landed yet, Wendy said. We were the only ones in town so far. Come quick! she said. Check out the gorgeous room!

"Okay," I said. "Okay, I'm hurrying!" In the background, more whooping and that laugh again, and Wendy hung up without saying good-bye. I dropped my phone on the chair and pulled off my dress, my leggings—I would never have dared to wear leggings a year ago. I didn't need a shower, I would just put on my contacts. I would wear eyeliner, I would wear red lipstick, I would wear a cowl neck dress, I would wear heels and perfume and run my fingers anxiously through my hair, coaxing it to stand up in spikes, swoop in front of my ears. I raced around the room, looking for the best source of light, for Q-tips to erase an eyeliner mistake, and I was finally ready. All the lights were on, the curtains open. I stood in front of the full-length mirror. Were there any mistakes? Did I look like someone who should be wearing this dress, which clung to my breasts and my hips, and was a little short? Were my arms too big? Could you see the lumps of my stomach, where it looked like a mining company was excavating fat deposits? I smoothed down my dress, rebuckled my shoe, checked one eye, the other eye. Bulletproof eyeliner, bulletproof me.

Chicago feels like a real city, the way no other city but New York does. Chicago has that compact, upflung center, tall buildings covered in silver glass that reflects the sky. The streets carve canyons through the skyscrapers, so you feel small and protected when you wander down the sidewalks. Maybe also a little lost, but still so urban and sophisticated. There is a sense of pageantry and busyness about Chicago that is missing from most other cities, a rush, a feeling that everything is going on somewhere, led by someone. That anything could be happening, and you could be missing it. It's not a real city if you don't feel slightly off-balance, a little worried that you are always slightly behind. It's an anxious feeling, but it's also exhilarating, motivating. It pushes you forward, sending you hurrying to the next thing and the next and the next, taking everything you get and wanting everything you're given.

Chicago was a shot in the arm, after San Francisco.

At the hotel, I stood in the hallway, listening to the voices inside the room. I heard a burst of that laughter, and had the immediate impulse to assume that they were laughing about me. I shoved it down, checked my lipstick, powdered my nose, carefully brushed off the extra powder, closed my eyes, and knocked.

There were cheeses and crackers and spreads on the coffee table—"From Trader Joe's," Wendy said. It was the first thing I noticed. Ben, sitting on the couch, looked up at me.

"Hi," I said to him, but I didn't know how I managed to say it. "Well, hi," he said to me. I wanted to fill up a plate, to sit down on the floor and pull the platter close and fill up on chocolate-covered nuts and thick wedges of yellow cheese and small rounds of salami, because then I would have something to look at besides him, and I would have something to keep my jaw moving.

I wanted to keep looking at him, but I was afraid someone in the room would notice. I wanted to act as natural as possible. I wanted to turn to him and say something witty that would indicate very clearly that we were simply roommates, and I had never joked about having a torrid affair with him. His voice was as deep and round as the ring of a bell, and his eyes were blue.

I sat down next to him, theorizing that it would be easier to look at everyone in the room except him if I were sitting next to him. My mouth was moving, and we were laughing, and I was perfectly natural.

I met his eyes just for an instant and then reached over to the table for my cup. I took a long swig of my drink, and then another and another, and then Wendy herded us out the door and into a cab.

I was aware of him all the time, in the front seat chatting with the driver, laughing his booming laugh. He opened the door for us when we got to the bar, and I felt the brief touch of his hand on my waist as he stepped by me while I was introducing myself to Brenda, another friend who had come to meet us here. I was aware of the conversation he had with the bartender while we dragged the Formica-topped tables together and gathered enough seats and ordered drinks and got comfortable. I was aware of him when Wendy and I talked about what we were doing next and where we were going and who we were meeting and when. He was always in my peripheral vision, in the back of my mind. I spun around when he took the seat next to me, bent close to my ear, and said, "A whiskey girl, huh?"

I blinked at him. An instant of vertigo, gone in the next blink. "Always," I said, shifting a cigarette out of my pack and handing him my lighter, exactly as if I had done the same thing hundreds of times. He grinned at me as I leaned in and he flicked it on. I smiled at him, breathed out the smoke. "I can't drink beer," I said, gesturing at his pint. It was filled to the top with a dark beer that looked almost poisonous.

"Oh, I can drink beer," he said. He had dimples, one in his cheek, and one in his chin. I wanted to put the tip of my finger in them. The way he was looking at me. "Want to have a chugging contest?"

"I will sip like a lady, and watch you do all the work," I said. He kept smiling at me as he reached past me for my pack of cigarettes and tapped one out. "Hey!" I said, mock-outraged. "That's my lucky cigarette!" He had taken the one I had turned filter-side-down; I don't remember where I had picked up the habit.

"It's my lucky night," he said, and cocked his eyebrows at me. He knew how ridiculous he was, and I laughed. I turned my head when someone called my name across the table, but he was always there. I felt a line of heat down my arm where his body edged mine. It blazed when he glanced my way, when he shifted, when our knees bumped. I brushed my hand across his shoulder when I got up for another drink; I leaned into him, put my lips at his ear.

"Do you need another?" I said. He jumped. He leaned ever so slightly back into me.

"Well thank you so much," he said. "That's very kind of you."

Everything seemed so easy. I knew what to say, and he said all the right things, too. I leaned into every turn with absolute faith and conviction. There was a sense of speed and freedom, and I didn't think of anything else at all but that moment. I was relishing the feeling that comes when you know, without a doubt, that someone wants you.

I didn't remember the last time anything like this had ever happened to me. If it had ever happened to me.

I was on my third drink. One was enough to get me drunk, but I didn't feel anything except warmth and happiness. Monique was behind me, her arms tucked around my neck.

"Hellllloooo!" she said, with a kiss on my cheek, her bosoms pressed against my back. "Ben!" she said.

"Miss Monique!" he said. "My favorite!" He held out his hand and she grabbed it, shimmying down the aisle between tables and hugging him from behind.

"I don't think I'm your favorite anymore, huh, am I right?" She looked over at me expectantly with her chin on top of his head. He held her wrists and looked at me almost as expectantly.

"I'm working on it," I said, and raised my glass to them. He broke into that laugh, and Monique widened her eyes at me. I shrugged and tried to look innocent, and she made We Are Going to Talk eyes at me, and was off around the table saying hello to everyone. More friends came in, and people cheered, and there was hugging and talk about travel issues and hotels and how we got there and when.

Occasionally, Ben's hand would creep over to my cigarette pack and he'd steal another and laugh at my indignant look. I loved it. Of course I did. It was light out for a long while, and then it began to get dark outside. The bar was lit by the jukebox and low sconces that lined the walls. Someone took out a camera and began taking pictures, and the flash made everything brilliantly bright. I didn't immediately demand to look at the photos and then demand to delete any unflattering ones. Right then I didn't care anymore if I looked okay in a picture. I was absolutely satisfied to simply have a picture exist. It was a comfortable feeling that drifted by in a sea of other comfortable feelings, in the warm, dark bar, filling up with a comforting haze of noise and smoke.

I tugged Mo's sleeve and made my way to the back, dodging around people with their feet up on chairs and tables, men playing pool, and the couples making out. It felt like everyone was turning to watch me as I went by, and it felt like they were looking at me with interest. I caught the eye of a man in the corner, and he lifted his glass at me. I laughed, a quick burst like a firecracker, because it was so ridiculous. And it was ridiculous because maybe it wasn't a joke. I gave him a thumbs up as I passed by, and when a table of people laughed, I realized that I didn't assume, automatically and without pause, that they were laughing at me. I glanced over at them, a group of people so much younger than me glowing under the low lamp with their heads together, half-empty glasses in front of them, all focused on each other. They were unaware of anything but their happiness together at exactly that moment, and I knew how they felt. I understood what it meant to be self-contained, and to understand the world and be in it, instead of rubbed raw by it.

It was a one-person bathroom but I pulled Monique inside with me, pushed the door shut fast. I put my arms around her. She was wearing a fuzzy sweater, and I found myself plucking bits of fluff from her shoulder as she demanded, "Well?"

I leaned back and opened my mouth and shut it, and then laughed. I said, "Well, what?"

"What time is it in San Francisco?" she asked.

I turned to the mirror and pretended to care about my hair. "I love Chicago," I said, and then met her eyes in the mirror.

"I knew you'd love him," she said. "I love Ben!" Her eyes were huge and blue.

"I know," I said. "Shit," I said, in a heartfelt way.

"You're in trouble!"

"He's incredibly gorgeous. You didn't tell me that. He's exactly my type."

"I told you that."

"You did." I frowned at myself in the mirror.

"You can flirt with him," she said, seriously for a moment.

"I know," I said. "Oh, Monique. I think he likes me. He's flirting with me, too."

"Of course he likes you."

"I guess," I said. "I don't know." She nestled in next to me at the mirror.

"Little Jen," she said, and then stopped and put her arm around me. "Look at you! You're so small! You're like a tiny little thing!"

"I am not," I said automatically.

"Anyway," she said sternly. "It is okay! We are having a good time. You seemed so happy before."

"I'm happy," I said. "I'm just going to be happy."

"I endorse that plan," Monique said. "That's a wise plan."

"That's me," I said. "Wise."

We piled into a caravan of cabs and ended up at a bar with live band karaoke. Jake and Ben went shouting to the bar, and Wendy leaned over to me. "So what do you think?" she said. She looked over at Monique, back at me. "You love him, right?"

"I totally love him," I said.

"Who do you love? What are you talking about? What's going on? Can I love them, too?" Ben was at my shoulder, leaning into me, and Wendy was laughing.

"Go sing something," I said, pushing him off me and prodding him toward the stage.

"You want me to sing? I can sing. I can sing all night, baby girl." He tugged my earlobe and ambled toward the guy taking names.

"He's ridiculous," I said to Wendy. I knew my grin was just as ridiculous.

"It's part of his charm," she shouted as the music came up.

They called Wendy's name, and she pushed through the crowd and up to the stage. We all stood to shout her name and yell, "Woo!" We danced, and Ben was moving in the crowd. When he came up behind me I turned and threw my arms around his neck. He danced. He was a good dancer. He spun me out and back, and we moved until I couldn't breathe. I collapsed on him, yelled, "I'm going outside!" in his ear and pushed my way through the crowd. Someone held the door for me and I knew it was him, of course it was. There was so much power in that. New, strange, heady.

The rest of the night, I never lost track of him. Our group closed down the bar, and we were figuring out who was taking cabs where. Ben was standing with a handful of people who were taking off to get hot dogs, when my cab pulled away from the curb.

In our hotel room I thought about leaving my makeup on, just for an instant, just in case, and then immediately scrubbed it all off with a washcloth. I was pink and red and white and blotchy, and my glasses made everything seem a little imperfect and unappealing. I was hungry. I ordered room service. When it came I sat on the bed in my pajamas, watching cable television and working up the appetite to take a bite of my sandwich. There was pounding at the door, and when I opened it Ben was there with his carry-on bag over his shoulder, smiling at me.

"There you are," he said. "I had a hot dog! A Chicago hot dog. It was good." He drew the word *good* out into half a dozen syllables. He was smiling delightedly, like it had been the best night of his life. He dropped the bag right there in the foyer and put his arms around me, pulled me into him, and stepped us both backward into the room. He was so much larger than me, tall and broad and rock-steady. "And how are you, missy? Look at you, all ready for bed. You're so cute. And you wear glasses, too. My god." He pushed them up my nose and left his finger there for a moment. I ducked away.

"You want a club sandwich?"

"You got a club sandwich? From where?"

"Room service," I said. "I thought I was hungry, but I wasn't, by the time it showed up." I sat down at the end of my bed.

"That's an expensive mistake to make," he said. He lifted the bread gingerly to examine the congealed bacon and poked at it with the decorative toothpick.

"Maybe I'll have it for breakfast," I said.

"I'm sure you'll find something better for breakfast," he said. He hauled his bag off the floor and dropped it on the bed, started digging through it. "So, which bed are we sleeping in?" he said.

"I'm sleeping here," I said, patting my coverlet. "And that means you'll be over there," I said primly.

"What if I want to sleep there," he said. "What then?"

His crooked smile was chocolate-covered, dipped in sprinkles, rolled in nuts. Delicious. Somehow I said, "Life is full of difficulties."

"Or I could make you move," he said. He swooped down on me and lifted me off the end of the bed, and I panicked.

"No! No! Oh my god, no, you can't no, no, no." Struggling and kicking and clutching at him.

He settled me back down, but didn't let go. He smoothed my hair back. "Are you okay? What's wrong?"

"You can't lift me," I said. I didn't want to say, *You'll hurt yourself and I'll be embarrassed as soon as you notice that I'm not as tiny and delicate as you make me feel. That I'm not someone you want to be flirting with, someone you think is hot and confident and totally with it.*

"Are you kidding me? You're wee. I can lift you with one arm." He did, pulling me right up off the ground, lifting me over his head. I shrieked, and then shrieked again when he bounced me off the bed, but I was giggling. He sat down next to me on the bed and curled his fingers around my ankle. "You're a little bit crazy, you know that?" he said.

He flung himself down next to me, and I found myself turning over, putting my cheek on the pillow, looking at him. He looked back at me so seriously.

I thought, *I will just have this smallest taste. Just for this moment.*

We talked. I was tired, and still tipsy, and he was too, but we lay there for hours and talked about things until I forgot that I thought he was so beautiful and I forgot that when I was next to him I wanted to touch him and that I wanted him to touch me.

Which is a lie. I lay there and knew exactly how far he was from me, registered every shift, every deep sigh, was acutely aware of my breathing, my hands, my skin and his. His voice was a rumble deep in my chest. I liked him.

He reached over just a few inches and took my hand. He rubbed his thumb along my wrist, a soft brush. He slid his hand over the small of my back and rested his palm flat. His thumb, feathering across my skin. I fell asleep like that, relaxing into that tiny caress, into the feeling of being touched.

A rush like icy water and I sat up, caught my breath. He was asleep, and I had no idea what time it was. He looked about twelve years old, rumple-haired. I sat for a moment, just a moment longer, and then I gathered myself back in, all the parts of me that were weak and vulnerable and wicked and longing and tucked them away. I slipped out of his bed and back into my own. Cold sheets, shivering. I switched the light off and put the pillow over my head, and I was asleep so much more quickly than I deserved to be.

I didn't say anything to Monique all the next day. She and I and her boyfriend Ian went to breakfast at a Greek place, then the aquarium, then back to the hotel to get dressed for dinner, and all I wanted to do was confess. I wanted to tell someone what had happened. And then I got stuck on—what had happened, exactly?

There's the test. You know the test. It is infallible. You stop and ask yourself, in the dizzy heat of the moment with your heart pounding, or when you are alone again: *How would I feel if my significant other was doing this exact same thing? Had done this? How would it feel to know?*

I did not stop to ask myself, because I knew.

It wasn't real. It wasn't something I had ever felt before. And—and I could just let myself feel this way, just once, just for a while. Just a sliver of cake.

I dressed quickly, and hurried back down to the lobby—my dress was purple-pink, low-cut, snug-waisted, swirly-skirted. It had been hanging up on the back of the door since I had bought it, and I hadn't cut off the tag. It said "16." The dress was a size 16, and it wasn't important how I looked in it, because I felt spectacular. And I wanted to be seen. I wanted people to look at me, look me up and down. I wanted them to say, "Jen, you look incredible. Jen, you are spectacular. Jen, you are the prettiest of them all." I was feeling greedy. I was feeling cut loose.

Jake came through the lobby while I stood looking around for the bar. He looked me up and down. "You look amazing," he said.

I curtseyed. "I feel very pretty!" I said.

"As well you should!" he said in his slightly formal, gallant way.

I glanced behind him, and Ben was coming out of the elevator, wearing a T-shirt. They were both tall and ridiculously broad-shouldered in T-shirts and jeans.

"Are you guys not coming to dinner?" I caught Ben's eye, looked away quickly. Jake said they were going to a Cubs game, and that they'd meet us at the club later.

"For dancing?" I said. "Do you like to dance?" I said to Ben, who had come up next to Jake.

"You look amazing," Ben said.

People in our group started pouring out of the elevators and in through the front doors, and we had to leave immediately, or we were going to miss our reservations.

"Look," Monique said. "Look at this picture of you!" We were on a leather couch in the back of the club. It had started to get a little busier, but our group was still the biggest one at the bar. Monique held her camera out to me and we put our heads together, looking at the little LCD screen. "You look so good," Monique said. "And I have to tell you this," she said, putting the camera down in her lap, and turning to talk into my ear, so I could hear her over the music. "I keep looking at the pictures I'm taking of you, and I think, 'This is a good photo! She looks so skinny in this photo!' and then I look at the photo, and it's you."

I picked up the camera and called the photo back up. "That's what I really look like, you mean?" It was a good photo of me. I was smiling at dinner, and my jaw was sharp and my collarbones prominent and I had—cheekbones, maybe? And I was smiling and my arms looked strong. My shoulders looked narrow, my breasts still perky, my waist small, and it was me, there, in the photograph, this lovely girl who looked so happy, so undefeated, undefeatable. I looked so ordinary, like I had never had a problem in the world, like I would always be strong.

"I look like that," I said to Monique.

"You really do. That's you. That's how you look, all the time. I was afraid you'd be so different. That you'd totally change and I wouldn't recognize you, you know?" She put her head on my shoulder. "But you're you. You're just smaller."

I threw my arms around her and snuffled into her hair, pulled back. "Sorry, sorry. I'm crying on your head. I'm sorry!"

"Come on," she said. She hopped up and pulled me after her and we danced to eighties music that all seemed vaguely familiar. I danced and swung the skirt of my dress and spun and spun.

I once had a dream that I stood at the bottom of an endless flight of stairs. And I took the first step, and then the next, and then I was flying up the stairs effortlessly, each step after the other, climbing higher. I woke up exhilarated from that dream and never forgot that feeling. I woke up disappointed, because I knew I couldn't climb like that.

That night in Chicago I thought that if they didn't close the club, I'd never stop dancing. And if they did, I would dance all the way home, down the street, and up the boulevards. I could do that now. I could lead a parade, a marathon, a parade of reveling marathoners across the entire city, across the entire country, and never once stop for breath. When Ben came up behind me I knew it was him, and I spun around and wrapped my arms behind his neck, up on tiptoes, smiling at him.

"Did you miss me?" I said.

He lifted me up off the ground, and I laughed, and he said, "What do you think?" A spin and he slid me down and we were dancing. Happiness, that sense of lightness, his arm around my waist, and his head dipping down. He spun me out and spun me back in and it was effortless. We danced, and then we separated in the crowd, and we found each other again and again, came back together again like we had been always dancing together, like we had practiced it.

Together on the couch, arm to arm, talking to other people. This was good. This was fun. This was exactly what I needed. I was shouting that to Monique, sitting on my other side, and she was nodding her head vigorously. "You did," she said. "We all did!" I said. This was exactly what the doctor ordered, right? I got another drink, and when I came back I dropped myself in his lap and grinned at him. I didn't even worry that I was too heavy. He leaned over. Lips behind my ear. Monique looked at him, then locked eyes with me, wide and expectant.

He said, softly and deliberately, "I'm going to kiss you when we get back to the hotel."

I shivered. Closed my eyes for a brief moment.

Well? Monique said, without saying a word. I shrugged, and took a long sip of my drink.

"We're getting hot dogs!" Jake said, but Ben waved him off. We caught a cab, and the ride back was endless. Trembling heart skipping beats.

We didn't look at each other as we walked across the lobby. I leaned against the back of the elevator and watched the numbers tick up. He took my hand. We walked silently down the hallway, side by side and hand in hand. He let us in, and I moved into the room ahead of him. I stepped out of my heels and left them neatly lined up one next to the other. Unfastened my earrings, set each one down carefully on the desk side by side. I glanced over my shoulder and met his eyes, and then he was right behind me, pulling me around to him hard, his hand cupping the back of my neck. He kissed me like he had waited years for this. I lifted up on my toes and he kept kissing me, his hands running down my back and to my waist. He pulled me up against him and kissed me, and I kissed him back with my arms around his neck, holding on tight, hardly breathing, hardly thinking, thinking *yes, please.*

He lifted me up and up, kissing me still, and then I was falling down onto the bed, bouncing. I laughed and he was on the bed next to me, gathering me up and kissing me again and it felt like I was still laughing. He kissed along my jawline and down my neck and his hands skimmed along my sides. Suddenly I was aware and awake and tense. He lifted himself up on one elbow and looked at me.

"You're so gorgeous," he said, and I pulled his head down and I kissed him. He rolled onto his back and hauled me up on top of him like I was weightless. Straddling his hips, I let that rush of it flare down my spine. I kissed him again, smiled against his lips as he worked my dress down off my shoulders, left me in my black lace bra. I was so glad I was wearing a black lace bra.

"Gorgeous," he said, his hands on my waist, pulling me back down.

I let it happen. I reveled in it happening. I swam away from part of me that shrieked *wrong, wrong, wrong, selfish, wrong.* It wasn't my fault, it wasn't, it wasn't.

I flinched when his hand ran down my belly, aware of my body and how it must look to him, but he followed it with kisses that felt hot and I was there, right there and nowhere else.

the morning after . . . waffling and waffles . . . having a boyfriend

I woke up before he did and sprung from bed, ducking into the bathroom with an armful of clothes. I locked the door and sat on the lid of the toilet with my hands on my knees until I heard Ben moving in the next room. I climbed into the shower and stood there, waiting for something to occur to me. I didn't know how this worked, and I didn't know what I was supposed to think about myself.

I sat on the floor of the tub and let the water pour over me. I fit in the tub—there was so much room on either side of my hips. I ran my razor carefully over the bumps of my knees and the turns of my ankles as if everything depended on it. I stood and scrubbed with the little hotel soap, turning it over and over between my fingers. I smelled like flowers and lemons, and the towels were soft and huge and wrapped twice around me. Ben knocked on the door as I was pulling on my skirt and I said, "One second!" I hoped my voice sounded normal.

"Good morning," he said when I eased out of the bathroom and around him, dashing to the far end of the room.

"Good morning!" I said without looking at him. There was a brief silence, and then the bathroom door closed. The water ran and I thought I should escape while I could, but I couldn't find my shoes or my wallet or my key card. Then he came out of the bathroom and wrapped his arm around my waist and nuzzled my neck. I pulled away and I said, "I'm sorry."

"I'm not," he said. "Let's go to breakfast." There was that smile again, and his mouth pressing the side of my neck.

I opened my mouth. I closed my mouth. I could pretend for a little while. For a little while longer.

He held out his hand to me, and I curled my fingers around his, and hung on all the way down to the lobby.

There was a line at the restaurant. We bounced in the sunshine, a big group of us all starving. A woman came down the sidewalk offering freshly fried donut holes rolled in powdered sugar, and I took one from her tray, then took another as she passed back up the line. They were sweet, and melted in my mouth in a burst of sugary dough.

Ben stood at one side of the group, talking to Jake, and Monique saw that I was distracted and jumpy and filled with—glee. There was that feeling. A secret, terrible glee, an edging of gold all the way around my body that I was sure that anyone passing by could see.

She said, "Well? What happened last night?" and I contorted my face into all kinds of expressions, and I stammered and went from red, and she said, "What? What?"

"Nothing," I said. She looked skeptical. The line moved into the restaurant, and I moved forward, threading through the crowd until I was next to Ben because there wasn't much time left. He smiled down at me as we made our way over to the table, and then we sat next to each other. Everyone hung over, but happy. We all ordered enormous stacks of pancakes and waffles and blintzes. I ordered something covered entirely with whipped cream and fruit-flavored sugar and drank cup after cup of coffee, my leg pressed up against Ben's. I ate quickly and without thinking, and then I had to shove away from the table.

"Restroom," I said at the hostess stand. She pointed me down the stairs and I bolted casually—I did not know you could do that, bolt in a casual full-out run. I pounded down the stairs and punched open the door—*a single stall, oh, thank you for that*—and the door slammed behind me. I hunched over, sitting on the toilet, scared that there was someone out there who could hear the noises I was making, who would smell something awful sneaking under the crack of the door. I had wave after wave of cramps, sweat pouring down my face. I was panting, flushing, flushing, unable to move, clinging to my knees. Nothing ever changes, not really. Not me.

I was in there for—ever. I didn't know for how long. It finally felt safe to stand up, to flush again and wait one more time to flush, to wash my hands and make my way back upstairs.

When I pulled my chair out, Ben looked up at me. "Are you okay?" he said. "You were gone for a while."

I glanced over at Monique, back at Ben. "There was a line," I said. "Someone was in there forever."

"That's what we figured," Monique said, and my heart unclenched. I smiled at her and smiled at Ben and I sat and thought that I didn't know who I was, but he didn't, either.

Our group was breaking into pieces to fly back home in all directions. We raced to the hotel, because it was getting late. When the door of our room closed behind us, Ben spun me into his arms. I relaxed for a moment, then pushed away.

"We have to go," I said.

"Just one more minute," he said, backing me against the door, crooning into my ear. "We only have a few minutes more."

"We have to go," I said, letting him pull me back to the bed, falling back, absorbing the way he was looking at me, his voice, his hands. I wanted to cry.

"I'd like your number." He smiled. "Obviously." That voice. His voice stroked down the back of my neck. His thumb brushed over my cheekbone.

"Why?" I said. I was frozen solid. Terrified of myself. I sat up, scrambled over to the corner. I heard myself say, "This can't go anywhere."

When I looked up, he was staring at me. I had to look down again. "You know I have a boyfriend, right?" Nausea. I knelt and started shoving my clothes into my suitcase. He didn't say anything. "I'm sorry," I said. "I'm really sorry." I couldn't make myself look at him.

"Okay," he said.

"Okay?" I said.

"You have a boyfriend right now."

"I do," I said, confused.

He picked up my phone and dialed a number. His phone rang. He closed it, and looked at me.

"I can wait," he said, as if he knew something I didn't, and thought I was someone braver. Who owned up to her mistakes. Who changed her life. Not me.

Chapter 33

onederland, ho . . . baby, you're a firework . . .
lies like hits that just keep on coming

The day after I returned from Chicago, I stepped on the scale and saw that it read 199. I cried. They called that "Onederland" on the weight loss surgery boards—the weight, not the tears. Most people on those boards had never, in their conscious memories, weighed a number that started with a one. I was one of those people, and I was a typical weight loss surgery patient in every way—fat throughout the majority of my lifetime, unable to lose weight on my own, morbidly obese but healthy enough to undergo anesthesia, struggling with compliance because I had never undergone the recommended counseling. And when I had gotten down to a size that allowed me to sneakily fit into the rest of the population, I lost my shit entirely.

The theory is that people who overeat need something to fill the hole that not-overeating leaves behind, so they search madly for alternative methods. Another theory is that formerly obese people simply burst like a firework, explode into the world, race across the sky, and then fall to the earth in flames. They are fire, and they devour all the things that their brand-new life as a skinny person leaves in their path.

Another theory is that all the hormones once stored in obese people's fat get released, swirling in tide pools all through their bodies, leaving them helplessly flailing in the undertow.

And even yet another theory: Fat people got fat for a reason—they had no impulse control. And once there is no longer a focus for that lack of impulse control, once Oreos are out of the picture, there goes their id, pouring out in a tidal wave of joyfully self-destructive behavior.

They are all pretty much the same theory.

When I got home from Chicago, Andy was waiting for me in the apartment with the blanket ready on the couch and *Dr. Who* queued up on the TiVo. He said, "How was your trip! Did you have the best time?"

I dropped my bags and said, "You're here! Hi!"

"Hi," he said, just like everything was the way it was supposed to be—or at least the way it had always been.

"It was fun!" I said, rearranging my luggage. "I wish you had come," I said and I was not lying. He looked at me and I waited for him to know, to understand what I had done. I thought I must be vibrating with the truth of it. He hauled himself up off the futon and wrapped his arms around me. They went all the way around. He kissed the top of my head, and I froze.

I was so full of what happened—it was like I had been emptied out and refilled with molten electricity that kept sparking and burning and flaring up in my belly, shook my skin, and made me tremble. I didn't understand how someone could look at me and not just *see*. But if I kept my mouth shut, nothing had to change and we could go on as we were. That seemed like the safest and easiest thing for everyone, for all of us. The only thing I could possibly do.

My brother's wedding was in just a few weeks, and we had expensive plane tickets, and everything was already arranged. We had a hotel room in upstate New York, where the wedding was being held, and I had promised Andy that we'd have New York bagels and New York pizza. I had promised that we'd go to my brother's fancy restaurant and have a fancy meal. I had promised that we would have a wonderful time and the best vacation—and he hadn't had a vacation in years and years, and I couldn't ruin that. I wasn't willing to let my mistake just—upend everything, and make everyone miserable. I would choke it all down, the guilt and the embarrassment (I knew people knew), and the happiness (it wasn't *real* happiness, not really, it was just momentary giddiness), and I would hold it close as a good memory, as a secret alternate universe, and things would go on the way they had been, because that's what things had to do.

wedding trip . . . couple-fight! . . . my mother is astonished

Butterflies, that was the feeling. I had been worried that there was some kind of meltdown about to happen on the plane, that while I sat buckled into my seat (The seatbelt buckled! Without an extension! I'd never get over it) my stomach was going to rupture and shoot bile five feet into the air, splash on the bulkhead, and shower down on rows six through twelve. But it wasn't my usual intestinal disorder, for once—it was all fear.

My bridesmaid dress, a yellow linen sheath with a brocade sash, was tucked into my suitcase, doubled over and wrapped in plastic. The day I got it back from the tailor I tried it on with the shades drawn and the door locked, and turned and turned and turned in front of the mirror. I pulled out my silver wedges to see what they looked like with the dress and I examined my ankles and my knees and the shape of my waist and the size of my arms and my neck in the mirror.

I had looked at myself carefully, both close-up and farther away. I had come to the tentative conclusion that it was possible I'd be able to survive seeing my entire family for the first time in years—all my brother's childhood friends who hadn't seen me in even longer, all the people who thought of me as fat, or very fat, or obese—any of the sizes I had been throughout my life. All the people who couldn't imagine me being skinny, or even ordinary. I paced through the apartment in my dress, the crisp swing of the linen swishing, my shoes clomping. Were they slightly too large? Maybe they were too large. Could I walk in them? I could walk in them. Could I do this? I couldn't do this. There had to be some way to escape this. Why had I agreed to do this? I pulled off the dress and placed it carefully on the padded hanger, tugged the plastic down. My shoes lined up neatly beneath it. We'd be leaving in less than a week.

"Jen!" my brother said, jumping out of the car in the passenger pick-up lane. We hugged hard. I plucked at his collar, smoothed his T-shirt over his shoulders, patted his hair. I always had to look at him carefully, to align what he looked like in my head with the reality of him, tall and blond. He was always taller than I remembered, and always broader through the shoulders. He was always exactly the way I remembered, and completely different. Seeing him wiped away my anxiety, or some of it. He made me forget myself for a moment, and that was such a relief, that brief respite from that noise in my head and the constant tremor of self-consciousness that underlay everything with a quiet hum.

He shook Andy's hand, and he grabbed my bag, and I was home, sort of. I grew up in New York. I was happy to be back, but it had always felt too large and too hard to know. My brother could slip into the city without a ripple and get immediately caught up in the current, smooth and quick and confident. He led us to his car and Andy held the passenger-side door open for me. Ken navigated us back to his apartment in Park Slope, talking about the wedding.

"Are you nervous?" I said, because that's what you're supposed to say to a groom who is to be married in just two days.

"Of course not," he said, merging onto the highway. "I'm awesome."

"So you're not going to freak out and drive us to Taiwan then," Andy said from the backseat.

"Maybe," Ken said. "But not because I'm nervous."

Carrie was a blur, a flash through the apartment, but she paused when we came through the door. "Oh my god!" she said, startling me. I don't think I had ever actually understood the phrase *taken aback,* with its implication of being knocked back by the surprise of it, to a place you thought you had left behind for good. When Carrie exclaimed at the sight of me I really did take a slight step back, rocking in my shoes under the force of her astonishment. It took me a full second to realize what she was talking about, and why she would say that to me. I used to catalog the things people said to me as they started to realize I had lost weight, and then lost a lot of weight, and then lost most of the weight, but those comments had trailed off, and that sense of immediate feedback and gratification had gradually faded, not without some regret. I had been sad when I realized I had run out of people who would be amazed by my amazing physical transformation into something amazing and transformed.

Now I remembered the unholy combination of glee and embarrassment and eager, desperate longing for more praise—praise that belonged to my reconfigured digestive system, but I was totally happy to take credit for.

I wanted to hug Carrie a lot. Her eyes were wide and bright, and she looked at me from top to bottom. She looked delighted for me. "You look *fantastic,*" she said. She turned to Ken and elbowed him. "Doesn't she look *fantastic*? Your mom is going to *flip out.*"

"She really is," Ken said. "She's going to be all—" his voice switched to the falsetto we used for Mom's voice: "—*Jen. JEN. You. Look. WONDERFUL.*" He arranged his face into an "I'm about to weep" configuration, clutched his chest, and then enveloped me in a hug, fake-sobbing on my shoulder. We hung on to each other's shoulders and faux-wept while Carrie and Andy looked at each other.

"They're like that when they get together," Carrie said.

"We're pretty much the same person," I said, hanging on to my brother, still flush with bubbling glee. I danced around the room and

I wanted to *talk* about it, to tell them all about surgery and diets and losing weight, and how lucky I was to have experienced the spectrum of human physicality, and the emotions that were inexplicably caught up in my physical and psychological transformation, and etcetera, and etcetera, but I held it together, just barely. The wedding was more important than me. It was what we needed to focus on.

We helped Carrie put together their wedding favors—pretty folded and decorated boxes to house my brother's pastries. Carrie showed us her wedding planning binder, as thick as my forearm and crammed with papers and receipts and brochures and lists and scraps of fabric.

"Good Lord," I said. "I don't know how you did it. I couldn't do that."

"Wedding planning is complicated," Carrie said. "It's probably more complicated than marriage."

"Oh, I doubt that," Kenny said from the couch. Carrie threw him a smirk, and he raised his beer bottle to her. She leaned over and kissed him with their wedding album in her lap. They smiled at each other, a long, eyes-locked kind of look that I felt like I shouldn't be watching, because they didn't notice anyone watching.

When we were finished with the favors, we offered to take the two of them out for drinks. "No," Carrie said. "I'm too tired. And I still have a bunch more to do. You guys go."

"It's okay?" Kenny said. "I haven't seen my sister in a long time." I beamed at him from across the room.

"Go," she said, waving us out the door. So we took Kenny out to the bar and bought him shots. It was loud and so crowded it didn't feel like there were individual people there so much as a shifting wall of spandex jeans and spiked-up hair and band T-shirts. Everyone was bony and looked a little scruffy. The bar's walls and floors were all weathered gray plywood, and the ceiling was miles away and tic-tac-toed with hanging industrial pendants. They swayed in the wake of the rumbling shouts that rose up from the solid mass of drinkers.

We snagged a booth from a bunch of impossibly scrawny kids who had staggered out of it just as we pushed through the crowd. Now our empties covered the table.

"I don't usually drink this much," my brother said. He was staring off into the distance and wobbling gently.

"You're getting married!" Andy said. "You deserve to celebrate! You should drink all the beer! You should have more shots! You want another shot?"

"No, I don't think so," Kenny said unsteadily.

"Yeah!" I said, and Andy slid out of the booth and disappeared into the crowd of Brooklyn hipsters. It was hard to hear anything—guitars were jangling in the speakers above our booth, and balls rumbled and crashed on the bocce ball court at the back of the bar. The light was yellow and hazy, and my brother's face was wide open and flushed. He leaned forward over the table, and I leaned forward, too. We were going to have a moment, I could tell.

He said, "Jen." He tapped the table. "Jen. I don't like dark beers."

I patted his hand. "Andy's going to get you a light beer. Something hoppy."

"That's good! He's a good guy, Andy is."

I cupped my hand over the top of my glass, and I leaned forward again. "He is. But you know—"

Kenny was looking at me with that thousand-yard stare again. "What?" he said. "What? I do know. I know." He tapped his finger on his temple.

I sat back, and unexpectedly felt tears behind my eyes. "You're so drunk," I said. I laughed.

He blinked, and nodded slowly once, and then again. "Carrie is great," he said. "Grrr-eat."

"I know," I said. "I'm so happy for you guys. I really am."

When Andy came back, we all knocked back our whiskies. The guys made noises and wagged their tongues around and scrunched up their eyes.

"You guys suck," I said. The whiskey was a lava hot spring in my belly.

"I have to go," Kenny said, bouncing the shot glass on the table. "I have to go see Carrie." He hauled himself out of the booth and started to make his way to the rear of the bar. I caught him and spun him around, shoving him ahead of me like a snowplow, parting the drifts of people.

When we stumbled outside, the air was remarkably cool, and the sky was wide and close. The streets were dark, gates pulled down over the windows of tiny expensive boutiques and the shoe shineries that had been there for forty years. We started to make our way slowly down the sidewalk.

"I don't want to go yet!" Ken said. He walked from one edge of the sidewalk to the other, making incredibly slow forward progress.

"I'm going to go to bed," I said.

"I'll go! Let's go to this bar!" Andy waved his arms around and pointed at a weird Irish bar on the corner.

"You guys go," I said. "Give me your keys."

"Here are my keys, sister," Kenny said. "We're going to go have man time. We're going to go talk about women. That's what we're going to do."

I glanced at Andy, who was swaying slightly with a smile on his face. "Okay, you go tell Andy about women," I said.

"We're going to talk about drinks," Andy said, and they fell through the door into the bar. The door swung shut behind them, and I carefully crossed the street and went into the Dunkin' Donuts. I ordered a chocolate angel, and I was licking the last of the chocolate off my fingers before I got three doors down to Ken and Carrie's apartment. My fingers were sticky, and it was dark, and I kept dropping the key, again and again.

In the morning, my head thumped and thumped, and my cheeks were kind of white. Andy slept in, and Kenny was sitting at the computer in his boxer shorts. Carrie and I were supposed to go get manicures. I wished I had sunglasses.

"We'll be back," Carrie said, dropping a kiss on Ken's head.

"I love you," he said.

"I know," she said.

We ran for the bus and I dropped a handful of quarters into the token box. There was no room to sit, and all I wanted to do was sit. The sun felt like a flashlight directly in my eyes, which bulged out, each in turn, to the pounding rhythm of my headache.

Carrie said, "I hope we didn't keep you up last night," and I shook my head, a sort of confused bobble. She said, "We went outside so we wouldn't wake you."

"What?" I said.

"Ken and I had a big fight," she said. "I was up all night waiting for you guys. He said he wasn't going to be very late." Her face was very serene, and her hair curled across her forehead. She looked like a dark-eyed Botticelli cherub. Their babies were going to be so pretty. Guilt stabbed behind my bulging eyes.

"I'm sorry," I said. "It's my fault. I just haven't seen him for so long. For two years, almost. It was really nice to see him."

The bus lurched and swung around the corner, and she pointed out the dress shop that had sewn all of our bridesmaid dresses. I was still nervous about mine—I couldn't get the wrinkles out, and I was sure I looked like a sack of off-brand flour in it, even with the brocade sash doubled and knotted tight around my waist. All the other bridesmaids were wearing dresses in the same fabric and color, but we had a range of different styles and I was sure that there had been a right style to pick and a wrong style, and at the wedding I was going to learn I had failed the quiz.

Carrie yanked on the cord and the bus squealed to a stop at the next corner. The nail salon was fancy, all white and pink and spangled with shiny equipment. The pedicure chairs were raised, mosaic-tiled platforms covered in plush pink cushions, and when I extended my grubby feet into the bubbling ceramic bath, I was worried the water would foam up gray and dingy. I hoped I had shaved my legs smooth enough. I wished I had thought to brush my hair.

Carrie settled in next to me and smiled, a bright and sunny look. She chose a soft, pale pink, and I picked a glowing neon one. We handed them to the ladies who rolled over on their low stools and talked in quiet voices to each other, ignoring us. Carrie leaned back and closed her eyes.

"Tired?" I said inanely.

She rolled her head over to look at me. "We were up pretty late. Ken threw up all over the sidewalk."

"Oh geeze," I said. "Poor Ken."

She frowned. "That's what he gets for drinking so much." She leaned her head back again.

"We kept buying him drinks," I said. "It really was my fault."

"Oh, I was so mad at him. He was out all night drinking and I was home alone. He knew I was nervous."

"I'm sorry," I said lamely. "It was my fault. We just hadn't seen each other in a while." I trailed off.

She sighed. "He just has to understand, I'm the most important person here. I've got to be his priority. It's our wedding weekend. That's the most important thing." Her voice was sure and serious.

"You told him that," I said.

"We had such a big fight," she said. "I'm surprised you didn't hear us. I was yelling at him so loud and he was saying 'I don't feel so good.' And then he threw up and I was so mad at him again." She laughed. My stomach knotted at the idea.

"I'm sorry," I said.

"It's fine," she said. "He's really hung over today." She grinned in a way you would call impish, with her little pointed chin, and said, "Yes, thank you!" when the pedicurist held up the bottle silently to confirm her color choice. When Ken called, she smiled at his name on the caller ID, and when she picked up her voice was teasing and sweet and low. I sat with my head turned and pretended I couldn't hear her.

Once our toes dried we headed out the door and climbed into the minivan they had rented to lug all their baggage and supplies upstate. Andy was riding shotgun until Carrie opened the door and shooed him out. She climbed in next to my brother, who steered with one hand as she held the other.

When we pulled into the hotel parking lot, there was a sudden rush of activity—Ken and Carrie hopping out, doors opening, people barreling toward us, shouting and hugging and general hubbub.

I sat frozen in the backseat with my hand on the lock. No one had noticed us yet. "Do I look okay?" I asked Andy. He started to nod and say "Of course! You look great!" but I stopped him and said, "Seriously? Do I look okay? I don't want to get out." I wondered why I thought wearing camo-print Bermuda shorts was a good idea. I had been so high on the thought that I could wear shorts that I had bought every print Old Navy offered in my size. The problem, I thought, was that I wore them in public.

"You look great," Andy said. "Are you ready?"

The minivan's back hatch flew open, and there was a rush of hot air and sunshine and my brother hauling out boxes. "Come on, sister! Grab some bags."

I kept my head down and moved quickly toward the entrance with my arms full of bags. My mother appeared like a heat mirage.

"Andy?" she said, and he said, "Hi, Mrs. L!"

I found myself saying "Not to mention your daughter," and watched her face move swiftly from polite to puzzled to absolutely astonished. She didn't move at all, and then her arms were around me and the pile of packages in my arms. "Jen!" she said. "My Jen!"

"Are you crying?" I said, when she pulled away.

She lifted her glasses up and wiped at her face with the butt of her hand. "I'm allowed to cry," she said. "Look at you. You look beautiful.

I mean, you were always beautiful, but look at you. You just look—you look so beautiful."

I looked at Andy and looked at my mother, and looked around the lobby, afraid someone would overhear us. "Thank you," I said. "We have to check in. And I don't know where these go." I hoisted up the mess of bags in my arms.

"I almost didn't recognize you," she said. "Wait until your aunt sees you. She's going to be like, *whoa*. Oh, Jennifer."

"Hey, Ma," my brother said, sliding his arm around her shoulders. She beamed up at him.

"I'm going to put these at the front desk," I said to Ken, but I wasn't sure he heard me. I slipped away. I figured no one would recognize me if I didn't make eye contact, and no one did.

the wedding . . . surviving my family . . .
perspective . . . dancing alone

Carrie was radiant. My brother, who had been fidgety and panicked when the line of yellow bridesmaids went trooping down the aisle, went still when she appeared.

We shuffled into a smooth line under the branches of the wide-spread tree that flanked the altar. I didn't know the other bridesmaids very well, but they all seemed to know each other, and they were elegant and bright in their dresses. Until I had seen them, I had felt lovely and slim like a yellow flower. And now, next to them I was rumpled and wide. I marveled at perspective, and thought it was a wondrous thing. I didn't like it at all.

At the rehearsal dinner I had been not just a regular girl, but a regular *pretty* girl, the kind that old drunken uncles smiled at, and then leaned over to tell your mother, "She's a beauty. She's a beautiful girl! You've got some beautiful kids there, Mary!"

The rehearsal dinner was held at a little restaurant with an open bar, and all night, over and over, everyone told my mother how beautiful I was. I would be a liar if I said I didn't enjoy it. I was being congratulated for being so attractive. Most people there didn't know I had weighed 140 pounds more than this—most people there just thought I was a pretty girl in a dress. My aunt Evelyn yelled something in my ear about surgery, but I didn't hear exactly what she said. I didn't want to. She yelled, "Beautiful!" and I said, "Thank you!"

Andy was sitting at the bar chatting with the bartender, and I made my way across the room, smiling at the people who snatched at my arms or my skirt, and asking me if I was Ken's sister and telling me I was so pretty. I made it to the bar, and Andy turned on his stool and handed me a half a tumbler of whiskey.

"How's it going?" he said. "Are you surviving?"

"I'm surviving," I said. "I'm very pretty, you know."

"Cheers to that," he said, and clinked his shot glass to my glass, and we both drank. He was wearing a button-down shirt and a new pair of jeans. He smiled at me, and I was grateful to him in a painful rush of sentiment. I was grateful that he had flown here to deal with wedding madness and panic, to talk to my family, to meet people he'd never see again, to be rushed from place to place. I was grateful to him, and I loved his halo of wiry hair and sweet smile and his laugh, and I didn't want to break either of our hearts.

In my ear someone said, "Jen Larsen?" and then I felt hands at my waist. I jumped. It took me a moment to realize it was one of Ken's oldest friends, from back in Pennsylvania. Shawn who was shy, who knew me through my most awkward phase, that run of teenage years in which no human being on earth is attractive and some human beings (me among them) are painfully ugly. Shawn, who knew me when I was sad, ugly, and lonely, an eighth grader wearing button-down cotton shirts with pictures of teddy bears on them, because that's how little I knew about the world.

Shawn stood there with his hand on my hip, looking exactly the same as he had when he was a kid.

"Wow. Holy crap, you look just fantastic," he said.

"This is Shawn," I told Andy. "Shawn, this is my boyfriend, Andy."

"You're a lucky man," Shawn said, pumping Andy's hand up and down, both mocking and sincere.

"Don't I know it," Andy said.

At the wedding the next day, standing in front of a garden full of people, there were too many eyes and I felt that confidence shrinking.

My mother was beautiful in an icy blue dress that sparkled. Her hair was brushed sleek, and her eyes shone behind her glasses. She kept her hand on the chair next to her, which was empty except for a yellow rose—the chair my father ought to have been sitting in. She and my aunts were grouped together, large ladies in long and sparkling dresses. They looked like sisters, all of them together like that, in the shapes of their faces and the contours of their bodies, and the way they wore their fancy outfits as if they wished they were sweatpants. They all looked beautiful. I wondered if I still looked like I was part of the family, and how I would feel about the answer, either way.

When it was time, I pulled a folded piece of paper out of the neckline of my yellow dress and stepped up to the microphone. I said, "Sometimes clichés are clichés for a reason." I said something about true love and happily every after. I kept my eyes on the creases in the paper and focused on keeping my voice from shaking. My brother looked so serious and so grown-up, with his hands folded in front of him and a serene look on his face, like he knew exactly what he was doing and thought this was the best idea he had ever had. And then it was over and my brother and sister-in-law kissed and raced back down the aisle, hand in hand, disappearing back into the house where the reception was held. The photographer stopped the bridesmaid crew in the parlor, asking us to file into the side garden to pose near the bridges and streams and flowers, edged by low brick walls with dappled patterns of shade and sunlight. Ken and Carrie came out of the house behind us, and we trooped around the garden taking pictures.

"When are you getting married?" everyone kept asking me. "You've lost so much weight!" they kept saying. "Look at you in that dress!" "Yes," I said. I was skinny and amazing when I saw myself in the faces of my family.

When Ken and Carrie had their first dance, I sobbed, mascara staining the tips of my fingers when I wiped my eyes. He was a grown-up, and he was so happy, and I was so happy for him.

Andy sat outside, smoking cigarette after cigarette. He did not like social events. People wandered the reception room, from table to table, bending over and shouting in each other's ears. The room had a warm, gold glow that made everyone look like they were beautiful and in love.

"Are you next?" an aunt asked me. I said, "Don't ask Andy that!" My aunt Evelyn said, "Are you taking your vitamins? Some people die from this surgery." I went to the coat closet to dig a second pack of cigarettes out of my bag. I sat outside on the deck with Andy, and he went and got me more wine. A few minutes later, I went and got more wine, and then he got me another glass. When the DJ announced that we were dancing, I tried to pull Andy onto the floor, but he resisted.

"Uh-uh," he said. "I can't dance! You dance! Go!" He disappeared back onto the porch, and I stood still for a moment until my brother's best friend yanked me onto the floor. We started spinning in circles, arms in the air, and I got dizzy.

When I checked the time on my phone, there was a text.

Thinking about you.

Ben.

I'm at my brother's wedding, I wrote.

I wish I were there with you, he wrote.

I clicked my phone shut.

apologies . . . breaking up . . . walking out

I thought I could have a secret that made me wistful and sad, and still go on with my life. I thought I could have the kind of secret that wouldn't change my life at all. I thought I could wait for his birthday—no one should be broken up with right before their birthday. But when we got back from the wedding and things started to settle back into the rhythm of life, I realized I couldn't do it anymore. I realized I couldn't breathe inside the routines we had built around us. The terror of being alone was being eclipsed by something I couldn't even explain—guilt, certainly. Maybe a sense of possibility. Maybe a reckless need to finish what I had started, to tear everything down to the bare foundation. Maybe I couldn't be a whole different person until I was standing in the wreckage with dirty hands and a pounding heart.

We were sitting in the back garden of the bar where we had our first date. The sun was setting and it was getting damp and cold, and my heart was thumping so hard it was pushing the breath out of me in great whomps. I didn't know what I was going to say. I didn't know I was going to say it until I opened my mouth and said, "I don't think this. We. Are working. As a couple. A relationship."

Andy was very still. My heart vanished from my chest and the cavity collapsed inward.

I didn't say, *I didn't know what it was like to be pursued, and absolutely desirable.* I didn't say, *I have so many excuses and sometimes they sound so very reasonable and even forgivable.*

I didn't say, *We don't talk about the important things. For five years, we never have.* I didn't say, *You don't want to marry me. You don't want to move in with me. You don't want babies. You don't want* me.

I said, "I'm so sorry. I am so sorry."

He looked startled, for just the briefest instant, and then he looked serious and calm.

"I'm sorry," he said. He took my hand, and he looked at me, and he said, "I'm sorry. I love you. I'm sorry I couldn't."

I was swaying, and then my head was on his shoulder and I was sobbing. My heart was gone, and my breath wheezed through the hole it left in my chest. I said, "I'm so sorry. I'm so sorry."

"Don't be," he said. "It's my fault."

And I wasn't strong enough or brave enough to contradict him.

When he left, I sat there in the dark for the longest time before I could make myself gather up my things and push open the swinging door back into the bar.

"Andy paid," the bartender said cheerfully when I put a twenty dollar bill down on the bar, but I left it there, elbowed open the front door, and started walking.

job offer ahoy . . . confessions abound . . . being okay

As if I were being rewarded, the next morning I woke up to the phone ringing. Before I could formulate a thought about where I was or why my eyes stung, the manager at the ad agency I had interviewed at was offering me the job in the huge brick-and-stone building overlooking Chinatown. He offered me money I hadn't expected, and benefits, and the world on a tiny silver platter. I sat up in bed and politely asked for more, as if my skin had been left hollow by the fat that had disappeared, and an alien intelligence had crept inside. They gave it to me.

The agency was a building full of beautiful, thin, fashionable, and dynamic people, all of them so different from the comfortable librarians with soothing voices who had looked so distressed when I gave my notice that I wanted to leap out of my chair and run around the desk and say, *No! I'm sorry! I was only kidding! Let's turn this around. Let's crank the camera backward and we'll pretend it never happened.* But that had been impossible for a long time.

I still took up too much room, compared to these unreasonably skinny people and their highly polished skin. I was so tired of comparing myself to people. These people had no pores, and their hair always looked like it was being tossed casually around their slender shoulders and swan-like necks by an ocean breeze blowing directly out of the pages of a J.Crew catalog.

And I was—average. But why couldn't I have it too, that blonde and polished elegance? I just wanted to know what it was like. Just for a little while. I wanted someone to be jealous of me. I wanted to be hated because I was so hot. Because maybe that's what would finally do it.

Every day I went to work, squished into a seat on the crowded train. Every day I went out for a smoke break each hour and a half, and had a glass of wine with lunch, sometimes two. Every night, I stopped at a different corner store for a couple of bottles of wine. Every night I sat outside on the stone steps and smoked menthol lights and drank a water glass full of wine so I could sleep. I got used to the smell of my hands and the taste of my tongue. I got used to always feeling full and heavy in my head. Such a familiar feeling from so long ago, this sense of being in the wrong body, of being wrong, of desperately wanting something that was so impossible to have.

And yet here I was, in a whole new life. Not fat. I had *finally gotten what I wanted*. Every day I tried to drown that idea.

It felt like something had broken when Andy and I broke up. When I broke us up. I called Monique, and I said, "Things had been bad for a long time. Things had been bad for four years." I called friends I hadn't spoken to in months that had almost accumulated into years. I called my friend Katie and said, "I couldn't tell you. I couldn't tell anyone. And I couldn't talk to anyone. Do you understand?" And she said, "I wish you had told me. I am so glad you're okay." I called Karen and said, "I'm a cliché. I have turned into a cliché."

And she said, "No. You're not a cliché. It's not a cliché. Look, don't you think it started to happen so long ago, this urge you had to change your life? To make things different? To be different?"

I couldn't answer.

"The day you decided to go get weight loss surgery," she said. "That was the day you decided that your life needed a new direction, that you were going to make a difference for yourself. And everything you've done, it's just part of getting closer to that."

I stuffed my knuckles into my mouth and tried not to sob so loud I startled the upstairs neighbor.

I called all the people I never called, and I apologized in stumbling, halting ways. I confessed. Over and over I was banging my fists on the life I had constructed and watching it crack into pieces and collapse into dust. I confessed that I had hidden everything, and I confessed that I had lied about how great things were, and I confessed that I had *cheated*. And I had gotten what I wanted. I was living it, wasn't I?

My friends said, every single one of them, "I'm sorry." They said, "Are you okay? What can we do to help?"

I poured myself another glass of wine. I started smoking inside the apartment. I was a completely different person, and my life was completely different.

"What are you going to do now?" Monique asked. Her face was too serious. We were eating tiny cheeseburgers at Lime. I remembered I had a birthday celebration here, years ago. I had been wearing shoes with tiny heels, but I could barely walk in them. I clomped, and my feet hurt. I had ground those heels down to their nubs. But I remember feeling beautiful that night because I was wearing new jeans and red satin shoes. Evidence in the form of pictures exists. My face looks open and soft and happy.

"Move to Palm Springs and molest cabin boys, probably," I said. I took another handful of zucchini fries.

"Okay, before that," she said.

"I don't know," I said. "I think I should probably just sit around in a hair shirt for a while. Enjoy being myself. Is that what they say? Being by myself. Being with myself. Enjoy *me*. But I don't want to do that. I hate everything, and myself, and I'm miserable." My new policy was complete and total honesty. I would never lie again to the people I loved.

"Have you told Ben?"

"Ben, who?" I said, lying through my teeth. In my bag on the floor was my phone, and on my phone, in my outbox, was a text that read, *I broke up with my boyfriend.*

She rolled her eyes and we ordered more cocktails. I said, "I'm going to be a sassy single girl. I've never been one of those. I can probably do that now."

I didn't know how to do that.

I sat with Jen Wade at the bar and she said, "You have to stop thinking you need to say what people want to hear, and you have to stop thinking everyone needs to like you, and you have to stop thinking that you aren't important."

The creepy bartender came over and leaned an elbow on the bar. He waggled his scraggly eyebrows and said, "Do you lovely ladies need anything?"

"Just you telling us we're lovely," I said, cocking my head at him and smiling, stirring my straw in my whiskey.

Jen Wade kicked me.

"Ow!" I said.

"We're good," she said to him politely. "Thank you."

He moved down the bar and she sighed at me. "That's what I *meant*," she said in a low voice. "Do you see?"

I gazed at her patterned stockings for a moment, and then I said slowly, "I don't really want him to tell us we're lovely."

"Right," she said.

"Okay," I said.

"You're important. Your friends care when you disappear. You shouldn't disappear."

"Okay," I said. I wished a tear would drop into my drink, because that would be poetic. But tears just slid down my face and made me blotchy.

"Good for you," Josh and Leota both said. They sat across from me at the picnic table in the back of the bar, and they told me they were proud of me, as if they hadn't heard me confess everything I had done wrong.

"We love you," Leota said.

"We think you're the bomb, Jen Larsen," Josh said.

I could have a new life, I thought. I could figure this out. I could.

losing my face . . . secret surgery . . . clandestine cake

My first day at my new job, they took a headshot to put on the company directory. I stood in front of the white column in the lobby trying not to make a squinty face at the man with the gigantic camera. HR emailed it to me later that day. For a moment, I was honestly convinced that I had opened the wrong file.

When did my face get narrow? When did my chin get pointy? The line of my jaw was like the edge of a knife, and my nose was longer and more prominent—sharper, even, than I had imagined. I had a really big nose. My cheeks were gone, and left their bones behind, and the feeling in what was left of my stomach was like roller coaster riding,

You can lose weight, but how do you lose your face? I wanted to go digging in the couch cushions. I wanted it with a sudden, panicked, visceral need. I went to the mirror in the bathroom and stood there looking at myself, wondering how I'd missed it, until another ridiculously tiny blonde woman came in and glanced at me. I went back to my desk. There was my alien face, still on the screen. My head had been remolded like Jell-O. My eyes seemed larger. My head seemed longer. *My face had changed.*

There are two pictures of me, taken on Halloween, seven days before my weight loss surgery. In the photos, I weigh approximately 317 pounds, which is exactly ten pounds heavier than I had been when I last weighed in at my surgeon's office, when he told me I should lose about ten pounds before my surgery.

In the photos, it is Halloween, and just a week away from my surgery. I am a Devil in a Blue Dress. What I remember is that I felt cute. I felt really cute, and kind of clever—my hair was a violent red, and the little devil horns I wore were sparkly. My blue dress was from a local designer who designed specifically for fat women.

In the first picture I'm posing with Wendy. She's Hello Kitty, and she's wearing the same dress I am, only in pink. I am making the squinty-eyed constipated face with the squinched up lips that I always think makes me look sexy, but just makes me look—squinty-eyed and squinchy-lipped. My guts were going to be in a bucket in just a handful of days or so. But that's me right there. That is my face. That is the face of the person I am, inside my head. I have a head like an egg, but not as pointy at each end. My cheeks are full, and round into apples when I smile; my jaw is soft, but my chin is a little knob.

The second picture is a candid. It's taken from across the room. I'm happy, sitting next to Andy, gesturing as I laugh at something he's said. He isn't wearing a costume because he doesn't believe in Halloween. My hair is fiery, and my dress is blue and I am—enormous. I am physically wide. I am more than twice as wide as Andy is. Andy is ordinary-sized, maybe a little lean, and I am as big as more than two of him. You cannot see the whole of my body in the photo, but you can see how broad I am compared to him. The girth of my arms, the way my chin slopes in a gentle curve down into the thick column of my neck. Everything about me is round, and soft, and large. And it is a shock to me, every time I look at that photo, because *that is not me.* By which I mean, that is not the self in my head. And that couldn't be the self I walked around inside for I don't even know how long. That is not the body from inside which I talked, thought, flirted, lived my life. I never once thought I looked like that.

I didn't understand how I could look like that but not be that person, or how I could look like my employee headshot and not be that person, either. Constantly a stranger to myself, on either side of the scale.

But being on the skinny side was like getting away with something. At the ad agency, no one knew I used to be fat. Sometimes it felt as if not confessing that I used to be obese was lying. As if my current weight was a lie, because that's not really who I was. *I am actually a fat girl. I just don't look like one.*

I was starting to look less and less like one. I was disappearing. I was drinking every night, and smoking a pack a day. I kept losing weight. Over the course of three months, I was a size 14, then a 12, then a 10, an impossible size 10, but I didn't stop there. I dropped out of double digits, into single digits. I weighed 150 pounds, 140, 130. I was a size 4. And I ate. I played, *how much can my tiny stomach hold before I throw up?* I played, *let's see if I can break this surgery.* Let's see if I can fuck this up, too. But I kept losing weight.

That's how it is supposed to work, right? You get your guts scrambled, redesigned, *fixed*, and you lose weight no matter what you do to yourself or why. You lose weight no matter how fucked up you are, no matter how crazy you are. You lose weight with no sense of personal responsibility, without having to develop self-awareness, self-control, a sense of self. In fact, you go ahead and you lose your sense of self and your sense of stability and your way, along with two or three or four pounds a week. But it was okay, because I was so thin that people told me, "You're so tiny! Look at how small you are!"

I was *flaca*, Spanish for skinny; it also means weak, feeble. I was an XS, finally, finally, and then I couldn't lose any more. I had nothing left to lose. And it pissed me off, because how did some people get skinnier than that? Why did I have no upper limit, but a lower limit? Why wouldn't I be allowed to know what it was like to be truly, absolutely, perfectly thin? I wanted to lose weight until my skin collapsed inward and there was no longer any difference between my insides and my outsides. I wanted to be a size nothing.

It became a kind of a sick fascination, lying down and tracing the outline of my ribcage. Look, here are my ribs, here is the outline of my ribcage, all the way down to the bottom, here is the drop-off, that sharp ridge that collapses into soft belly. It made me feel that haunted-house kind of delighted squeamish. It was enthralling, this skeleton which I never noticed before. I was a science project. When I was fat I had hips and rolls instead of angles and knobs, but the curious, horrified fascination was the same. How could being fat and being skinny be so much alike?

But my stomach still hung down, soft and white and wrinkled, like an ancient, over-washed towel pinned to my navel. My thighs sagged. My knees were wrinkled. The idea of being naked in front of someone now was just as awful as it was 180 pounds ago. I cried with my tits in the hands of an elderly Vietnamese bra fitter at Nordstrom.

"Not C," she said decisively. "Not B. A. 34 A." The bras at that size were beautiful scraps of lace, but I cried as I tried them on, because my breasts were gone.

All the weight I had ever gained had fallen off me like it had never been there in the first place, like I could just forget I had ever been anything but too skinny. But it felt like getting away with something whenever I said "yes!" firmly and decisively to the barista when she asked if I wanted whipped cream on my hot chocolate, instead of hemming and hawing about it to make it clear I was embarrassed about the calorie expenditure. Now I got away with piling a grocery cart full of frozen pizzas and quarts of ice cream and sacks of cookies. I got away with wearing leggings.

I was skinny, and I was allowed to wear what I wanted and eat crap all I wanted because of that. I felt guilty for getting away with it. Elated that I could get away with it. Like I'd been initiated, finally, into some secret conspiracy of skinny people.

At work, clients sent us huge gift baskets of chocolates or donuts or gourmet banana bread. Women with their glossy hair and their expensive shoes and tiny pants, men in their tight polo shirts and skinny jeans and shiny belts, they all brought salads for lunch in stacks of Tupperware containers for maximum freshness. Account directors and project managers and studio people—they'd carefully assemble their salads on a large glass plate, add a sprinkle of flaxseeds, and set a small dish of fat-free vinaigrette on the side of the plate, while at their elbow would be a three-foot chocolate Easter bunny. They'd turn and march out of the kitchen without even looking at the city block worth of dark gourmet chocolate staring at them.

Or sometimes they'd glance over at an entire platter of hand-assembled sandwich cookies, dipped in powdered gold, while they were carefully slicing their braised tofu on top of a leaf, and they'd say, almost regretfully, as if it were a real problem, "Oh, that looks so good." Almost apologetically, "I only want a *taste*, though. Just a taste." And they'd take a knife and actually carefully, surgically remove a thumb-wide section from a cookie smaller than a drink coaster. Some afternoons I'd come into the kitchen and there would be an entire platter filled with donuts, each with just a chunk neatly removed because someone only wanted a *taste*. The tiny galley kitchen was always busy, people rushing in and out with giant mugs of coffee fueling their creative rampages, and everyone only wanted a taste. They were happy, and skinny. Why didn't they want more?

When an email went out—*gift in the kitchen, leftovers from a meeting, I have brought in the bounty from my chocolate tree and wish to share it with all of you on the fifth floor*, I had to stop myself from bolting from my chair. Free food has always been a kind of trigger, a siren song, an irresistible invitation. If I didn't fall on the free food and devour it immediately, when would it come around again? How could I miss this golden opportunity, which might never return?

Me, rushing to the kitchen. Alone, looking at the half of a cake sitting there in a throne of crumbs, wondering how big a slice I could take and how quickly I could smuggle it out and back. I'd need a napkin to hide it. I'd need a really big knife. I'd need a smaller plate, so no one could tell that I was toting around half of a half of a cake.

One Friday I was digging a blade through that day's cake, carving out a piece as wide as my hand, when an account manager walked in. You could tell by the shoes.

"Oh!" she said. "Cake! How nice. There's always so much junk around here." She opened the fridge, tossed back her hair, and plucked out a low-fat yogurt.

"I know!" I said. And I was skinny, but I still found myself saying, "I haven't eaten all day. And I could use the sugar rush, you know?"

I should have said, "I am hungry, and I like cake." I should have said that when I weighed three hundred pounds. That would have been so hard to do. But now it should be much so much easier to say.

But this woman (a size zero, I would bet half my slice of cake) was having low-fat yogurt for dessert, and she was eyeing the cake like calories were contagious, and I was lying so that she thought I was like her. I plopped my enormous slice onto my plate. It bled strawberry all over the counter. I licked my fingers, thought about scooping up the stray piece of frosting left behind—technically part of my slice, so it belonged to me anyway—but I got control of myself.

I was ashamed for wanting cake, and she was horrified by the idea of wanting cake. I was a fat girl, and she was a skinny woman, and we were both crazy.

"I don't know how you do it, girl," she said. She rummaged around for a spoon in the mess of a silverware drawer. "Stay so skinny and eat like that."

I was wearing my new matchstick plaid jeans and bronze heels and a silk cami. No one would know I had gotten surgical intervention unless I told them. Instead, I lied. When someone asked me, how can you eat whatever you want? How do you stay so skinny? I would shrug.

But sometimes, sometimes, I would bring up the fact that I had lost 180 pounds, just to see the looks on their faces—*You? Never! Not possible! Look how slender you are!* and then, *How did you do it?*

Every single time, I lied. I said, "a lot of protein," mostly, and tried to change the subject. I mean, that was totally true, right? It just left out some tiny details. Insignificant details. Details like, I had once hated myself and my body so much I got surgery to change who I was. Details I didn't like remembering.

"Oh! Well," I said brightly to my skinny coworker. I covered over my slice with a napkin and grabbed my fork. "Have a good afternoon!" I bolted.

I thought I finally understood it—why some thin people were so angry at fat people for being fat. They thought fat people were breaking the rules. They assumed fat people got to eat the cake. They assumed that fat people never turned down anything. They assumed that fat people slept in a bed of ham with a pillow of bacon and never said no to seconds or shared their dessert, and they thought *that's not fair*, and they were probably as angry at fat people for being able to eat as fat people were angry at skinny people for being able to be thin.

And I was briefly, incandescently angry, because I should have been able to eat whatever I wanted. I shouldn't have been sneaking cake.

And I knew I would still rather be skinny in this wreck of a body than have stayed fat in that wreck, because life was so much easier here.

losing my shit . . . falling out of cabs . . . spanked by a stranger . . . the breaking point

I was saying *yes* blindly to anything that came along, because any kind of change would be a next step. Any kind of next would be a not-now. I had to keep going because eventually I'd end up somewhere. I knew, in a vague way, that I couldn't go on going to work and comparing myself to blonde women who were six feet tall and then going home and smoking a pack of cigarettes while I finished a bottle of wine. I thought, *What would a normal person do?* I said yes to an engagement party invite. When was the last time I had been to a party? Chicago didn't count. And Chicago was so long ago.

I walked to the party through the mist of fog, toward the ocean. I stopped at a corner store for a bottle of champagne to bring. When I rang the doorbell, Heather swung open the door and said "Oh, my god!" She said, "You look amazing!" but I was not glowing and pink-cheeked like she was, newly engaged and beautiful. Behind her a house full of people buzzed and laughed, and I thrust the bottle of champagne at her. "Congratulations!" I said. I could feel my heart thumping.

Heather took the champagne and put her arms around me and then tucked me into the crook of her elbow, leading me into the kitchen. She always had a way of seeming quietly delighted, as if under the surface she was crackling with a bright and brilliant electricity that made her hair curl into that riot of blonde ringlets. She took my coat and disappeared before I could stop her, or follow her like a baby duckling, and I was standing in the kitchen with people I thought I should know, or had known, and a totally blank mind. How did you talk to people at a party? *Alcohol,* I thought, and I made my way to the bar, smiling at the people who glanced at me as I passed. I poured myself a tumbler of whiskey and drank it quickly, pretending to be making my way across the living room to an important engagement on the other side. I stood nervously by the window in the hallway, wondering when I could make my way back. I tried to stand up straight, wondering what I looked like. I touched my stomach, smoothing down the fabric of my dress, plucking it away from my skin, tugging it down, straightening it. I wrapped my fingers around my glass and tried to not let go.

When Heather appeared near the bar I swam through the crowd back to her, taking the long way around so that no one who was watching me would see me crisscrossing aimlessly. My glass was empty, and I poured another one, taller this time, and then flung myself on Heather's mercy. She laughed at the things I said. Heather was younger than me, and her friend, sitting in the chair next to her, was even younger. Practically a baby. He laughed at the things I said, too. Heather sat on the couch, and I knelt next to the couch, next to her friend's chair. I leaned forward when I talked to him, and he watched me with the most curious look on his face. I never caught his name. I smiled up at him, and I watched him flutter and spin. I tilted my head, and he shifted. I said, "Yes, please," when he asked if I wanted another drink, and he watched every sip. He watched me talk to Heather. When she left, I stayed. He got me another drink, and when I stood, he did, too.

"I'll come with you," he said, when I told him I was going downstairs to smoke, and I just smiled at him and turned, carrying my drink with me.

He put his hand over mine when he lit my cigarette. His face flared up. I took another sip of my drink, and another, and I thought, *This is what I want, this child with his hand on the brick wall behind my head, leaning in toward me.* I tossed my cigarette into the gutter, and turned to open the door. He had his hand on it before I did, and held it for me. I raced up the stairs in front of him and pushed through the crowd, leaving him behind. I gathered my coat, I left my drink on the windowsill, and I slipped back out of the door alone. At home, Fang circled the coffee table, alarmed by the noises I was making. He knocked over my wine glass and I left it there, spreading red and wet across the parquet floor.

"I should date," I told Sage at our work Christmas party. "I am young and reasonably attractive—"

"*So* reasonable," I thought Sage said. The terrible DJ music echoed horribly in the enormous warehouse. We had made our way upstairs to find some breathing room and a bar that was less crowded, and we found a bored bartender who decided to make all of our drinks doubles. I was two in, and everything was warm and bright and beautiful, like tall, beautiful, bright Sage, who I wanted so badly to like me. She was very much herself, sure and assured, unafraid to say *no,* or *screw you,* or *back off.* Sage was incontrovertibly Sage, the way all my friends seemed to be incontrovertibly themselves. I would ask them their secrets, I thought. I would have another drink.

A bouncer came up the stairs and nodded to us. He was slight and narrow-shouldered, with slicked-back hair. He was wearing an earpiece. I wanted to pluck it from his head and direct the whole party.

"Oh, hi!" I said. I waved. "Are you our manly protector-type person?" I twinkled at him and he seemed startled.

"Sure I am," he said. "But you ladies should behave yourselves, anyhow."

"We never do," I said, and turned back to Sage, who was rolling her eyes.

"I'm totally practicing," I said. "I am honing my skills."

"Honey," she said. "There are better—what do you call them. Knife sharpeners." She was a little drunk, too.

"Hey! Photobooth!" I said. "Let's do the photobooth!" I grabbed my drink and sloshed over to the booth in the corner. It was empty, and it didn't seem to take any coins. I hit a couple of buttons and looked at the screen confusedly. It started flashing, and I straightened up and smiled just like a professional model. I was adorable. Adorable! When I flipped the curtain back, the booth didn't spit out any pictures, and Sage was gone. I would find her again. In the meantime, I would just go outside and smoke. I could stay out there and smoke all night if I wanted.

It was pouring, so I huddled with a crew of smokers in cocktail dresses and elaborate eyeliner. Meanwhile, I had forgotten to put on mascara, which made me feel oddly naked, and my hair was so bad I had, in desperation, thrust a clip in my bangs and hoped for the best. I had changed out of my high heels and into a pair of vaguely sensible pumps. I smoked furiously and watched the other guests sparkle at each other. It wasn't even clear why I was there at the holiday party. I only knew the people in my department, and I wasn't even sure that any of them were still there. It was still raining, pouring, and the gutters were ankle-deep creeks, but I would finish my cigarette, and maybe by then it would have let up, and I would get my coat and go home where it was warm.

"You look cold," the bouncer said, the same bouncer from upstairs. He wore an ankle-length leather duster, which made me sad for him.

"I need a fabulous coat like yours," I said. "But I wouldn't look as cute in it."

I heard myself saying the words, and I couldn't make myself stop.

He looked surprised, and then he grinned at me. "No, you'd look cuter."

"Maybe," I said, "If I didn't wear anything under it."

I could drown myself in one of the gutters. I could put a cigarette out in my eye. I could just let the words keep pouring out of my mouth, the way the drinks had poured into it. He sidled closer to me, and he said things about how cute I was and how awesome I was. He asked me all about the party, and told me about how he was actually a party planner and he was doing this as a favor for a friend.

I said, "I need another drink," and he said, "Let me escort you." He put the tips of his fingers at the small of my back and guided me through the crowd, stiff-arming drunken packs of ad executives. He told the bartender, "Take care of this gorgeous girl," and he winked at me and was gone, and I thought maybe I should go, because I wanted to scrub off the heat his fingerprints had left behind. I wanted to go home. I pushed back through the crowd, which was harder to do without a short bouncer, and I shoved money into the tip jar when the coat check person brought me my still-damp wool coat.

The bouncer was back outside when I shouldered my way through the shouting people who gathered around the front entrance. He saw me and hauled me over to his corner of the smoking area.

"Did you get your drink?" he said, smiling down at me like I belonged to him.

"I did!" I chirped. "But now I have to head out. I am—it's late and I'm, you know."

His face slumped, all of it falling down around his chin. "So soon?" he said. "Do you have to?"

"Really," I said. And then, "I'm sorry! I'm going to go catch a cab."

"I'll hail it for you, sweetheart. But first." He took out his phone. "Call me," he said.

"Can't you just write it down? I don't know where my phone is," I lied.

He smiled in a very satisfied way and pulled a marker out of his jacket pocket. He put the marker in my hand and smoothed his jacket up his wrist. I wrote my number in messy strokes. My real number, for some reason, because I was afraid he'd quiz me on it. He tugged his sleeve down.

"Tomorrow," he said.

I didn't remember if he had ever told me his name, or if I had told him mine.

"Come on, now," he said. "I'll get you home."

"So he hailed me a cab," I said. "One of those minivan cabs with the sliding doors. It's pouring out. He hauls the door open, and I grab the roof and kind of yank myself up, but my shoes slip because the step is wet, and then my hands slip because the roof is wet, and I land on my back in the gutter."

"No," Monique said. Her eyes were huge. We were at our monthly dinner party, a little bit early, and I was leaning back on the couch, looking up at the high ceiling of Jen Wade's living room. I folded my hands on my belly.

"Yes," I said to the ceiling. "And I lay there for a second, in five inches of water, just stunned. He yelled and he pulled me up, and he kept asking, 'Are you okay? Are you okay?' and I was just kind of laughing, because what are you supposed to do when someone watches you fall out of a cab and into a ditch?"

"Probably die," Monique said.

"He still called me the next day."

"Who did?" Jen Wade said, coming back into the room.

"Jen's new boyfriend," Monique said.

"He's not my new boyfriend," I said. "My real new boyfriend is the guy I met at Kezar last night. He told me all about how he was working his way through *The Joy of Cooking*, and then invited me back to try his infused vodka."

"He did not," Monique said, and Jen Wade laughed.

"He did," I said. "So I said, 'Sure!'"

"What?" Mo said. "You didn't."

I shrugged. "And when we got there he poured me a glass and it was awful, so I didn't drink it. When I leaned over to put it down on the coffee table, he grabbed me and kissed me. Which was *awful*. He was all pointy tongue. And then!"

"There's more?"

"Of course," I said. "He told me, 'Do you know what I've been thinking all night?' and a part of me is totally thinking, 'Oh no, he's going to confess his love for me.' And instead he says, 'I've been thinking about you sucking my cock.' And then I started to stand up to—I don't know. Pretend to look at his bookshelves or go to the bathroom or something, and he grabbed me again and hauled me over his lap. And he spanked me." I laughed, but they weren't laughing.

Jen Wade said, "Jen, he could have hurt you. Did you know this guy?"

"No," I said. "I mean, I wasn't—he seemed okay. He seemed kind of strange, but okay?"

"You just met him at a bar," Monique said.

"He was a regular, so—anyway. Then I told him I had to go, and he said, 'But I was hoping you'd stay and blow me all night.' And I said 'Okay, bye!'"

They still weren't laughing. "I'm glad you left," Monique said.

"I don't remember if I gave him my number," I said. "But I don't think he remembers my name, anyway."

"That will make it awkward when he shows up at your house and tries to spank you," Jen Wade said, and I laughed, and they did too, and I took a long swallow of wine. I could imagine exactly what they thought of me. Another long swallow.

"So I'm not really handling this really well?" I said. It was a very quiet question, and they didn't hear it.

The doorbell rang and I ran to the bathroom. I was flushed red, with a sharp needle-prick feeling from my scalp to my forehead down to the top of my chest. I gripped the edges of the sink and I tried to breathe steadily, patiently, waiting for one breath to finish before I took another, and another, and another, and another.

"Hi," he said. He picked up before I could panic and hang up. It was chilly out, and my shoes were too tight, but I was walking because I was so full from dinner. I couldn't stand and wait for the train. I couldn't stand still. I paced from streetlight to streetlight, light to dark to light, up the narrow corridor of tall buildings toward Market Street.

I pressed the phone to my ear and said, "Hi. It's me."

"I know," he said.

"I don't know what I'm doing," I said. "I don't know how to do this."

"You do," Ben said.

"I can't."

"You can."

My breathing was loud against the mouthpiece of the phone.

Brave. Certain. Happy. One of us believed it.

"Okay," I said. "Okay."

my mother, myself . . . ruby Tuesdaylicious . . . the truth in photographs

My mother has always been fat, and I had always been fat. And my mother, because she is my mother and has known me all my life, knows that some of my choices have been pretty stupid. She seems as astonished as I secretly am when things turn out, when consequences spring up rose-like and smelling sweet, when things don't go to hell. She is not expecting things to go wrong, not necessarily. She is not waiting for my inevitable failure. What she's doing is squeezing her eyes shut and gripping the armrests as I swing by on my trapeze far overhead, just beneath the pointed top of the tent, unbuckling my safety harness and doing shots of tequila.

When we talk, I hear mostly relief in her voice. In my voice I hear an overwhelming urge to convince her that I am okay, that everything is just perfect. It sounds not unlike I'm trying to convince myself. But that's just because I'm never really sure, not about anything. And one of the things I hate the most is having other people see my insecurity, which always feels like a lack of strength.

When my mom asked me to come visit, when she said I should stay for the weekend because she missed me, I was almost afraid to go. But

I went, because she is my mother, and sometimes, when you've hit rock bottom, you need your mother.

"Are you hungry?" she said in the car on the way out of the airport. "We'll get dinner. It'll be my treat." She took me to Ruby Tuesday's, off the freeway. It was busy, and we had to wait in the plush, hotel-like lobby. She settled down into the suede chair in the corner. She set her bag on the wide mound of her belly and wrapped her arms around it. She had been sitting like that for as long as I had remembered. She had always looked exactly like she did right that moment, a series of overlapping concentric circles like a Picasso, large and soft and tapering down to tiny, delicate feet in black leather tennis shoes. She wore stretchy pants and pink socks and had perfectly manicured long nails with little starfishes painted on each thumb, a crystal on each of her pinkie nails. A white sweep of hair. My mom. I sat down next to her and put my head on her shoulder.

There is something comforting about Ruby Tuesday's. It is perfectly bland, in beige and muted colors. Over-padded benches, silverware wrapped up snug inside paper napkins, a laminated menu with pictures. We both ordered healthy things without consulting each other. I wanted her to think I was healthy. She wanted me to think she was healthy. We both looked at the basket of rolls in between us. I took one, and a pat of butter.

"Do you remember," I said, "Daddy telling me to only butter one piece of toast? And then I was supposed to press them together."

"When did he do that?" my mother said. She took a roll, too. "I don't remember that." Her rings flashed under the low-hanging pendant light.

"I think that's the only time he ever said anything about my weight." I covered my roll with the entire pat of butter, and took a big bite. "Did he ever say anything to you?"

"He never did," she said. Her glasses were reflecting the light of the outside sign, and she wasn't really looking at me. "He loved my butt. He would have said 'junk in the trunk!'"

"Mom!" I said.

"What? It's true." Her cheeks were round and pink when she smiled. "Your father thought I was hot stuff. But he was the one with a tight butt."

"Okay, we're done with that subject now," I said, and took another roll, and she did, too. When I put my fork down halfway through my fish entrée, she put her fork down, too.

"They give you so much," she said.

"Mom, you don't have to—"

"What?" she said, smoothing out her napkin and folding it neatly next to her plate.

"Nothing," I said.

"I missed you." Her eyes were shining at me across the table.

"I know. I missed you too, Mom." I nodded at her plate. "Is your rice good?"

"It's very good." She picked up her fork. "They make it very good here."

We took pictures when we got back to the house. On the living room couch next to my mother, my head on her yielding shoulder. She always smelled like baby powder. My aunt took a picture, and then tilted her head back to peer through her glasses at the screen. "Another one, Mary," she said. "Don't make such a stupid face."

"I'm not!" my mother said. She settled her hands over her belly. "Jennifer's the important one in the picture, anyway. I look terrible."

"No you don't," I said. "Hey! Hey, put your glasses back on!" And the flash went off.

She sent the email before I even landed. I still smelled like cross-country travel and tiredness. The cat circled around my feet, dug his claws into my knee, and I yelped and scooped him onto my lap.

I miss you, my mother wrote. *It was wonderful to see you. My beautiful daughter. I am so proud. Attached are pictures.* I double clicked, and my face burst onto the screen.

I am leaning toward my mother, smiling. She looks proud, and she is not wearing her glasses. She looks just like my mom. She is wider than I am, and I am taller than she is. My arms protrude from the short sleeves of my blouse, and they look scrawny. I look small on the squashy brown couch. I look small, exactly like my mother, nothing at all like my mother. People might call her fat, but she is my mom. My mom-shaped mom, who is mom-sized.

I thought, maybe it was possible that the same thing was true about me. That I looked like Jen. That I was Jen-shaped and Jen-sized.

She sent more photos, from the wedding so long ago I could barely remember it. In the photograph, I am smiling. I am standing there straight, in the garden of the country house, a cool green wash of foliage behind me, a cool blue sky, and the sun is bright on my hair.

My skin was so bare and exposed that day—my arms, my knees, down to my ankles and strappy shoes. My sternum, my collarbones, the sweep of my neck and my shoulder blades were bare, too. So much skin, and none of it perfect, none of it flawless.

I clicked through the rest of the photos and then came back to the bridesmaid photo. A girl in the sun. If I looked closely, I could point out every flaw and bump and problem. But as I sat there, I realized that I was that girl in the picture, and that was a pleasurable thought. That I could just be that girl. It didn't have to be a transitional state. I didn't have to be someone who used to be too fat, or someone who worried too much about being skinny. I could be that girl. The steady stream of awareness of my body and my size and my shape could slow down to a trickle, a murmur I could tune out easily.

I could have a drink without thinking—needing—to finish the whole bottle. I could have a bite of something sweet without feeling like I needed to swallow the entire cake whole or I'd be missing something. I could call Monique and we could drink cocktails and talk about the essential, vital, important things, and gossip about the unimportant things. I could call Katie and sit with her on her back patio and drink wine, talking about our writing, and the future, and the definition of success.

I could accept a compliment—you're perfect, someone could say, and I could just say thank you, without any obligation or gratitude. Someone could demand something of me—something as small as a "smile, beautiful," on the street, and I could say *no*. I could even say *back off.*

I could think, *I am happy, but this is not enough,* and that could be a wonderful thing.

Those moments of presence, of being in the present, could maybe become days at a time; weeks, months, years. A lifetime worth of it. It could take a long time. Far longer than it did to lose the weight. But it could happen.

Weight loss stories are supposed to have very definitive endings— I reached my goal! I have triumphed! There go the harmonicas, and here comes the hero of our story, wearing a slinky dress in size whatever, thrilled with herself and thrilled with her accomplishments and thrilled with the brand-new body that is her ticket to a happy drive into the horizon and the setting sun, as hot as she all-of-a-sudden believes she is.

Then the credits roll and you are dabbing away a little tear and pressing your fist to your heart, because it is throbbing with the beauty of it all, so hard it might just thump right out of your chest.

I had kept waiting for the credits to roll, I think. I was tired of waiting.

I said, *fuck this.* I bought a bike.

A bike was for someone who was healthy. Someone athletic and happy and fit. Somehow, bikes only belonged to people who weren't afraid, and now I had one.

Sometimes when I swung my leg over the bar and settled into the seat, in that moment of uncertainty—will I topple this time, or will I push off and find myself moving smoothly, perfectly balanced between the earth and the sky?—I remembered being a kid, and wondering how I looked from behind. Wondering about the absurd picture I must be making, the narrow seat, the wide ass. I hadn't been happy. I hadn't thought I could ride a bike. How long had I spent thinking that I couldn't do things until I was skinny? How much of my life had I wasted, how much of this kind of soaring joy, flying down a hill recklessly with all my worries streaming behind me, had I missed? Why had I spent so long hating myself, and why had I spent so long waiting?

I was sad for that girl on the bike when I was a kid, the teenager staying home from the school dances because she was afraid, the young adult taking whatever was offered to her, whether she wanted it or not, because she was afraid she'd never get another chance. The adult who had moved across the country and went to graduate school and wrote a book, but thought it wasn't good enough, thought *she* wasn't good enough because her pants size was wrong. So many years of my "before."

But now I had so many years of my "after" to live. It didn't matter anymore that I couldn't have figured this out sooner, because here I was pushing off and rushing forward. I wished I had known it was possible earlier. I wished I had known that I could have been happy, that I could have asked for more. I wished I had listened to the people who told me it was possible, to the people who had lived the possibility.

I bought a bike and I discovered the joy of a furious pedal to the top of a hill, and then the coast down the hill that whipped the sweat away from my forehead and neck. That feeling of flying. The wheels spun, and I breathed in the chill in the air and pumped the pedals harder, leaving that all behind, growing smaller and smaller, then vanishing into the horizon.

I rode my bike to the bar to meet Andy.

Let's hang out, I wrote in my email, three months after we had broken up. I missed my best friend. I sent it with a hiccup of my heart.

Okay! he said, and I realized I was luckier than I had ever believed.

We sat shoulder to shoulder and we talked as comfortably as we ever had, and there was a sadness, there. A sense of loss, and a sense of relief. Release, even. Gratitude.

"I can't believe you rode your bike here," he said. He tipped his whiskey into his mouth, threw his head back, and grimaced.

"What, you thought I'd die horribly in traffic? I know I'm going to! It's kind of exciting."

"Well, no. I hope you don't die in traffic. We're not going to talk about that. I mean, why bike when you can sit on a comfortable bus?"

"Buses aren't very comfortable."

"Well, no. But you know what I mean."

I knew what he meant. But the bike was important. I was stronger— my legs were solid. I was more mobile, more active, more a part of the world. I still ate Oreos, but I liked to think that I was eating fewer Oreos. The truce with my stomach was an uneasy one, frequently broken, but it had become an inextricable part of my life. My uncertain, unreliable stomach came from the same place this new strength did, this feeling that I could pump my bike up any hill in San Francisco, and laugh all the way back down with the wind tearing through my hair.

I had the good parts with me, and if I couldn't leave the bad things behind, then that was going to have to be okay. That was going to be my life.

Andy bought me a drink, and then I bought him a drink, and I was drunk enough to say, "I'm sorry."

He put his arm around me, and to my relief, he said, "I know." He said, "It's okay."

He didn't have to do that; I didn't really deserve it. But there it was.

Tipsy, giddy, I rode my bike through the dark. I passed the park, and through the trees I heard the quiet roar of a crowd watching a free concert. The sprinklers had come on, and the grass and the earth were wet, and the air was cool. I realized that this was exactly what summer has always smelled like to me. This fresh and wet, clean and earthy smell was exactly perfect and exactly right, my childhood rushing at me through the dark.

I pumped the pedals harder and shot through the intersection and laughed, because there's no way my mother would have let me go riding around the streets at night, and I felt everything that was good about being an adult mixed with everything that was good about being a kid. The perfect smell of a childhood summer, racing through the dark on my bike, completely and totally independent and boundless and free.

That happiness buoyed me up the hill and through the dark streets, and I thought of other happinesses, the things that override the difficult parts, at least for a while. The things that make the difficult parts okay.

I was grateful for the size and shape of my body. I was skinnier than some of my friends, and fatter than other of my friends. I was able to ride my bike. I was ready to think about things that had nothing to do with my body.

I pedaled hard, and the wind was cold through my hair, and I thought of the pleasure of being creative, of starting with nothing palpable and ending up with something real that you have spun out of nothing at all. The heat of the sun, which melts all the way through you, and the icy cold from the air conditioner, which slices you thin and shakes you awake.

Ice pops. Feather pillows. Anticipation. Ice cream. A fat black cat who follows you from room to room. Chilled white wine; the transition from day to dusk to night. Night-lights, an overcast sky, a fully lit skyscraper; a completely black and winding canyon road at one in the morning. Waking up and realizing you're exactly where you want to be, and not having to move for hours.

Finished manuscripts. Emails full of good news. Phone calls that end in *I love you*. Hilarious text messages. Trashy novels. Bubble baths. Soy candles. Real bacon for breakfast. Purring. Body heat. A sense of accomplishment. A sense of perspective. A sense of acceptance and the peace that follows afterward. Deciding that something is none of your business, and the accompanying giddy freedom of that.

Reading for hours, napping, a memory-foam mattress, the slant of sun on a polished wooden floor, the first sip of an iced latte, Legos, coloring books, crocheting a scarf. Chopping celery, a rib at a time. The smell of paper. A full bookshelf. The library. The perfect compliment.

The perfect and perfectly timed pun. Shopping for dresses, opening a big check, making lists, having a game plan. Remembering something you swore you wouldn't forget, remembering something you had forgotten. Remembering happiness.

Taking the good parts with me, and leaving the bad things behind. Wanting more.

Streetlight to streetlight, I pedaled home.

a sparrow . . . saying no . . . a thousand
nautical miles

When I showed up at Idle Hand, the tattoo parlor where Iggy worked, he showed me his drawing traced out in delicate pencil lines. A sparrow, in flight.

"It's perfect," I said.

"Go get a drink," Iggy said. "I'll be about a half hour."

Molotov's was empty except for me and some tattooed kids sitting in one of the vinyl booths at the back of the room. At the bar, on a stool as rickety as mine, was a guy who introduced himself as Lou. He was three seats over, but scooted down next to me.

"No thank you," I told him, when he started to pull out his wallet. "I'm good." He stayed, though, and he asked me questions, nursing his beer. It was as bright as it ever got in there, light pouring in through the tall windows that lined the front and making the red walls glow. Being in a bar during the day was always disconcerting.

"So!" Lou said. "A tattoo!" He raised his glass to me, and we toasted. "A sparrow!" he said. "What does it symbolize?"

"Well," I said. I spun my glass around on the bar, pushed it away, pulled it back to me. "Beauty. Freedom? And—" I didn't really want to talk about it. I hadn't entirely articulated it to myself—I just knew what I wanted, and I knew where it belonged on my body. I knew why, too, but couldn't explain it. I didn't want to explain it to Lou. I shrugged. "Luck," I said.

"Wrong," Lou said. "A sparrow is what sailors get when they have traveled five thousand nautical miles." He nodded sagely. "Safe journey there, and safe journey home."

I asked the bartender for another drink, and Lou tried to pay for it again. He wanted to come sit with me while I got it. "I'm good company!" he said.

"No," I said. "No thank you," actually. But no.

He stayed at the bar, and I went back to the tattoo parlor. I hopped up on the padded table and rolled up my jeans.

There was always that moment of hesitation before a tattoo, before the needle came down, when I remembered that bright bloom of pain that focused into a burn, when I wanted to jump up and run. I held tight to the sides of the table and I breathed in through my nose. Iggy bent close and the needle touched down. It was like I remembered it, every single time.

The blood was running down my foot, between my toes, and my foot was twitching in jumps and jerks, spasming so that I yanked it out of Iggy's hands time and again. He steadied my foot against his knee, and he held on firmly. His lines were perfect and sure.

"You're doing really well!" Iggy said. "You've come a long way."

I used to make low, keening noises and whine a lot, which is the favorite thing of every tattoo artist. This time I kept my jaw clenched and my mouth shut. My foot shimmied and shook every time he struck a nerve, and I apologized each time. I clung to the edge of the padded table, tried to stay still.

"I'm so sorry," I said again. I didn't recognize my voice.

"That's right," he said. "I can't work with this, with your nervous system. Get it under control and then come back to me." He grinned at me.

My toe vibrated. The Pogues were playing loud. He hunched over my foot. He dipped the needle in the thimble of black ink and dragged another perfect line down through my skin. Things began to seem washed out, pale, and glittery. I hunched my shoulders, trying to hold on tight.

"Are you okay?" He glanced up at me, and then flicked the tattoo gun off, snapped his gloves into the garbage can. Then I only heard his voice. "Let's get you down here. You need a break. Careful. That's right, sit right here. Lean back a bit, there. I'll be right back."

It didn't seem like he had moved at all, but then I was holding a can of Coke, a candy bar that had green nougat. I looked at it for a long time. He said, "Gross, right? It's all we have. Eat it. Drink some soda. Bring your blood sugar back up, you were about to pass out."

The soda was perfectly sweet. I wanted to fold the candy into my mouth and let it fill up my entire head. I slumped down and tried to breathe around my mouth full of chocolate. "I'm okay," I mumbled. I swallowed. "I'm sorry. I don't know what's wrong. I ate before I came. I've done this before, right? I'm sorry."

He put the garbage can in front of me and a cold compress on my neck and forehead. "No. Don't apologize," he said. "It happens. It's nothing you can help."

"I'm embarrassed," I said. "I'm tougher than that."

"Who cares?" he said. "You're doing fine. You're doing better than a lot of people. You're okay."

"Okay," I said. "I'm ready."

"You sure?" He put his hand on my shoulder. "I don't want you passing out on me."

"I won't," I said. "I'm tough. I can take anything."

Full-body shivers. I felt hollow-boned, as if I could float away. I held on, because that's what I did in situations like this. I held on tight and I didn't let go and I for sure didn't let myself give in and fall apart. I held on tight as he dragged the needle through my skin, which was so close to the bone and nerves now. My feet had been fat, at one point—how does that happen, that you gain weight in your feet? They had once had a padding of fat and that was gone now. You could see tendons, veins right below the surface. I clung to the table and tried not to cry.

The last twenty minutes of my tattoo hurt everywhere in my body, up through my foot and along the sides of my legs. The pain leapt up into my spine and dug into the back of my neck and the top of my head. I breathed in through my mouth, out through my nose, and held onto the table because it was the only thing left in the world.

Iggy flicked off the gun. "There," he said.

It was beautiful.

I sat on the table under the overhead lights as Iggy bandaged up my foot, my sparrow. My bird in flight. I was exhilarated. Burning, buzzing in the wash of endorphins. Ready to travel five thousand nautical miles.

Epilogue

And they all lived happily ever after, the end.

It's been about five years since I had weight loss surgery. Maybe six? Somewhere around there. And in my desk there's still a stack, about as thick as a ream of printer paper, of folders with all the documentation and medical records and instructions and manuals and permission slips and checklists and diagrams and insurance bills and medical bills and leaflets and pamphlets. Weight loss surgery involves a lot of paperwork, and I saved all of it like I'm afraid there's going to be an open-book test and I'd really regret having spent an hour shredding everything.

If there were any kind of test about weight loss surgery, though, I'd fail it. I had memorized the basic spiel about what weight loss surgery entails, but I never really understood it. I know you're supposed to primarily eat protein, but I don't remember the amounts, and as for the final word on eating fat, I don't think I ever really waited around to hear it. I also still have no idea how to pronounce *duodenal*. Doo-odd-en-all? Duo-dennal? Something like that. I had it switched. Whatever the fuck that means.

What it boils down to: An uncertain number of years ago, an unclear procedure was performed on unconfirmed areas of my digestive system, and subsequently, though I was unsure about and unprepared for what I was supposed to eat and when and where and how and to what extent, I lost a lot of weight. I lost all of the weight. I lost so much weight that people were starting to say "Jen, where did your weight go? Do you need us to help you find it? Here is a sandwich."

What I learned: Being skinny is far, far easier in this world than being fat, and being skinny does not solve all your problems.

I don't think I gained weight in order to hide from the world—I think that weight and size are much more complex issues than that. But I think it was comfortable and easy to let fat be my whole problem. And when I was left with no fat but plenty of problems, I was the only one left to blame. It's like I had cleaned out the flooded basement, which is great and all, but now I had to actually address the cause of the flooding, and it was harder than you think. It's so much harder than I was led to believe.

I spent too much time trying to forget the person I was and just trying to be happy and thankful that I wasn't that person anymore, and that is one of the most terrible ways to live.

The final tally: I lost 180 pounds. At the lightest I was 130 pounds, was a size 4, and had no boobs. Right now I'm about 165 pounds (no, no—a quick trip to the scale mid-sentence tells me I'm actually 168) and a size 10.

Generally, I am happy. I don't stand out, and I can fit just about anywhere, in this world that's built for a specific size of person. I can breathe more easily and walk more easily; I have even been known to break out into a run. Things have been good, in a lot of ways. So many ways. And I've learned to be grateful for the woman I was, who was strong and brave and beautiful and powerful, who I treated so poorly and who I dishonored by trying frantically, in a panic, to wipe out.

I have never regretted getting weight loss surgery. I deeply, absolutely regret all the years I spent stupidly hating myself for being fat, and for waiting for my life to start and things to get better once I found a way to not be fat anymore. I wasn't strong enough to stay the size I was and learn to be happy in my body; I wasn't brave enough to address the physical and emotional realities attached to being fat in a world that doesn't like fat people.

Whatever size and shape you are, it is absolutely vital that you are happy with yourself. I cannot tell you how important it is to accept the person you are and to find peace with what you look like. Diet, exercise, weight loss surgery. Self-actualization, self-acceptance, Health at Every Size—you are strong enough and smart enough to figure out what you can do, what will help you become—not a magically skinny person, but a healthy, happy person who doesn't give a damn what other people think about your body.

If you think you need to lose weight to be happy with yourself and in your skin, please be healthy. Please do it mindfully. Please do as I say and not as I did—that could be the epigraph of this book. Please consider your options, and understand the consequences of every choice you make. Please be true to the person you are right now and everything you've ever accomplished.

This is what I've learned, in the end: It's an ongoing process, whatever size you are, whatever path you choose. I am still struggling with it. Every single goddamn day, I struggle with it. I struggle to be healthy, to be happy, to be a person I like, to be a person I am proud to be, inside and out, whatever size I am. I fail more often than I can tell you. But the more I try, the easier it gets.

Here are some important resources:

Body image and self-esteem:

- The mission of the International Size Acceptance Association (ISAA) is to promote size acceptance and fight size discrimination throughout the world by means of advocacy and visible, lawful actions. ISAA defines size discrimination as any action which places people at a disadvantage simply because of their size. ISAA defines size acceptance as acceptance of self and others without regard to weight or body size. www.size-acceptance.org

- Health at Every Size is based on the premise that the best way to improve health is to honor your body. It supports people in adopting good health habits for the sake of health and well-being rather than for weight control. www.haescommunity.org

- The National Eating Disorders Association (NEDA) is a non-profit organization dedicated to supporting individuals and families affected by eating disorders. NEDA campaigns for prevention, improved access to quality treatment, and increased research funding to better understand and treat eating disorders. www.nationaleatingdisorders.org

- The Love Your Body campaign challenges the message that a woman's value is best measured through her willingness and ability to embody current beauty standards. http://loveyourbody.nowfoundation.org

- BodyPositive looks at ways we can feel good in the bodies we have. Remember, your body hears everything you think. www.bodypositive.com

Some important books to check out:

- *Lessons from the Fat-o-sphere: Quit Dieting and Declare a Truce with Your Body,* Kate Harding and Marianne Kirby

- *FAT!SO?: Because You Don't Have to Apologize for Your Size,* Marilyn Wann

- *Fat Chicks Rule!: How To Survive in a Thin-Centric World,* Lara Frater

Food and physical fitness:

- Theresa Bakker is a personal trainer who is also fat, and she combines her knowledge of fitness training with a keen understanding of clients who are struggling with weight-related shame and judgment. In other words, she gets it. Her mission in life is to spread the word that people of all sizes are capable of improving their lives through good nutrition and regular physical activity. **www.biggirlsworkout.com**

- The "Food for Thought" Pyramid is designed to offer a more balanced focus on enhancing your own health, supporting the health of others, and improving the overall health of your community. **www.food-for-thought-pyramid.com**

- Be Nourished encourages a non-diet approach to food, weight, and health. It offers workshops, classes, and retreats to tackle sensitive topics like conscious eating, body acceptance, and hunger awareness. Be Nourished also provides counseling, yoga, and massage therapy to holistically complement the supportive atmosphere it believes is needed to realize long-term body acceptance, the ability to eat intuitively, and the power to be psychologically and physically nourished. **www.benourished.org**

- The National Sustainable Agriculture Coalition supports small- and mid-size family farms and works to ensure access to healthy, nutritious foods for everyone. **http://sustainableagriculture.net**

Weight loss surgery:

These websites, written by other weight-loss surgery patients, honestly explore real life after weight loss surgery:

- All forms of weight loss surgery, including gastric bypass, are major procedures that can pose serious risks and side effects, and

each surgery also requires you to make healthy changes and get regular exercise. WebMD offers a guide to making a decision about weight loss surgery.
www.webmd.com/diet/weight-loss-surgery/surgery-for-you

- ObesityHelp offers guidance for those seeking weight loss solutions. It provides a comprehensive program of support and education as well as assistance in locating resources.
www.obesityhelp.com

- Melting Mama's and her husband both had gastric bypass surgery in 2004. Her blog is a realistic, snarky and honest look at long-term life after weight loss surgery. **www.meltingmama.net**

- The Bariatric Bad Girls Club is a social network for weight loss surgery patients where members find support and tools for advocacy. Real women share the good, the bad, and the ugly of everyday life after weight loss surgery, including matters from which others shy away. The BBGC emphasizes education and self-advocacy for bariatric patients.
www.facebook.com/groups/bbgirlclub

- Shelley had RNY gastric bypass surgery in June 2006. She writes a funny, honest blog about her ongoing struggle with her weight, her body image, and the psychological issues that led to her original weight gain.
http://theworldaccordingtoeggface.blogspot.com

Acknowledgments

My father gave me my artsy streak, along with my inability to talk about my feelings. I miss him, but I don't want to talk about it. My mother gave me her deeply emotional side, her butt, and her support, no matter what stupid-ass thing I wanted to do next.

My brother, Ken Larsen, without whom I would have never known the feeling of ultimate, supreme power, has grown up to be one of the most amazing people I know. (He was later smart enough to marry Carrie Ellman. She has taught me an astonishing amount about self-confidence and assertiveness by example, and she is a real Larsen.) When this book arrives, a baby Larsen will have arrived, too—and I am so grateful to be an aunt. Thank you.

When I was old enough to flee home for college, Rodrigo Trujillo gave me more than a place to stay—he gave me a lifelong family. He is my oldest and dearest friend, and I don't know what I'd do without him. He didn't even grumble, much, when I moved to San Francisco, fleeing an ex-boyfriend and looking for a reason to live. (And in the first draft of this book, he was a bounty hunter named Bonesaw.) Thank you.

In grad school at USF, I found incredible instructors who were patient with my various writing-related breakdowns: Lisa Harper, Lewis Buzbee, and Jane Anne Staw, in particular. I would have stopped writing, in despair, without you. Thank you. (I think.)

I also met writers who were far more talented and disciplined and hard working than I, who became some of my greatest friends, allies, and supporters, who listened to this story and forgave me for my flaws, who read terrible drafts of this book and made them so much better than I ever could have alone: Katie "katydid" Flynn, Josh Mohr, and Leota Higgins. Thank you.

San Francisco is where I struggled to figure out who I was and what the fuck I was doing. And where I was lucky enough to have Jen Wade, who is short, Shannon Kokoska, who is hilarious, and Kieca Mahoney, who is not perky. They are incredible women, and were my friends even when I didn't deserve it. Thank you.

I didn't—don't—deserve a lot of the luck in my life. And yet I somehow ended up with Alex as a friend. He instilled in me my appreciation for Manhattans, enjoys my comedy stylings, and was there for me always, no matter what. Thank you.

Monique van den Berg, my lesbian life partner, is an amazing and tireless cheerleader, gives incredibly vital feedback, lets me go on and on even when I am at my craziest, and reminds me that I am no Robert Penn Warren. Thank you, Mrs. van den Cullen. I will always be your porky princess. (WINK.)

Iggy Vans at Idle Hand in San Francisco is an exceptional artist. He designed and inked me with the beautiful tattoos that changed my body, and that I get compliments on every day. Thank you.

The only reason this book exists is because one day, not long after my weight loss surgery, I got an email from Susan Kaplow at Condé Nast telling me I had something to say and should do so as a blogger on the brand-new website she was starting. Sarah McColl and Ricky Marston were the reason that website, Elastic Waist, was so professional, Wendy Wimmer raised the level of discourse and was a comrade in arms, and our amazing readers showed me that my story was worthwhile. Thank you.

When I said "forget this blogging thing, I'm gonna write me a book," the stupidly talented Jennette Fulda and Wendy McClure kept me as sane as I ever get throughout the proposal and submission process. Their above-and-beyond generosity and patience and understanding was staggering and I am grateful.

Karen Meisner is both the ultimate source of the title and the person who talked me through the panic. She is the only reason I could write the manuscript. She is one of the most generous and thoughtful humans I have ever been lucky enough to know and adore, and to my great fortune she has always believed in me. I love her completely, but especially her butt. Thank you.

Laura Ross and Cheryl Pientka, my awesome agents, believed in the book throughout the long and painful process, and wonderful, enthusiastic Brooke Warner at Seal took a chance on it. Elke Barter made the cover gorgeous beyond my dreams, and Theresa Noll and Julie Pinkerton did brilliant jobs of wrestling my messy prose into submission—and believe me, I know how much that can suck. Any mistakes that remain are my own. Thank you.

Eben Brinson Smith III changed my life, and made me realize I could change for the better. For that I will always be grateful. I love you, and thank you.

This book is true to the best of my knowledge and ability. And in some ways it is an apology. But mostly it is a thank you to all the people in my life who have supported me and loved me and kicked my ass when I needed it and celebrated with me. Thank you.

About the Author

Jen Larsen is a writer, editor, and proofreader living for less in Ogden, Utah. You can find her at jenlarsen.net.

before, 2006

after, 2010

Selected Titles from Seal Press

By women. For women.

Half-Assed: A Weight-Loss Memoir, by Jennette Fulda. $15.95, 978-1-58005-233-7. Pastaqueen.com blogger Jennette Fulda's satisfyingly inspirational memoir about the challenges and triumphs of losing half of her 372 pounds.

Something Spectacular: The True Story of One Rockette's Battle with Bulimia, by Greta Gleissner. $16.00, 978-1-58005-415-7. A piercing, powerful account of one woman's struggle with bulimia, self-image, and sexuality, set against the backdrop of professional dancing.

Pale Girl Speaks: A Year Uncovered, by Hillary Fogelson. $16.00, 978-1-58005-444-7. An edgy, funny memoir about a woman who became angry and self-absorbed when she was diagnosed with melanoma—until her father was diagnosed with the same skin cancer, and she had to learn to lead by example and let go of her fear.

Licking the Spoon: A Memoir of Food, Family, and Identity, by Candace Walsh. $16.00, 978-1-58005-391-4. The story of how—accompanied by pivotal recipes, cookbooks, culinary movements, and guides—one woman learned that you cannot only recover but blossom after a comically horrible childhood if you just have the right recipes, a little luck, and an appetite for life's next meal.

Dancing at the Shame Prom: Sharing the Stories That Kept Us Small, edited by Amy Ferris and Hollye Dexter. $16.00, 978-1-58005-416-4. A collection of funny, sad, poignant, miraculous, life-changing, and jaw-dropping secrets for readers to gawk at, empathize with, and laugh about—in the hopes that they will be inspired to share their secret burdens as well.

We Hope You Like This Song: An Overly Honest Story about Friendship, Death, and Mix Tapes, by Bree Housley. $16.00, 978-1-58005-431-7. Bree Housley's sweet, quirky, and hilarious tribute to her lifelong friend, and her chronicle of how she honored her after her premature death.

SealPress.com
Facebook.com/SealPress
@SealPress